THE DEAD
DO NOT DIE

THE DEAD DO NOT DIE

"Exterminate All the Brutes" and *Terra Nullius*

Sven Lindqvist

THE NEW PRESS

NEW YORK
LONDON

Published in the United States by The New Press, New York, 2014
Distributed by Perseus Distribution

CIP data available
ISBN 978-1-59558-989-7 (pbk)
ISBN 978-1-62097-003-4 (e-book)

The New Press publishes books that promote and enrich public discussion and
understanding of the issues vital to our democracy and to a more equitable world.
These books are made possible by the enthusiasm of our readers; the support of a
committed group of donors, large and small; the collaboration of our many partners
in the independent media and the not-for-profit sector; booksellers, who often hand-
sell New Press books; librarians; and above all by our authors.

www.thenewpress.com

Composition by dix!
This book was set in Scala

Printed in the United States of America

CONTENTS

Introduction by Adam Hochschild   vii

"Exterminate All the Brutes"   1

Terra Nullius   187

INTRODUCTION

Like many of the most original writers, Sven Lindqvist is hard to pi-
geonhole. He is not exactly a historian, for his graduate degree is in
literature. He is not exactly a travel writer, for he has little interest in
the colorful details that make a place seem exotic; he always wants
to direct our attention back to our own culture. He is not exactly a
journalist, for when he travels to far points on the globe, he is less
likely to interview anyone than to tell us about his own dreams. His
work does not come in predictable neatly tied packages: he travels
through Africa meditating on Joseph Conrad's *Heart of Darkness* but
never reaches the Congo; he goes all the way to Australia to write
powerfully about what its native peoples endured but chooses not to
interview a single Aborigine. And, for that matter, he's not someone
on whom I, or almost any American writer, can have the last word,
for the great majority of his thirty-three books have not been translated from Swedish.

If there is an English-language writer whom Lindqvist reminds
me of, it might be James Agee: also uncategorizable, also working in
many genres, also at times forcing painful detail on his admirers—
his masterwork *Let Us Now Praise Famous Men* is not easy bedtime
reading. Yet that book changed and expanded forever our sense
of how to see the world, and, at its best, so does the work of Sven
Lindqvist.

If you asked most Americans or Europeans, for example, to date
the great tragic turning points of the modern era, they might say
1914, when World War I began and we saw the toll industrialized
slaughter could take, or 1945, when the United States carried this to

a new level by dropping two atom bombs on Japanese cities. If you asked Lindqvist, I think he would say 1898 and 1911. Why?

These dates, too, have to do with industrialized warfare; the difference is where the victims were. The year 1898 saw the Battle of Omdurman, during which a small force of British and colonial troops, Winston Churchill among them, in a few hours killed more than ten thousand Sudanese and wounded another sixteen thousand, many fatally, most of them falling victim to half a million bullets fired by Hiram Maxim's latest machine guns. It was the first large-scale demonstration of what this horrific new weapon could do. Thirteen years later, on November 1, 1911, during another long-forgotten war, an Italian lieutenant named Giulio Cavotti leaned out of his open-cockpit airplane and dropped several hand grenades on two oases near Tripoli, Libya. It was the world's first aerial bombardment.

In both cases, of course, the victims Lindqvist draws our attention to were colonial peoples. This, I think, is the insight and the driving passion at the core of the two books in this volume and of several of his others, particularly the remarkable *A History of Bombing*—where he traces the genealogy of British terror-bombing of German cities in World War II back to similar targeting of civilians in a colonial war in Iraq more than twenty years earlier. To read *"Exterminate All the Brutes", A History of Bombing,* or *Terra Nullius* is to be reminded of how incredibly Eurocentric a view of the world most mainstream historians have. We are accustomed to thinking—in the famous phrase of British foreign secretary Sir Edward Grey—of "the lamps . . . going out all over Europe" in 1914 as a catastrophic war began and forget that they were extinguished decades earlier for people on other continents as they experienced European conquest.

Almost all of us educated in North America or Europe grew up learning that there were two great totalitarian systems of modern times, each with fantasies of exterminating its enemies: Nazism and Communism. Lindqvist reminds us that there was a third: European colonialism. And, most provocatively, he makes connections between it and one of the others.

"Exterminate All the Brutes" takes us deep into the history of
Western consciousness in a search for the sources of the very *idea*
of extermination and finds it in many unexpected places. An early
"kindergarten for European imperialism," for example, was the Canary Islands, where some five hundred years ago diseases and weapons brought by conquering Spaniards reduced an estimated eighty
thousand indigenous inhabitants to zero in less than a century.
How many people who have visited these lovely islands as tourists
ever learned this? Not me. Lindqvist also introduces us to Lord Wolseley, eventually commander in chief of the British army at the time
of Omdurman, who, in this era when British wars were colonial
ones, spoke of "the rapture-giving delight which the attack upon an
enemy affords. . . . All other sensations are but as the tinkling of a
doorbell in comparison with the throbbing of Big Ben." Then there
is the nineteenth-century birth of scientific racism, which eagerly
twisted Darwin's discoveries to justify the idea that "inferior" races
were fated to disappear from the Earth, just like species of plants
and animals gone extinct—and implied that there was no sin involved in helping them on their way.

And finally, along came plenty of thinkers and politicians who
saw this as inevitable. In 1898, the year of Omdurman, one of them
declared, "One can roughly divide the nations of the world into the
living and the dying." Who said this? Lord Salisbury, prime minister of Britain. And then comes Lindqvist's most provocative and
unexpected discovery: a German thinker, Friedrich Ratzel, an ar-
dent enthusiast of colonialism, believed that there was a "demonic
necessity" for the "superior race" to see to it that "peoples of inferior
culture" die out. And who were these inferior people? They included
"the stunted hunting people in the African interior" (tens of thousands of whom were wiped out in 1904 in the notorious German
genocide of the Herero people of today's Namibia), Gypsies—and
Jews. Hitler had a copy of Ratzel's book with him in 1924, when he
was in prison writing *Mein Kampf.*

"Hitler himself," writes Lindqvist, "was driven throughout his
political career by a fanatical anti-Semitism with roots in a tradition
of over a thousand years, which had often led to killing and even to

mass murder of Jews. But the step from mass murder to genocide was not taken until the anti-Semitic tradition met the tradition of genocide arising during Europe's expansion in America, Australia, Africa, and Asia."

Can we prove this beyond doubt? Not without knowing exactly what was in Hitler's mind. But I defy anyone to read *"Exterminate All the Brutes"* and not see the Holocaust in a somewhat different light and the Jews, as Lindqvist suggests, as the Africans of Europe. His bold contention has riled some more traditional scholars, deeply wedded to the idea of the Holocaust's uniqueness. Unique it certainly was in scale, technology, and speed, but Lindqvist makes us realize that it was but one of an appalling series of attempts—the others almost all outside of Europe—to exterminate an entire people from the face of the Earth.

Terra Nullius has also not been without its critics, chief among them white Australians who feel that all this history of the shameful treatment of Aboriginal peoples is familiar news by now. To some extent that's true, but unfortunately, as Lindqvist shows us, not true enough. The achievement of this book, while more complex, again includes reminding us of how people in a country we normally consider enlightened thought so much like Nazis. What would we say, for instance, about a German theorist who, a mere half-dozen years before Hitler took power, wrote, "The survival of the Jews will only cause trouble"? We'd say that this person paved the way to Auschwitz. In *Terra Nullius,* Lindqvist introduces us to George H.L.F. Pitt-Rivers, a British anthropologist, who wrote in 1927 of Australia, "The survival of the natives will only cause trouble." By contrast, Pitt-Rivers added, "there is no native problem in Tasmania . . . for the very good reason that the Tasmanians are no longer alive to create a problem." Hauntingly, Lindqvist quotes an earlier report from similarly minded researchers who described the typical Aborigine as "a naked, hirsute savage, with a type of features occasionally pronouncedly Jewish."

In other ways as well, Lindqvist subtly examines how white Britons and Australians have looked at Aborigines, showing us how their perceptions and theories are so often a projection of white fantasies. Because women used the same form of address for a husband's brother as for him, for example, early anthropologists theorized that the Aborigines practiced group sex, with brothers owning all women in common. Because Aborigines (unlike whites) used no corporal punishment on their children, their child-rearing was judged inexcusably lax, and their children, half-castes in particular, were often seized and taken from them, in order to be reared in state institutions in ways less "primitive."

Above all, whites eagerly promoted the reassuring illusion that because so much of central and western Australia looked like desert, it couldn't possibly belong to anyone and so was *terra nullius*—no one's land. "There was little appetite for admitting that . . . every stone, every bush, and every water hole had its specific owner and custodian, its sacred history and religious significance." It was far more convenient to believe that the land was no one's, which meant it could be used for everything from open-pit mining to testing long-range missiles and British atomic bombs.

Lindqvist's work leaves you changed. *"Exterminate All the Brutes"* first made me fully aware of one of the real-life models for Joseph Conrad's Mr. Kurtz and, for a book I was then writing, set me looking for more. Two books later, I found myself writing about the Battle of Omdurman. And no one who reads *A History of Bombing* will ever again feel that the Allies of World War II fought the "Good War." Lindqvist opens a world to us, a world with its comforting myths stripped away. You read him at your own risk.

—Adam Hochschild

"EXTERMINATE ALL THE BRUTES"

One Man's Odyssey into the Heart of Darkness and the Origins of European Genocide

Sven Lindqvist

Translated by Joan Tate

To Olof Lagercrantz
who traveled with *Heart of Darkness*
and Etienne Glaser
who was Adolf in *Hitler's Childhood*

All Jews and Negroes ought really to be exterminated.
We shall be victorious. The other races will disappear and
die out.

White Aryan Resistance, Sweden, 1991

You may wipe us out, but the children of the stars can never
be dogs.

Somabulano, Rhodesia, 1896

CONTENTS

Preface   9

PART I

To In Salah   13

An Outpost of Progress   22

To Ksar Marabtine   40

PART II

Gods of Arms   47

To Tam   78

The Friends   83

PART III

To Arlit   99

Cuvier's Discovery   105

To Agadez   115

PART IV

The Birth of Racism   131

Lebensraum, Todesraum   150

To Zinder   168

Notes   181

PREFACE

This is a story, not a contribution to historical research. It is the story of a man traveling by bus through the Saharan desert and, at the same time, traveling by computer through the history of the concept of extermination. In small, sand-ridden desert hotels, his study closes in on one sentence in Joseph Conrad's *Heart of Darkness*: "Exterminate all the brutes."

Why did Kurtz end his report on the civilizing task of the white man in Africa with these words? What did they mean to Conrad and his contemporaries? Why did Conrad make them stand out as a summary of all the high-flown rhetoric on Europe's responsibilities to the peoples of other continents?

I thought I had the answer to these questions when in 1949, at the age of seventeen, I first read *Heart of Darkness*. Behind the "black shadows of disease and starvation" in the Grove of Death I saw in my mind's eye the emaciated survivors of the German death camps, which had been liberated only a few years earlier. I read Conrad as a prophetic author who had foreseen all the horrors that were to come.

Hannah Arendt knew better. She saw that Conrad was writing about the genocides of his own time. In her first book, *The Origins of Totalitarianism* (1951), she showed how imperialism necessitated racism as the only possible excuse for its deeds. "Lying under anybody's nose were many of the elements which gathered together could create a totalitarian government on the basis of racism."

Her thesis that Nazism and Communism were of the same stock has been well remembered. However, many forget that she also held the "terrible massacres" and "wild murdering" of European imperialists responsible for "the triumphant introduction of such means of pacification into ordinary, respectable foreign policies," thereby fathering totalitarianism and its genocides.

In the first volume of *The Holocaust in Historical Context* (1994), Steven T. Katz has begun a demonstration of the "phenomenological uniqueness" of the Holocaust. On some of his seven hundred pages, he speaks with contempt for those who have instead emphasized the similarities. Sometimes, though, he is more tolerant and says, "Their approach might be called, nonpejoratively, a paradigm of similarity; mine, in contrast, is a paradigm of distinctiveness."

The two approaches seem to me equally valid and complementary. My desert traveler, employing a paradigm of similarity, finds that Europe's destruction of the "inferior races" of four continents prepared the ground for Hitler's destruction of six million Jews in Europe.

Each of these genocides had, of course, its own unique characteristics. However, two events need not be identical for one of them to facilitate the other. European world expansion, accompanied as it was by a shameless defense of extermination, created habits of thought and political precedents that made way for new outrages, finally culminating in the most horrendous of them all: the Holocaust.

PART I

To In Salah

You already know enough. So do I. It is not knowledge we lack. What is missing is the courage to understand what we know and to draw conclusions.

Tademait, "desert of deserts," is the deadest area of the Sahara. No sign of vegetation. Life all but extinct. The ground is covered with that black, shiny desert varnish the heat has pressed out of the stone.

The night bus, the only one between El Goléa and In Salah, with a little luck, takes seven hours. You fight your way to a seat in competition with a dozen or so soldiers in crude army boots who have learned their queuing technique in the close-combat school of the Algerian army in Sidi-bel-Abbès. Anyone carrying under one arm the core of European thought stored on an old-fashioned computer is obviously handicapped.

At the turnoff toward Timmimoun, hot potato soup and bread are served through a hole in the wall. Then the shattered asphalt comes to an end and the bus continues through roadless desert.

It is pure rodeo. The bus behaves like a young bronco. With windows rattling and springs screeching, it rocks, stamps, and leaps forward, and every jolt is transmitted to the hard disk I have on my lap as well as to the stack of swaying building blocks that are my spinal disks. When it is no longer possible to sit, I hang on to the roof rack or squat down.

This is what I had feared. This is what I have longed for.

The night is fantastic beneath the moon. Hour after hour, the white desert pours past: stone and sand, stone and gravel, gravel and sand—all gleaming like snow. Hour after hour. Nothing happens until a signal suddenly flares up in the darkness as a sign for one of the passengers to stop the bus, get off, and start walking, straight out into the desert.

The sound of his footsteps disappears into the sand. He himself disappears. We also disappear into the white darkness.

3

The core of European thought? Yes, there is one sentence, a short simple sentence, only a few words, summing up the history of our continent, our humanity, our biosphere, from Holocene[1] to Holocaust.

It says nothing about Europe as the original home on earth of humanism, democracy, and welfare. It says nothing about everything we are quite rightly proud of. It simply tells the truth we prefer to forget.

I have studied that sentence for several years. I have collected quantities of material that I never have time to go through. I would like to disappear into this desert, where no one can reach me, where I have all the time in the world, to disappear and not return until I have understood what I already know.

4

I get off in In Salah.

The moon is no longer shining. The bus takes its light with it and vanishes. The darkness all round me is compact.

It was outside In Salah that the Scottish explorer Alexander Gordon Laing was attacked and robbed. He had five saber cuts on the crown of his head and three on the left temple. One on his left cheekbone fractured his jawbone and divided his ear. A dreadful gash in his neck scratched his windpipe, a bullet in his hip grazed his spine, five saber cuts on his right arm and hand, three fingers broken, the wrist bones cut through, and so on.[2]

Somewhere far away in the darkness is a glimpse of a fire. I start lugging my heavy word processor and my even heavier suitcase in the direction of the light.

Banks of red wind-driven sand cross the road, the loose sand gathering into drifts on the slope. I take ten steps, then ten more. The light does not come any nearer.

Laing was attacked in January 1825. But fear is timeless. In the seventeenth century, Thomas Hobbes was just as frightened of solitude, of the night and death, as I am. "Some men are of so cruel a nature," he said to his friend Aubrey, "as to take a delight in killing men more than you should to kill a bird."[3]

The fire still seems just as distant. Shall I dump the computer and suitcase in order to be able to move on more easily? No, I sit down in the dust to await the dawn.

Down there, close to the ground, a breeze suddenly brings the fragrance of burning wood.

Do desert scents seem so strong because they are so rare? Is the desert firewood more concentrated, so it burns more fragrantly? What is sure is that the fire that seems so distant to the eye suddenly reaches my nose.

I get up and struggle on.

When I finally reach the men crouching around the fire, it is with a great feeling of victory.

Greet them. Ask them. And am told that I am going completely the wrong way. There is nothing to do but turn back, they say.

I follow my tracks back to the place where I got off the bus. Then I go south in the same darkness.

5

"Fear always remains," says Conrad. "A man may destroy everything within himself, love and hate and belief, and even doubt, but as long as he clings to life, he cannot destroy fear."[4]

Hobbes would have agreed. In that they shake hands across the centuries.

Why do I travel so much when I am so terribly frightened of traveling?

Perhaps in fear we seek an increased perception of life, a more potent form of existence? I am frightened, therefore I exist. The more frightened I am, the more I exist?

6

There is only one hotel in In Salah, the large and expensive state-owned Tidikelt Hotel, which, when I finally find it, has nothing to offer except a small, dark, icy cold room in which the heating devices have long since ceased functioning.

Things are just as usual in the Sahara: the smell of strong disinfectant, the screech of the door's unoiled hinge, the blind half torn down. I recognize so well the rickety table, its fourth leg too short, and the film of sand on the surface of the table, on the pillow and the washbowl. I recognize the tap that slowly starts dripping when you turn it full on, until after filling half a glass it gives up with a weary sigh. I recognize the bed made up with such military firmness that it never allows for feet, anyhow not at an angle from legs, and anchors half the bedclothes under the bed so that the blanket only reaches your navel all to preserve the bed linen's virginity.

OK, perhaps one has to travel. But why exactly here?

7

The sound of heavy blows from a club, falling on the larynx. A crackling sound like eggshells, and then a gurgling when they desperately try to get some air.

Toward morning I wake at last, still in my outdoor clothes. The bed is red with the sand I have brought with me from the bus. Each blow still crushes a larynx. The last one will crush mine.

8

The hotel is embedded in drifting sand, alone by a deserted road across a deserted plain. I plod out into the deep sand. The sun hammers down relentlessly. The light is as blinding as darkness. The air against my face is like thin ice crackling.

It takes half an hour to walk to the post office, which is equally far from the bank and the market. The old town huddles together, inaccessible to sun and sandstorms, but the new town is spread out thinly, with modern town planning doing its best to maximize the desolation of the Sahara.

The reddish brown clay facades of the center of town are enlivened by white pillars and portals, white pinnacles and copings. The style is called Sudanese, black, after *"Bled es sudan,"* the country of the blacks. In actual fact, it is an imaginary style, created by the French for the 1900 Great Exhibition in Paris, then planted out here in the Sahara. The modern town is gray International Style concrete.

The wind is blowing from the east. I have it stinging in my face as I return to the hotel, where long-distance truck drivers and foreigners dominate, all on their way "upward" or "downward," as if on a staircase. All of them inquire of the others about the road, about gas, about equipment, all of them occupied with the thought of moving on as quickly as possible.

I tape the map up on the wall and consider the distances. It is 170 miles to the nearest oasis in the west, Reggane. It is 240 miles of desert road to the nearest oasis in the north, El Goléa, from which I have just come. It is 250 miles as the crow flies to the nearest oasis in the east, Bordj Omar Driss. It is 400 miles to the nearest oasis in the south, Tamanrasset. It is 600 miles as the crow flies to the nearest sea, the Mediterranean, and 800 miles as the crow flies to the nearest river, the Niger. It is 900 miles to the sea in the west. Eastward the sea is so far away, it doesn't matter.

Every time I see the distances surrounding me, every time I realize that here, at the zero point of the desert, is where I am, a stab of delight goes through my body. That is why I stay.

9

If I could only get the computer to work! The question is whether it has survived the jolting and the dust. The disks are no larger than postcards. I have a hundred of them, in airtight packs, a whole library that together weighs no more than a single book.

At any time I can go anywhere in history, from the dawn of

paleontology, when Thomas Jefferson still found it unfathomable that one single species could disappear out of the economy of nature, to today's realization that 99.99 percent of all species have died out, most of them in a few mass exterminations that came close to wiping out all life. [5]

The disk weighs five grams. I put it in the slot and switch on. The screen flares up and the sentence I have been investigating for so long glows up at me in the darkness of the room.

The word Europe comes from a Semitic word that simply means "darkness." [6] The sentence glowing there on the screen is truly European. The thought was long on its way before finally being put into words at the turn of the century (1898–1899) by a Polish writer who often thought in French but wrote in English: Joseph Conrad.

Kurtz, the main character in Conrad's *Heart of Darkness*, completes his essay on the civilizing task of the white man among the savages of Africa with a postscript summarizing the true content of his high-flown rhetoric.

It is this sentence radiating toward me now on the screen: "Exterminate all the brutes."

10

The Latin *extermino* means "drive over the border," *terminus*, "exile, banish, exclude." Hence the English *exterminate*, which means "drive over the border to death, banish from life."

Swedish has no direct equivalent. Swedes have to say *utrota*, although that is really quite a different word, "root out," which in English is *extirpate*, from the Latin *stirps*, "root, tribe, family."

In both English and Swedish, the object of the action is seldom a single individual, but usually whole groups, such as quitchgrass, rats, or people. Brutes, of course, reduces the object to its mere animal status.

Africans have been called beasts ever since the very first contacts, when Europeans described them as "rude and beastlie," "like to brute beasts," and "more brutish than the beasts they hunt." [7]

II

Some years ago, I thought I had found the source of Conrad's phrase in the great liberal philosopher Herbert Spencer.

He writes in *Social Statics* (1850) that imperialism has served civilization by clearing the inferior races off the earth. "The forces which are working out the great scheme of perfect happiness, taking no account of incidental suffering, exterminate such sections of mankind as stand in their way. . . . Be he human or be he brute—the hindrance must be got rid of." [8]

Here were both the civilizing rhetoric of Kurtz and the two key words *exterminate* and *brute*, and the human being was expressly placed on an equal footing with the animal as an object for extermination.

I thought I had made a neat little scholarly discovery, worthy of being taken up one day as a footnote in the history of literature, Kurtz's sentence "explained" by Spencer's fantasies of annihilation. They in their turn, I thought, were personal eccentricities, perhaps explained by the fact that all Spencer's siblings had died when he was a child. A calm and comforting conclusion.

12

It soon turned out that Spencer was by no means alone in his interpretation. It was common and, during the second half of the nineteenth century, became even more common, so that the German philosopher Eduard von Hartmann was able to write the following in the second volume of his *Philosophy of the Unconscious*, which Conrad read in an English translation: "As little as a favor is done the dog whose tail is to be cut off, when one cuts it off gradually inch by inch, so little is their humanity in artificially prolonging the death struggles of savages who are on the verge of extinction. . . . The true philanthropist, if he has comprehended the natural law of anthropological evolution, cannot avoid desiring an acceleration of the last convulsion, and labor for that end." [9]

At the time, it was almost a platitude Hartmann had put into words. Neither he nor Spencer were personally inhuman. But their Europe was.

The idea of extermination lies no farther from the heart of humanism than Buchenwald lies from the Goethehaus in Weimar. That insight has been almost completely repressed, even by the Germans, who have been made sole scapegoats for ideas of extermination that are actually a common European heritage.

13

A battle over the living past is going on at present in Germany. This *Historikerstreit*, as they call it, concerns the question: Is the Nazi extermination of the Jews unique or not?

The German historian Ernst Nolte has called "the so-called extermination of the Jews by the Third Reich" "a reaction or a distorted copy and not an original action." The original was, according to Nolte, the extermination of the Kulaks in the Soviet Union and Stalin's purges in the 1930s. They were what Hitler copied.

The idea that the extermination of the Kulaks *caused* the extermination of the Jews seems to have been abandoned, and many people emphasize that all historical events are unique and not copies of each other. But they can be compared. Thus both likenesses and differences arise between the extermination of the Jews and other mass murders, from the massacre of the Armenians at the beginning of the 1900s to the more recent atrocities of Pol Pot.

But in this debate no one mentions the German extermination of the Herero people in southwest Africa during Hitler's childhood. No one mentions the corresponding genocide by the French, the British, or the Americans. No one points out that during Hitler's childhood, a major element in the European view of mankind was the conviction that "inferior races" were by nature condemned to extinction: the true compassion of the superior races consisted in helping them on the way.

All German historians participating in this debate seem to look in the same direction. None looks to the west. But Hitler did. What

Hitler wished to create when he sought *Lebensraum* in the east was a continental equivalent of the British Empire. It was in the British and other western European peoples that he found the models, of which the extermination of the Jews is, in Nolte's words, "a distorted copy." [10]

An Outpost of Progress

"Exterminating All the Niggers"

14

On June 22, 1897, the same year *Lebensraum* was born in Germany, British expansionist policy reached its peak.[11] The greatest empire in the history of the world celebrated itself with unequaled arrogance.

Representatives of all the peoples and territories subjugated by the British, almost a quarter of the earth and its inhabitants, gathered in London to pay tribute to Queen Victoria on the sixtieth anniversary of her ascension to the throne.[12]

At the time there was a journal called *Cosmopolis*, which was aimed at cultivated people all over Europe, with untranslated contributions in German, French, and English.

To this cultivated European audience, Queen Victoria was compared with Darius, Alexander the Great, and Augustus, but none of these emperors of antiquity was able to demonstrate such expansion as Victoria had.

Her empire had grown by three and a half million square miles and a hundred and fifty million subjects. It had caught up with and surpassed China, which, with her four hundred millions had hitherto been considered the most populous realm in the world.

Perhaps the other great powers in Europe had not sufficiently understood the military strength of the British Empire, it was said. There was more fighting instinct and military spirit in the British than in any other nation. As far as the navy was concerned, the empire had not only superiority, but supremacy over the high seas.

The British had not let themselves be intoxicated by their successes, but maintained a humble recognition that these results—perhaps unparalleled in history—were due to the grace and favor of Almighty God.

Also, of course, to the person of the queen. The moral strength of her character could not perhaps be measured with scientific precision, but its influence was obviously enormous.

"Today's ceremony," said one commentator, "means more, they think, than any triumph that has ever been celebrated: more national vitality, more commerce, more reclamation of wilderness, more suppression of savagery, more peace, more liberty. This is not bombast, it is statistic . . ."

"The British nation seemed deliberately to determine to regard its vast power, its colonising success, its vital unity, its world-wide territory, and to glory in them."

"We were never so strong, the shouts meant. Let all the world realise that we mean to be not less so in the future."

Cosmopolis's German and French contributors joined in the chorus of rejoicing. So the story introducing the journal's jubilee issue has an unprecedented shock effect.

15

The story is about two Europeans, Kayerts and Carlier, who have been dumped by a cynical company director at a small trading post by the great river.

Their reading matter is a yellowed newspaper that praises in high-flown language "our colonial expansion." As in the jubilee issue of *Cosmopolis*, the colonies are made out to be sacred work in the service of Civilization. The article extolled the merits of those bringing light, faith, and trade to "the dark places" of the earth.

At first the two companions believe these fine words. But gradually they discover that words are nothing but "sounds." The sounds lack content outside the society that created them. As long as there is a policeman on the street corner, as long as there is food to buy in the shops, as long as the general public sees you—only then do your sounds constitute morality. Conscience presumes society.

But soon Kayerts and Carlier are ready to do trade in slaves and mass murder. When supplies run out, they quarrel over a lump of sugar. Kayerts flees for his life in the belief that Carlier is after

him with a gun. When they suddenly bump into each other, Kayerts shoots in self-defense and does not realize until later that in his
panic he has killed an unarmed man.

But what does that matter? Concepts such as "virtue" and
"crime" are nothing but sounds. People die every day by the thousands, Kayerts thinks, as he sits by the body of his companion, perhaps by hundreds of thousands—who knows? One more or less was
of little importance—at least not to a thinking creature.

He, Kayerts, is a thinking creature. Hitherto, like the rest of
mankind, he has gone around believing a lot of nonsense. Now for
the first time he is really thinking. Now he knows and draws the
conclusion from what he knows.

When morning comes, the mist is shattered by an inhuman, vi-
brating shriek. The company steamer, which both men have been
waiting for for months, has returned.

The director of the great Civilization Company goes ashore and
finds Kayerts hanging from the cross on his predecessor's grave. He
is hanging, it seems, to attention, but even in death sticks out his
tongue at his managing director.

16

Not only at the director. Kayerts is sticking out his swollen black
tongue at the whole of the jubilee celebrations going on in the newspaper columns around the story, at all of the triumphant imperial
ideology.

It was natural that Joseph Conrad's "An Outpost of Progress," at
its first publication in Cosmopolis, should have been seen as a comment on the jubilee. But it had been written the year before, in July
1896, during Conrad's honeymoon in Brittany. It was one of Conrad's very first short stories.

The material was based on his own stay in the Congo. He had
traveled upriver on one of the company's steamers himself, seeing
the small trading posts and hearing his fellow passengers' stories.
One of them happened to be called Keyaerts.[13]

Conrad had had this material for six years. Why did he write his story just at that moment? The Congo debate did not start seriously for another six years, in 1903. What happened in July 1896 that made Conrad interrupt both his honeymoon and the novel he was writing and instead write a story about the Congo?

17

I have moved. I now rent a cheap room in the closed Badjouda Hotel opposite the entrance to the market, and I eat at Ben Hachem Moulay's Friends' Restaurant. At dusk I sit under the trees on the main street, drink coffee with milk, and watch people passing by.

A hundred years ago the market in In Salah was the liveliest meeting place in the Sahara. Slaves from the south were exchanged for grain, dates, and industrial goods from the north. The slaves did not even have to be kept in captivity: to flee from In Salah meant certain death in the desert. The few who nevertheless made the attempt were easily captured and punished. They had their testicles crushed, their Achilles tendons slashed, then were left behind.

In this once renowned market, today only a few imported vegetables are to be found, already drooping on arrival, and shoddy textiles clashing in angry, poisonous colors. The market's literary offerings feature part two of classical masterpieces such as *Don Quixote* and Mme. de Staël's book on Germany. Presumably, part one has been delivered to some other oasis, since it wouldn't be fair to allow the same oasis both parts of a sought-after book.

The only really interesting thing the market has to offer is fossilized wood, the remnants of gigantic trees that died out millions of years ago and were buried in the sand. Silicon acid has turned the wood into stone; then, as the sand moved on, the stone was uncovered and landed in the market.

It is prohibited to take fossilized-wood pieces larger than a clenched fist. But even in a clenched fist there is plenty of space for the Sahara's verdant forests. My piece is on the table here, misleadingly like living wood, charged with the fragrance of rain-wet leaves and the soughing of leafy treetops.

18

When Father came home from work when I was small, he would first of all go in to see Grandmother.

Mother did not like this and felt betrayed every time.

Was the love between mother and son stronger and more real than that uniting man and wife? Father was Grandmother's favorite son, the son she was carrying when her husband died, the son she bore as a lone parent. And my father, who had never seen his own father, had placed all his love in her.

Mother sensed this. So did I. I myself liked Grandmother best. In her powerlessness as an old woman, I recognized my own powerlessness as a child.

Grandmother smelled. A strong sweetish-sour odor came from her room and her body. Mother loathed that smell, particularly at table, and Grandmother knew it. She ate in the kitchen.

Now and again, Mother used to raid Grandmother's room to try to remove the actual source of the smell. She was doomed to failure, as the smell came from Grandmother herself. But every time, Mother cleared out "a whole lot of rubbish Grandmother's accumulated around her" and threw it away to get rid of the smell.

Father could not protect Grandmother from this. After all, it was true that she smelled. He could not deny the smell, nor that the smell meant dirt and that dirt had to go. The logic was irrefutable. Father could only delay and tone down the actions when Grandmother tearfully begged for mercy. The rest was up to me.

Grandmother was the seamstress of the house, and in a bundle under her bed she kept a whole library of patches and leftover pieces of cloth she called oddments. When I was very small I loved playing with these rags. I made a man out of a piece of Father's striped nightshirt, a woman out of Mother's pink silk blouse. Grandmother helped me. Together, we made animals as well as people.

So I understood perfectly how desperate Grandmother was when the "rubbish" was to go. Mother's attempt to keep the place clean was to me a loveless outrage, perfectly in keeping with those I myself was exposed to. So I rummaged in the bin for Grandmother's things and hid them among my own until the danger had passed.

In that way I also saved a yellowed book called *In the Shade of the Palms*.

19

In my childhood home, the books were arranged so that unbound books were kept to the left of the bookcase, clothbound books in the middle, and half-bound books farthest to the right.

The books were placed thus with company in mind. "Company" meant everyone who did not belong to the family. If company stopped in the doorway, they could see only a little bit of the bookcase and might then think that all the books were half-bound with gold lettering on the spines. If they came into the room, they might then think that all the books at least were bound. Only if the guests came right into the room could they see the unbound books farthest to the left.

Among the half-bound books was one called *Three Years in the Congo* (1887). In it, three Swedish officers related their experiences in the service of King Leopold.

An experienced traveler in Africa had advised Lieutenant Pagels to take the *chicotte* as his best friend, the whip made of raw hippopotamus hide, "which at every blow slashes bloody runes."

It may sound cruel to European ears, said Pagels, but he knew from experience that it was true. Particularly important was to seem coldly unmoved while administering a flogging: "If you have to order physical punishment to a savage, have this punishment carried out with not a muscle in your face betraying your feelings."

Lieutenant Gleerup relates in his report how he flogged his bearers until he passed out in an attack of fever, then how tenderly the recently flogged men cared for him, covering him with their white cloths and looking after him as if he were a child, and how he lay with his head in the lap of one of the men while another ran down into the steep valley to fetch water for him, so that he soon recovered and was once again able to wield the whip.

But only individual blacks behaved like this. The complete opposite was true of "the savage in general."

Pagels had tried in vain to find a single good side to the savage. "Should I be at death's door and a glass of water were enough to save my life, no savage would bring me that water if I could not pay him for his trouble."

Morality, love, friendship—all such things are lacking in the savage, said Pagels. The savage respects nothing but brute strength. He regards friendliness as stupidity. So one should never show a savage any friendship.

It was a gigantic task the young Congo state had taken on, if the great civilizing assignment were to be crowned with victory, says Pagels, who called down the blessings of the Lord on the noble, sacrificing friend of mankind, the high-minded prince, ruler of the Congo, His Majesty Leopold II, leader of these strivings.

On September 30, 1886, the reports of these three officers were laid before the Swedish Anthropological and Geographical Society in the banqueting hall of the Grand Hotel, in the presence of His Majesty the King, His Royal Highness the Crown Prince, and their Highnesses the Grand Dukes of Gotland, Vestergötland, and Nerike.

No one raised any objections. On the contrary. The chairman of the society, Professor Baron von Düben, stated: "It is with pride we hear that these gentlemen travelers in the Congo, throughout toil, battles, and privations in that inhospitable country, have always managed to hold high the prestige of the name of Sweden."

Such was the truth in the half-bound book foremost in the bookcase. But among the unbound books in the corner was another truth which smelled of Grandmother.

20

Right up to 1966, Swedish parents had the legal right to thrash their children. In many European countries, that right still applies. Even today in France it is possible to buy a special leather whip for the chastisement of wives and children, what the French call a *martinet* and the English the cat-o'-nine-tails.

In my parents' home, the birch was used. On exceptional occasions, my mother took me with her to the forest to cut osiers. Her face was then exactly as Pagels said it should be, not a muscle betraying her feelings.

I avoided all looks and gazed down at my black rubber boots. We went to the old sports ground, where willows grew on the edge of the forest. Mother cut one osier after another and tried them out by striking a few whistling blows in the air. Then she gave them to me. I carried them all the way home, filled with one single thought: Please don't let anyone see us.

The shame was the worst punishment.

And the waiting.

The whole day passed waiting for Father to come home. When he came, he knew nothing. I could see that on his face, which was just as usual. He was about to go in to Grandmother when Mother stopped him and told him about the terrible thing that had happened.

I was sent to bed. I lay there waiting, while they talked. I knew what they were saying about me.

Then they came into the room, both their faces cold, empty, and hostile. Mother held the cane. Father asked me if it was true. Had I really behaved so badly at the Christmas party? Had I used swearwords? Had I blasphemed and taken God's name in vain?

"Yes," I breathed.

Inside me I could see the girls' terrified delight and feel the warm glow of my arrogance as I sat there at the party surrounded by admiring friends and saying all those forbidden words—which still went on resounding within me when Father took the cane and started beating. "Fucking pissgod, fucking shitgod, fucking damned cunt who sneaked . . . bloody, bloody, bloody . . ."

Unlike Mother, Father had not been working himself up all day. He had started from cold, and at first he gave an impression that it was only with extreme reluctance he was doling out this "physical punishment," as Pagels called it.

I could not see his face as he beat me, nor could he see mine. But I could hear from the way he was breathing that something happened to him as he crossed the threshold into violence.

I imagined he was ashamed of hurting me so, that the shame had gone over into rage that made him strike even harder than he had intended. But perhaps it was my own shame I wrongly read into his actions.

I did know for certain only that people are seized with a kind of madness when they take to violence. The violence carries them along, transforms them, and makes them—even afterward, when it's all over—unrecognizable.

21

The book I saved from destruction, *In the Shade of the Palms* (1907), was written by a missionary, Edward Wilhelm Sjöblom. He arrived in the Congo on July 31, 1892. On August 20, he saw his first corpse.

In his diary, we see him on his travels by steamer up the Congo to choose a suitable place for his mission station. As early as his first day on board, he witnesses a flogging with the hippo-hide whip Lieutenant Pagels had so warmly recommended. All the white men on board are in agreement. "Only the whip can civilize the black."

At a Catholic mission, they have three hundred boys taken prisoner during the war between the state and the natives. They were now to be handed over to the state to be trained as soldiers.

The steamer is delayed while one of the boys is captured. He is bound to the steam engine where the heat is greatest. Sjöblom notes:

> The captain often showed the boy the *chicotte*, but made him wait all day before letting him taste it.
>
> However, the moment of suffering came. I tried to count the lashes and think they were about sixty, apart from the kicks to his head and back. The captain smiled with satisfaction when he saw the boy's thin garb soaked with blood. The

boy lay there on deck in his torment, wriggling like a worm, and every time the captain or one of the trading agents passed him by, he was given a kick or several. . . . I had to witness all this in silence.

At dinner, they talked of their exploits concerning the treatment of the blacks. They mentioned one of their equals who had flogged three of his men so mercilessly that they had died as a result. This was reckoned to be valor. One of them said: "The best of them is not too good to die like a pig."

22

Grandmother never got that book back. I kept it where it was, well hidden in the corner for unbound books.

23

How would Pagels have reacted had he gone back and been able to see what Sjöblom was now seeing?

Perhaps the diary of E.J. Glave provides the answer.[14] Here is no gentle missionary speaking. From the very start Glave is in agreement that the natives must be treated "with the utmost severity" and that their villages must be attacked "if they won't work in some way for the good of the land."

"It is no crime but a kindness to make them work. . . . The measures adopted are severe, but the native cannot be satisfactorily handled by coaxing; he must be governed by force."

That was Glave's starting point. He is an old Congo hand, one of the first to serve Stanley. But when in January 1895 he returns to the Congo, he comes across a brutality that revolts him. What finally shatters his loyalty are scenes of torture very similar to those Sjöblom had witnessed:

The *chicotte* of raw hippo hide, especially a new one, trimmed like a corkscrew and with edges like knife blades, is a terrible

weapon, and a few blows bring blood. Not more than twenty-
five blows should be given unless the offense is very serious.

Though we persuade ourselves that the African's skin is
very tough, it needs an extraordinary constitution to withstand the terrible punishment of one hundred blows; generally the victim is in a state of insensibility after twenty-five
or thirty blows. At the first blow, he yells abominably; then
quiets down, and is a mere groaning, quivering body till the
operation is over. . . .

It is bad enough, the flogging of men, but far worse this
punishment inflicted on women and children. Small boys
of ten or twelve with excitable, hot-tempered masters, are often most harshly treated. . . . I conscientiously believe that a
man who receives one hundred blows is often nearly killed
and has his spirit broken for life.

24

This was the turning point, for Glave as it was for Sjöblom. After
that entry in his diary, he becomes more and more critical of the
regime.

At the beginning of March 1895, Glave comes to Equator, the
station where Sjöblom is a missionary, the station Glave himself had
helped found.

"Formerly the natives were well treated," he writes,

but now expeditions have been sent in every direction, forcing natives to make rubber and bring it into the stations.
The state is perpetrating its fiendish policy in order to obtain
profit.

War has been waged all through the district of Equator,
and thousands of people have been killed and homes destroyed. It was not necessary in the olden times, when white
men had no force at all. This forced commerce is depopulat-
ing the country.

As Sjöblom had been, Glave was transported together with a boatload of small boys who had been captured to be brought up by the state:

> Left Equator at eleven o'clock this morning after taking on a cargo of one hundred small slaves, principally seven- or eight-year-old boys, with a few girls among the batch, all stolen from the natives.
>
> They talk of philanthropy and civilisation! Where it is I do not know.
>
> Of the *libérés*, brought down the river, many die. They are badly cared for: no clothes to wear in the rainy season, sleep where there is no shelter, and no attention when sick. The one hundred youngsters on board are ill cared for by the state; most of them are quite naked, with no covering for the night. Their offence is that their fathers and brothers fought for a little independence.

But when Glave, having completed his journey, is back among Belgians and his own countrymen, he is influenced by group pressure and smooths over his criticisms. His final judgment is mild: "We must not condemn the young Congo Free State too hastily or too harshly. They have opened up the country, established a certain administration, and beaten the Arabs in the treatment of the natives. Their commercial transactions need remedying, it is true."

It is the same final judgment made on Kurtz in *Heart of Darkness*: his trading methods were unsound and had to be abandoned.

25

Through his work as a missionary, Sjöblom comes into much closer contact with the natives than Glave does. Day after day, he notes down new examples of arbitrary killing.

On February 1, 1895, his sermon is interrupted by a soldier seizing an old man and accusing him of not having collected enough rubber. Sjöblom asks the soldier to wait until the service is over. But the soldier simply drags the old man a few steps to one side, puts the muzzle of his rifle to the man's temple, and fires. Sjöblom writes:

A small boy of about nine is ordered by the soldier to cut off the dead man's hand, which, with some other hands taken previously in a similar way, are then the following day handed over to the commissioner as signs of the victory of civilization.

Oh, if only the civilized world knew the way hundreds, even thousands are murdered, villages destroyed, and surviving natives have to drag their lives along in the worst slavery. . . .

26

In 1887, the Scottish surgeon J.B. Dunlop hit upon the idea of equipping his small son's bicycle with an inflatable rubber tube. The bicycle tire was patented in 1888. During the years to follow, the demand for rubber multiplied. That was the explanation for the increasing brutalization of the regime in the Congo which is reflected in the diaries of Sjöblom and Glave.

Belgium's king, Leopold II, issued a decree on September 29, 1891, which gave his representatives in the Congo a monopoly on "trade" in rubber and ivory. By the same decree, natives were obliged to supply both rubber and labor, which in practice meant no trading was necessary.[15]

Leopold's representatives simply requisitioned labor, rubber, and ivory from the natives, without payment. Those who refused had their villages burned down, their children murdered, and their hands cut off.

These methods at first led to a dramatic increase in profitability. Profits were used, among other things, to build some of the hideous monuments still disfiguring Brussels: the Arcades du Cinquantenaire, the Palais de Laeken, the Château d'Ardennes. Few people today remember how many amputated hands these monuments cost.

In the mid-1890s, this murky secret of rubber was still unknown. Glave would have been able to tell it, but he died in Matadi in 1895. Only Sjöblom and some of his colleagues knew what was happening and opposed the terror. In vain did they report the outrages to higher authority. As a last resort, they decided to appeal to world opinion.

Sjöblom wrote strong, factual articles in *Weckoposten*, the Swedish Baptist newspaper. He also wrote reports in English and sent them to the Congo Balolo Mission in London.[16]

The result was a small, almost unnoticeable comment in the mission society's monthly magazine, *Regions Beyond*: "Very serious disturbance amongst the natives, on account of the imposed traffic in india-rubber, has led to wholesale slaughter in several districts. . . . Official inquiry is being made as to the allegations against Free State administration in Equatorville. We want more, however, than investigation; the crying need is for redress. But the question is how to obtain this without a public *exposé?*"[17]

27

Charles Dilke knew how to read between the lines. He was an ex-cabinet secretary and member of the committee of the Aborigines Protection Society. With explicit reference to that brief report in *Regions Beyond*, he took up the situation in the Congo and wrote a sharp article under the heading "Civilisation in Africa."[18]

The article was the first sign that responsible circles in Great Britain had taken note of the missionaries' reports. It was published to reach a European readership in the newly started journal *Cosmopolis*, in which it appeared in July 1896, the same month Conrad wrote "An Outpost of Progress" and submitted it to—*Cosmopolis*.

Ten years have gone by, writes Dilke, since the ratification of the Berlin treaty that created the State of Congo. High-flown declamations in Brussels and Berlin had manifest themselves in the form of "the ivory stealing, the village burning, the flogging and shooting that are going on in the heart of Africa now."

In Conrad's story it is the declamations in the yellowed

newspaper that take the visible form of ivory stealing, slave trade, and murder.

The old forms of government, Dilke writes, have broken down and no new ones created. Spaces in Africa are so vast, the climate and solitude so intolerable to Europeans, nothing good can be expected of European rule.

In Conrad's story it is just the distances, the climate, and the solitude that break down the two Europeans. Most of all the solitude, for that entails also an inner abandonment, Conrad writes; they lost something that previously "had kept the wilderness from interfering with their hearts."

What? Yes, "the images of home, the memory of people like them, of men who thought and felt as they used to think and feel, receded into distances made indistinct by the glare of unclouded sunshine."

Solitude erased society from within them, and left behind fear, mistrust, and violence.

Taxation in Africa cannot pay for an administration of the same quality as in India, writes Dilke. Even democratic governments have occasionally to hand over responsibility to sheer adventurers. Even worse is when the Niger Company and the Congo state rule over vast populations in enormous territories utterly out of sight from public opinion.

Conrad's two rogues had acquired their ivory through the slave trade. "Who will talk, if we hold our tongues? There is nobody here." No, that was the root of the trouble, says the narrator. There was nobody there and being "left alone with their own weakness," men can get up to anything.

Dilke's article reminded readers of what man in situations of that kind could do. It refers to the extermination of Native Americans in the United States, of the Hottentots in South Africa, of the inhabitants of the South Sea Islands, and of the natives of Australia. A similar extermination was going on in the Congo.

This theme can also be found in Conrad's story. It is Carlier who speaks of the necessity of "exterminating all the niggers" in order finally to make the country habitable.

Dilke's article is a draft of Conrad's story, which in its turn is a draft of *Heart of Darkness* published two years later. And Carlier's *"exterminating all the niggers"* is the first draft of Kurtz's *"exterminate all the brutes."*

28

In May 1897, Sjöblom himself went to London and, although very ill, appeared at a meeting arranged by the Aborigines Protection Society. Dilke was chairman.

With his intense gravity and dry, detailed, rather pedantic way of speaking, Sjöblom made a great impression, and his testimony on the mass murders in the Congo received widespread publicity.

The debate that broke out in the press forced King Leopold II to intervene personally. In June and July 1897, he went to London and Stockholm to convince Queen Victoria and King Oscar II that Sjöblom's accusations were unfounded.

As a result of King Leopold's visit, leading Swedish papers carried long, critical articles on the Congo. But Leopold had greater success in London, where the preparations for the imperial jubilee were well underway; Queen Victoria had other things to think about than a few baskets of amputated hands in the Congo.

The great powers had little desire to interfere with Leopold's genocide, for they themselves had similar skeletons in their cupboards. Great Britain did not intervene until ten years later, when an organized movement called the Congo Reform Movement made it politically impossible for the government to remain passive.

It made no difference when Glave's diary in all its hideousness was published by *The Century Magazine* in September 1897. Nor did it make any difference when Sjöblom took the matter up in new articles. The Congo debate of 1897 was forgotten. The jubilee had erased it.

In 1898, the Congo received almost entirely favorable publicity, most of all in connection with the opening of the railway between Matadi and Leopoldville, which gave rise to widespread reports in illustrated magazines. Not a word was said on all the lives the railway had cost.

29

That is, not until the Royal Statistical Society held their annual meeting on December 13, 1898, when the society's chairman, Leonard Courtney, spoke on the theme "an experiment in commercial expansion." [19]

A private person, King Leopold II had been made by the great powers ruler over what was estimated at anywhere from eleven to twenty-eight million natives in an area as large as the whole of Europe—that was the experiment. Referring to a series of Belgian sources, Courtney described the way the administration and commercial exploitation in the Congo were interwoven. With the help of Glave's diary, he described the violence the system had created.

This is what Glave had written from Stanley Falls ("The Inner Station" in *Heart of Darkness*):

> The Arabs in the employ of the state are compelled to bring in ivory and rubber and are permitted to employ any measures considered necessary to obtain this result. They employ the same means as in the days gone by, when Tippu Tip was one of the masters of the situation. They raid villages, take slaves, and give them back for ivory. The state has not suppressed slavery, but established a monopoly by driving out the Arab and Wangwana competitors.
>
> The state soldiers are constantly stealing, and sometimes the natives are so persecuted, they resent this by killing and eating their tormentors. Recently the state post on the Lomani lost two men killed and eaten by the natives. Arabs were sent to punish the natives; many women and children were taken and twenty-one heads were brought to the Falls and have been used by Captain Rom as a decoration around a flower bed in front of his house!

According to a report in the *Saturday Review*, this is how Courtney rendered Glave's account:

The Belgians have replaced the slavery they found by a system of servitude at least as objectionable. Of what certain Belgians can do in the way of barbarity Englishmen are painfully aware. Mr. Courtney mentions an instance of a Captain Rom, who ornamented his flower beds with heads of twenty-one natives killed in a punitive expedition. This is the Belgian idea of the most effectual method of promoting the civilisation of the Congo.

Perhaps Conrad had read Glave's diary when it was published in September 1897. In that case, he was again reminded of it. Perhaps he came across the information in Glave's diary for the first time. We do not know. What is certain is that he was able to read in his favorite paper, the *Saturday Review*, on Saturday, December 17, 1898, how Captain Rom ornamented his garden.

On Sunday, December 18, he started writing *Heart of Darkness*, the story in which Marlow turns his binoculars on Kurtz's house and catches sight of those heads—black, dried, sunken, the eyes closed, the result of their owner's motto: *"Exterminate all the brutes."*

To Ksar Marabtine

30

In Salah is really called *Ain Salah*, which means "the salty spring" or, literally, "the salty eye" (the spring is the eye of the desert).

Water taken today from great depths still tastes of salt and is clouded by an average of 2.5 grams of dry substance per liter, some liters scarcely transparent.

Rainfall is fourteen millimeters per annum, but in fact rain falls every fifth or every tenth year. On the other hand, sandstorms are common, particularly in the spring. On an average, there are fifty-five days of sandstorm each year.

The summers are hot. 133°F in the shade has been measured. Winters are primarily marked by the sharp difference between sun and shade. A stone in the shade is too cold to sit on, a stone in the sun, too hot.

The light cuts like a knife. I draw breath and hold my hand in front of my face as I go from one patch of shade to another.

The best moments are the hour before and after sunset. The sun at last stops stabbing at your eyes, but a pleasing warmth still remains in your body, in objects, in the air.

31

In Salah is one of the rare African examples of *foggara* culture.[20] The word *foggara* is said to derive from the Arabic words for "dig" and "poor." It signifies the same kind of underground aqueducts that are called *kanats* in Persian. According to Arab chroniclers, a certain Malik El Monsour brought the *foggara* into North Africa in the eleventh century. His descendants live in El Mansour in Touat and call themselves Barmaka. They are specialists in *foggara* construction.

The *foggara* of the Sahara are often between two and six miles long. Together, there have been over eighteen hundred miles of them in the Sahara. You could walk upright in the galleries, which were sometimes fifteen to twenty feet high. The wells could be 120 feet deep, and the work was always carried out by slaves. Every time slavery was abolished, it remained in the tunnels, under another name.

It is a kind of mining, though the vein of ore is a vein of water. Work is carried out with a small short-handled mining pickax. The shaft is three square feet at the surface of the ground, and when down to the sandstone layer, the hole is reduced to two feet, just large enough to maneuver the pickax.

The waste is hauled up by an assistant and spread around the hole, so on the surface of the ground *foggara* look like rows of molehills.

When the well gets down to the layers of water-bearing sandstone, the tunneling starts. In the darkness of these tunnels, the digger easily loses direction. This is where his art is tested.

On the surface it looks as if *foggara* were dead straight, but underground, they are winding. The tunneler has to dig so that his tunnel connects with the tunnel from another shaft. Sufficient incline is also necessary, enough to keep the water running without prematurely using up the difference in height which has to extend the whole way.

When the French conquered In Salah—on New Year's eve between the nineteenth and twentieth centuries—the *foggara* had already started running dry. They have gradually been replaced by deep wells, but irrigation is still carried out at night to avoid evaporation. Every consumer of water has his star; when that star appears in the sky, it is a sign that his turn to have water has come. Those who are waiting for their star spend the night by the well. They are called the children of the stars.

32

One of the four quarters of In Salah is called Ksar Marabtine. There is not much to see there—ground, houses, sky, all have the same dust color. Only the burial places with their mysterious whitewashed *marabouts* glow suggestively in all the monochrome color of dust. Death is the only festive thing in life.

Rows of children sit on stones with slates on their laps, chanting the Koran. A man walks past kicking an empty bowl. Another man has fallen asleep in the dust, sleeping with his arms outstretched as if for an embrace and does not even hear the rattling bowl as it rumbles past.

The gym consists of one great hall with a very high roof. In the far corner is a dark changing room and a spiral staircase up to the balcony, where you warm up with jump ropes or gymnastics while looking over the hall.

It is all familiar, but somewhat primitive. The mirrors are few and small. The benches are wooden and not adjustable. The weight-lifting machines use rope instead of steel wires, but in order to hold, the ropes have to be so thick that the friction on return leaves no work left for the muscles. Otherwise everything is as usual—the smell of sweaty bodies, the clank of metal, the cries and groans.

I go down into the hall and am at once lucky enough to inherit a barbell, a narrow black barbell with loose weights.

Three times ten behind my head, three times ten up to my chin, and three times ten on the biceps. Then I abandon the barbell for some dumbbells that have just come free. I stand waiting for a moment, a dumbbell in each hand, looking around for a bench. A man invites me to "wedge between" on his bench and we do three times ten butterfly swings, although his dumbbells are twice as heavy.

The stand's black-steel tubing forms a little basket above my face as I lie on the bench and lift. A ten-year-old is just loading weights onto a barbell. I help him, and then we alternate; he three times ten, me three times twenty. Then he is satisfied.

A tall Arab with a white scar on his left cheek suggests we double the weights. Now I'm the one doing three times ten and he three times twenty. Then he doubles again, but I am satisfied.

So it goes on. One of the weight machines has slightly thinner ropes, which really do offer resistance in both directions. I work it three times fifteen behind my head. There are no rowing machines. The leg machines look rickety and risky, so I refrain. There's still a great deal to do.

The dreams and visions that came to me when I first started

training are rare nowadays. I dream in bed, not in the gym. But my thoughts clarify. Maybe that provides nothing new. But what I already know comes closer.

33

"Seven!"

Suitably exhausted, I am sitting on one of the low benches outside Chez Brahim sipping at a glass of tea brewed from fresh green mint.

The training loosens up the hard surface of the mind, opens the pores of self and afterward it is particularly pleasant to sit here watching passersby.

"Seven! Seven!"

In Salah has twenty-five thousand inhabitants, most of them black. I have seen many of them so often that we have begun nodding to each other. Nonetheless, I start with surprise when I realize that "Seven" must be me, Sven.

The name jerks me out of my anonymity, as if out of a dream. I look incredulously around—and catch sight of the happy Turiner I got to know in Algiers, the man who drives from Turin to Cameroon several times a year and regards the Sahara as nothing but an unfortunate traffic obstacle.

He has just greased the front of his Mercedes with Vaseline and now wants me to help him put drops of a transparent fluid into his turned-up eye—both measures intended to protect sensitive surfaces from the wear and tear of the sand. He will sweep on south early the next morning, driving as long as the light lasts, then sleep in the car.

"Can I come with you?"

"No," he says. "Your word processor and suitcase are too heavy. If you're going to Tam by car you have to be light."

His reply really suits me quite well. At the moment, my *foggara* work on the computer disk seems more tempting than continuing my geographical journey.

Hitherto I have shown that "exterminate all the brutes" is

connected with the interrupted Congo debate of 1896–97, with Dilke's and Glave's contributions in particular.

But the sentence also has another background in time. When, in 1898, Joseph Conrad was writing about the unemployed sea captain Marlow seeking a job as skipper in Africa, he was building on memories of the autumn of 1889, when he himself, the unemployed sea captain Jósef Konrad Korzeniowski, aged thirty-one, was applying for a post as skipper on the Congo river.

My hypothesis is that if you want to understand *Heart of Darkness*, you have to see the connection between December 1889 and December 1898.

So the next morning I am again sitting at my computer, a towel spread over the seat of my chair, wearing nothing but a thin Chinese undervest and a pair of short Chinese underpants, ready to go on.

PART II

Gods of Arms

"With the Might as of a Deity"

34

The great world event of the autumn of 1889 was Stanley's return after a three-year expedition into the interior of Africa. Stanley had saved Emin Pasha from the Dervishes.[21]

"The Dervishes" was the nickname of an Islamic movement that successfully resisted the English in the Sudan. The Mahdists, as they were also called, took Khartoum in January 1885. Relief arrived two days too late to save General Gordon. It was the most humiliating defeat the British Empire suffered in Africa.

But at the end of 1886, a courier reached Zanzibar with the message that one of Gordon's provincial governors, Emin Pasha, was still holding out in the remote interior of Sudan and was requesting relief.

The government hesitated, but some large companies made Emin Pasha's situation an excuse to equip an expedition, the main aim of which was to turn Emin's province into a company-ruled British colony.

Stanley was asked to take command. The man who saved Livingstone was to crown his career by repeating the exploit. "Dr. Emin, I presume."

35

But like Huckleberry Finn when he saved Jim, Stanley thought it too simple just to go straight on up to Emin and give him the arms and ammunition he had requested.

Instead, he led the expedition from Zanzibar, rounding the whole of Africa to the mouth of the Congo, past the steaming waterfalls, up to the navigable upper stretch of the river. There, with the help of King Leopold's boats and the slave hunter Tippu Tip's bearers, he hoped to be able to ship hundreds of tons of military matériel from the Congo to Sudan through Ituri, the much-feared "forest of death," where as yet no white man had set foot.

There were, of course, no boats. There were no bearers. Stanley had to leave most of the military matériel behind in the Congo and hurry on himself with an advance force.

Stanley was stocky, lower-class, as muscular as a garbageman and scarred by years and experience. As his deputy he chose an elegant young aristocrat, Major Bartellot, soft as silk, handsome as a lush tenor—but with no experience of Africa. Why?

Stanley detested the English upper class and measured himself by it. Perhaps he hoped to see such an upper-class creature broken by the jungle, see him lose his fine manner, lose his superior confidence, his self-control, thus throwing greater light on Stanley's own capacity as a man and leader.

Bartellot was indeed broken. Left behind as leader of the rear guard, he tried in vain to keep discipline with terrible daily floggings. His racism flourished, he became more and more isolated and hated, and was finally killed.

36

Meanwhile Stanley is struggling on in the suffocating heat, moisture dripping from the trees, sweat soaking clothing, hunger a torment, diarrhea, festering sores, and rats gnawing at sleeping men's feet.

The inhabitants of the forest are frightened. They refuse to trade or act as guides. Stanley has no time for anything else but violence. To acquire food for his expedition, he murders defenseless people on their way to market and shoots unarmed men in order to get their canoes.

Perhaps that was necessary to get there. But was it necessary to get there? Everyone had advised him against taking the route he did. Only his own aspirations required that he should do the impossible, which in its turn required murder—murder to acquire a goat or a few bunches of bananas.

Shackleton, explorer of the South Pole, was not so vain. Rather than sacrifice lives, he swallowed his pride and turned back. Stanley goes on leaving heaps of corpses in his wake.

One of the most horrific scenes: Stanley has a young bearer hanged for "desertion." The bearers had taken on the job of marching across East Africa's dry savanna. Stanley had taken them into this dripping primeval forest, where half of them had already died. He's only a boy, hungry and a long way from home, the others plead. But Stanley is unrelenting. He could not afford, he thought, to show the slightest sign of weakness now.

He was possibly right in that. But he had deliberately put himself in a situation in which killing was the only way out.

Ragged, starving, evil-smelling, tormented by fever and boils, stumbling at every step, the survivors finally reach the shores of Lake Albert.

Emin arrives with his steamer to receive them. He is wearing his dazzling white uniform. He is in good health, calm, rested. He brings with him cloth, blankets, soap, tobacco, and provisions for his rescuer. Just who is rescuing whom?

37

The Mahdists have left Emin's distant province in peace for five years. But rumors of Stanley's expedition challenge them to attack. Stanley returns to the Congo to fetch the rest of the expedition. The Mahdists immediately conquer the whole province except the capital, where Emin's men mutiny.

Soon the only hope is for Stanley to return and halt the disaster he himself has triggered off. Day after day, they all wait impatiently for Stanley to arrive with machine guns, rifles, and ammunition.

Instead, Stanley again comes stumbling in the lead of a bunch of skeletons shaking with fever. They have lost the arms and ammunition and are scarcely in a state to defend themselves, far less to overcome ten thousand screaming Dervishes.

Nevertheless, Emin wants to stay. He pleads with Stanley to let him return to his province and try to defend it. But Stanley cannot allow that. For in that way his own failure would have been far too obvious. He had not been able to provide anything Emin had requested, and he had simply made the situation worse.

But by taking Emin with him to the coast, even if by force, Stanley hoped to decide just what news was to be telegraphed all over the world. "Emin saved!" Emin was the trophy that was to turn Stanley's defeat into a media victory.

The coup succeeded. It was the only thing in the whole expedition that did succeed—getting the general public to rejoice.

In the moment of triumph, no one was interested in examining the details. Stanley had once again done what no one else had been able to do. That became an established fact in the minds of the public. So the victory was at least for the moment a reality—whatever it had cost, whatever it actually contained.

38

When the unemployed sea captain Korzeniowski, whom we know as Joseph Conrad, came to Brussels in November 1889, to be interviewed by Albert Thys, the director of Société Belge du Haut-Congo, the city was in the throes of Stanley-fever. It was known that Stanley was on his way to the coast, but he still had not arrived.

On December 4, when Stanley triumphantly brought Emin to Bagamoyo, Conrad was back in London. The press hummed for weeks with homage to the great hero of civilization.

In January 1890, Stanley arrived in Cairo, where he started writing his version of the story of the expedition. For the first time in sixteen years, Conrad returned to Poland and spent two months in his childhood Kazimierowka.

Meanwhile Stanley had finished *In Darkest Africa* and returned to Europe.

On April 20, he went to Brussels, where he was met with ovationlike tributes. At King Leopold's welcoming banquet, all four corners of the hall were decorated with a pyramid of flowers from

The noble Emin Pasha, as he looked while everyone was awaiting his rescue. *Illustrated London News*, November 30, 1889

which hundreds of elephant tusks protruded. The festivities went on for five days.

Meanwhile Conrad was on his way back from Poland. He arrived in Brussels on the 29th, while the Stanley festivities were still on everyone's lips. He met Albert Thys and was appointed and ordered to leave at once for the Congo. Conrad went on to London, where he made preparations for his Congo trip while the Stanley celebrations were at a pitch.

Stanley had arrived in Dover on April 26. He was taken by special train to London, where a huge crowd was waiting. On May 3, he spoke in St. James's Hall to thousands of people, including the royal family. He was awarded honorary degrees by both Oxford and Cambridge. Then countrywide celebrations took place.

Conrad was not present for all of them. On May 6, when Stanley was received in audience by Queen Victoria, Conrad returned to Brussels, and on May 10 he boarded a ship for Africa.

39

Conrad was on his way to Stanley's Africa.

Stanley was sixteen years older than Conrad. Like Conrad, he had grown up motherless. Like Conrad, he had been adopted by a benevolent father figure. Conrad was fourteen when Stanley found Livingstone and became world famous. At fifteen, Conrad ran away to sea, just as Stanley had done. Like Stanley, Conrad changed his name, his home country, and his identity.

Now with all the homage still echoing in his ears, he was on his way to Stanley's Congo—knowing nothing about the murky reality behind the Stanley legend.

40

On June 28, 1890 (the same day Conrad left Matadi at the mouth of the Congo to set off on foot to Stanleyville further upriver), Stanley's *In Darkest Africa* came out.

The book was an enormous success and sold 150,000 copies.

But it did not attract only flattering attention. Bartellot's father published his son's diaries to defend him against Stanley. During the autumn, all the European participants in the expedition published their own versions of what had happened. In November and December 1890, while Conrad was seriously ill in an African village, the English newspapers almost daily printed articles for and against Stanley.

During his eight months in Africa, Conrad found that reality differed glaringly from the grandiose speeches he had heard before his departure. When he returned to London at the New Year, 1891, sick and disillusioned, even opinion at home had begun to shift.

The discussion continued all through 1891. The most careful and detailed criticism was made by Fox Bourne in *The Other Side of the Emin Pasha Expedition* (1891). When everything had been said, a great silence settled over Stanley and his expedition, most of all about Emin Pasha.

41

In Africa Stanley had already discovered to his alarm that the man for whom he had sacrificed so many lives was no noble pasha but a stubborn Jew from Silesia.

Stanley was able to make Emin go with him, but could not make him appear in public. Emin protested during the return journey by maintaining total silence. During the actual welcoming banquet in Bagamoyo, he disappeared unnoticed from the table and was found on the paving stones below the balcony with his skull cracked. He was taken to the hospital while Stanley continued on his triumphal procession.

When, in April 1890, Stanley was being honored in Brussels and London as Emin's savior, Emin lay forgotten in a hospital in Bagamoyo. One night, he slipped out and, half-blind and half-deaf, started walking back to "his" province.

By October 1892, the Stanley fever in Europe was definitely over. By then Emin had also managed to get back home. The Dervishes found him and cut his throat.

A few years previously, his "rescue" had aroused hysterical attention in Europe. Now his death went unnoticed.

42

Six years later, in October 1898, George Schweizer's *Emin Pasha, His life and work, compiled from his journals, letters, scientific notes and from official documents* was published in London. In it the story of Emin was told for the first time from his own point of view.

The book was advertised and reviewed exhaustively through October and November. In December, Conrad sat down to write *Heart of Darkness*.

Just as Stanley traveled up the Congo to rescue Emin, in Conrad's story Marlow travels up the river to rescue Kurtz. But Kurtz does not wish to be rescued. He disappears into the darkness and tries to creep back to "his" people. Emin had also done that.

Kurtz is no portrait of Emin. On the contrary, everything sympathetic in Emin can be found in Marlow, the rescuer in Conrad's story. The monster is Kurtz, the man to be saved, who resembles Stanley.

Stanley also had an "intended," Dolly, who was told the untruth she desired. Just as the whole of the white world was told the lies they desired.

When Marlow lies to Kurtz's "intended" at the end of Conrad's story, he not only does what Stanley himself did, but also what official Britain and the general public were doing while Conrad was writing the story. They were lying.

43

History loves repetition. In the autumn of 1898, Stanley returned for a second time, now under the name of Kitchener.[22]

General Horatio Herbert Kitchener, called "the Sirdar," had done what Stanley had not managed to do. He had defeated the Dervishes and "saved" Sudan.

On October 27, 1898, he arrived in Dover. Just as when Stanley

THE DARK SIDE OF CAMPAIGNING IN THE SOUDAN: DESPATCHING WOUNDED DERVISHES

Above: "The Dark Side of the Sudanese Campaign: The Liquidation of Wounded Dervishes." Below: "The Reason." *The Graphic*, October 1, 1898

returned, great crowds had gathered to honor him. Just like Stanley, he was taken in a special train to London and granted an audience with Queen Victoria. At the welcoming luncheon, he maintained that the victory over the Dervishes had opened the whole length of the Nile valley "to the civilizing influences of commercial enterprise."

That was precisely what Stanley had said about the Congo River.

The following five weeks became a whirl of celebrations. In Cambridge, where Stanley had received his honorary degree, Kitchener received his on November 24. Some academics who had opposed the award were thrown fully clothed into the river while fireworks were let off in honor of the Sirdar. He went on to Edinburgh, where he received an honorary degree on November 28. Then countrywide celebrations took place.

A more exact copy of Stanley's return could hardly have been achieved. In the same issue of the newspaper that advertised and reviewed the book on Emin Pasha's journals, the book that showed how hollow the delirium had been the previous time—in the same issue the rejoicing of the people again resounded, cheers ringing out and empty phrases echoing.

Few questioned the victory at Omdurman. Few wondered how it came about that eleven thousand Sudanese were killed while the British lost only forty-eight men. No one asked why few or none survived of the sixteen thousand wounded Sudanese.[23]

But at Pent Farm in Kent, a Polish writer in exile interrupted the novel he was writing and instead started writing the story about Kurtz.

44

I go out into the sun, and as I draw breath, the hot air rushes into my mouth just as food often did when I was small and in far too much of a hurry to wait until it had cooled. Where now is that glass of cold milk that every breath demands?

45

At the battle of Omdurman, the entire Sudanese army was annihilated without once having got their enemy within gunshot.

The art of killing from a distance became a European specialty very early on. The arms race between coastal states of Europe in the seventeenth century created fleets that were capable of achieving strategic goals far away from the home country. Their cannons could shatter hitherto impregnable fortresses and were even more effective against defenseless villages.

Preindustrial Europe had little that was in demand in the rest of the world. Our most important export was force. All over the rest of the world, we were regarded at the time as nomadic warriors in the style of the Mongols and the Tartars. They reigned supreme from the backs of horses, we from the decks of ships.[24]

Our cannons met little resistance among the peoples who were more advanced than we were. The Moguls in India had no ships able to withstand artillery fire or carry heavy guns. Instead of building up a fleet, the Moguls chose to purchase defense services from European states, which thus were soon in a position to take over the part of rulers in India.

The Chinese had discovered gunpowder in the tenth century and had cast the first cannon in the middle of the thirteenth. But they felt so safe in their part of the world that, from the middle of the sixteenth century onward, they refrained from participating in the naval arms race.

Thus the backward and poorly resourced Europe of the sixteenth century acquired a monopoly on oceangoing ships with guns capable of spreading death and destruction across huge distances. Europeans became the gods of cannons that killed long before the weapons of their opponents could reach them.

Three hundred years later, those gods had conquered a third of the world. Ultimately, their realm rested on the power of their ships' guns.

46

But most of the inhabited world at the beginning of the nineteenth century lay out of reach of naval artillery.

So it was a discovery of great military significance when Robert Fulton got the first steam-driven boat to head up the Hudson River. Soon hundreds of steamers were to be found on the rivers of Europe. In the middle of the nineteenth century, steamers started carrying European cannons deep into the interior of Asia and Africa. With that a new epoch in the history of imperialism was introduced.[25]

This became a new epoch in the history of racism. Too many Europeans interpreted military superiority as intellectual and even biological superiority.

Nemesis is the name of the Greek goddess of revenge, the punisher of pride and arrogance. With profound historical irony, that was the name of the first steamer in 1842 to tow British warships up the Yellow River and the Great Canal in the direction of Peking.

Soon steamers were no longer used as tugs of the fleet, but were equipped with artillery of their own. The "gunboat" became a symbol of imperialism on all the major African rivers—the Nile, the Niger, and the Congo—making it possible for Europeans to control huge, hitherto inaccessible areas by force of arms.

The steamer was portrayed as a bearer of light and righteousness. If the creator of the steam engine in his heaven is able to look down on the success of his discovery here on earth, wrote Macgregor Laird in *Narrative of an Expedition into the Interior of Africa by the River Niger* (1837), then hardly any application of it would give him greater satisfaction than to see hundreds of steamers "carrying the glad tidings of 'peace and goodwill toward men' to the dark places of the earth which are now filled with cruelty."

That was the official rhetoric. At Omdurman it was demonstrated that the gunboat also had the ability to annihilate its opponents from a safe distance.

47

Until the middle of the nineteenth century, small arms in the third world were able to measure up to those of Europe. The standard weapon was a muzzle-loaded, smooth-bored flintlock musket, which was also manufactured by village smiths in Africa.

The musket was a frightening weapon for those hearing it for the first time. But its range was only a hundred yards. It took at least a minute to load the gun between each shot. Even in dry weather, three shots out of ten failed, and in wet weather the muskets ceased functioning altogether.

A skilled archer still fired more quickly, more surely, and further. He was inferior only in his ability to shoot through armor.

So the colonial wars of the first half of the nineteenth century were lengthy and expensive. Although the French had an army of a hundred thousand men in Algeria, they advanced only very slowly, as the arms of the infantry on both sides were quite comparable.

But with the percussion cap came a musket that failed only five shots in a thousand, and then accuracy improved with grooved barrels.

In 1853, the British began replacing their old muskets with Enfield rifles, effective at a range of five hundred yards and firing more quickly because the bullet was enclosed in a paper cartridge. The French brought in a similar rifle. Both were used first in the colonies.

But these weapons were still slow and difficult to handle. They emitted puffs of smoke, which revealed where the marksman was, and the sensitive paper cartridges absorbed the damp. The soldier also had to stand up while reloading.

Prussia replaced its muzzle loaders with the breech-loaded Dreyse rifle. This was tested for the first time in 1866 in the Prusso-Austrian war over hegemony in Germany. During the battle of Sadowa, the Prussians lay on the ground and with their Dreyse rifles fired seven shots in the time it took the Austrians, standing up, to load and fire one shot. The outcome was obvious.

A race now began between European states to replace muskets

with breech loaders. The British developed the paper cartridge into a brass cartridge, which protected the gunpowder during transport, kept in the smoke fumes when the shot was fired, and hurled the bullet three times as far as the Dreyse rifle did.

In 1869, the British abandoned the Enfield and went over to the Martini-Henry, the first really good weapon of the new generation: swift, accurate, insensitive to damp and jolts. The French came next with their Gras rifle, and the Prussians with the Mauser.

Thus Europeans were superior to every conceivable opponent from other continents. The gods of arms conquered another third of the world.

48

The new arms made it possible even for a lone European traveler in Africa to practice almost unlimited brutality and go unpunished. The founder of the German East Africa colony, Carl Peters, describes in *New Light on Dark Africa* (1891) how he forced the Vagogo people into submission.

The chieftain's son came to Peters's camp and placed himself "quite unembarrassed" in the entrance of Peters's tent. "At my order to remove himself, he only replied with a wide grin and, quite untroubled, remained where he was."

Peters then has him flogged with the hippo whip. At his screams, the Vagogo warriors come racing in to try to free him. Peters fires "into the heap" and kills one of them.

Half an hour later, the Sultan sends a messenger requesting peace. Peters's reply: "The Sultan shall have peace, but eternal peace. I shall show the Vagogo what the Germans are! Plunder the villages, throw fire into the houses, and smash everything that will not burn."

The houses turned out to be difficult to burn and had to be destroyed with axes. Meanwhile the Vagogo gather and try to defend their homes. Peters says to his men:

"I shall show you what kind of mob we have here before us. Stay here, and alone I shall put the Vagogo to flight."

With these words, I walked toward them shouting hurrah, and hundreds of them ran like a flock of sheep.

I do not mention this in any way to make out our own circumstances as anything heroic, but only to show what kind of people these Africans in general are and what exaggerated ideas people in Europe have of their fighting abilities and the means required for their suppression.

At about three, I marched further south toward the other villages. The same spectacle everywhere! After brief resistance, the Vagogo took flight, torches were thrown into the houses, and axes worked to destroy all that the fire did not achieve. So by half past four twelve villages had been burned down. . . . My gun had become so hot from so much firing I could hardly hold it.

Before Peters leaves the villages, he has the Vagogo told that now they know him a little better. He intends to stay as long as any one of them is still alive, any village is still standing, and any ox remains to be taken away.

The Sultan then asks to hear the conditions for peace.

"Tell the Sultan I do not wish for any peace with him. The Vagogo are liars and must be eliminated from the earth. But if the Sultan wishes to be slave to the Germans, then he and his people may possibly be allowed to live."

At dawn, the Sultan sends thirty-six oxen and other gifts. "I then persuaded myself to grant him a treaty in which he was placed under German supremacy."

With the aid of these new weapons, colonial conquests became unprecedentedly cost-effective. In many cases, expenses were largely limited to the cartridges needed for the killings.

Carl Peters was appointed German commissioner over the areas he had conquered. In the spring of 1897, he was brought to court in Berlin. His trial caused a scandal and received a great deal of attention even in the British press. He was found guilty of the murder of a black mistress. What was actually being condemned was not the murder but the sexual relationship. The innumerable murders

Peters had committed during the conquest of the German East Africa colony were considered quite natural and went unpunished.[26]

49

A new generation of weapons quickly followed: rifles with repeater mechanisms. In 1885, the Frenchman Paul Vieille discovered nitroglycerin, which exploded without smoke or ash, and this meant the soldiers could remain invisible as they fired. Other advantages were its greater explosive effect and relative insensitivity to damp. The musket's caliber, nineteen millimeters, could be reduced to eight millimeters, which dramatically increased the accuracy of the weapon.

The automatic rifle also came with the smokeless nitroglycerin. Hiram S. Maxim manufactured an automatic weapon that was light to carry and fired eleven bullets a second. The British supplied their colonial troops with automatic weapons early on. They were used against the Ashanti in 1874 and in Egypt in 1884.

At the same time, with the Bessemer method and other new processes, steel had become so cheap, it could be used for the manufacture of arms on a large scale. In Africa and Asia, on the other hand, local smiths could no longer make copies of the new weapons, as they had none of the necessary material, industrially manufactured steel.

At the end of the 1890s, the revolution of the rifle was complete. All European infantrymen could now fire lying down without being spotted, in all weathers, fifteen shots in as many seconds at targets up to a distance of a thousand yards.

The new cartridges were particularly good for use in tropical climates. But, on "savages," the bullet did not always have the desired effect, for they often continued their charges even after being hit four or five times. The answer became the dumdum bullet, named after the factory in Dum Dum outside Calcutta and patented in 1897. The lead core of the dumdum bullet explodes the casing, causing large painful wounds that do not heal well.

The use of dumdum bullets between "civilized" states was

prohibited. They were reserved for big-game hunting and colonial wars.

At Omdurman in 1898 the whole new European arsenal was tested—gunboats, automatic weapons, repeater rifles, and dumdum bullets—against a numerically superior and very determined enemy.

One of the most cheerful depicters of war, Winston Churchill, later winner of the Nobel Prize for Literature, was the war correspondent of *The Morning Post*. He has described the battle in *My Early Life* (1930), the first volume of his autobiography.

50

"Nothing like the battle of Omdurman will ever be seen again," Churchill writes. "It was the last link in the long chain of those spectacular conflicts whose vivid and majestic splendour has done so much to invest war with glamour."

Thanks to steamboats and a newly laid railway line, even out in the desert, Europeans were well supplied with provisions of every kind. Churchill observed

> many bottles of inviting appearance and large dishes of bully beef and mixed pickles. This grateful sight arising as if by enchantment in the wilderness on the verge of battle filled my heart with a degree of thankfulness far exceeding what one usually experiences when regular Grace is said.
>
> I attacked the bully beef and cool drink with concentrated attention. Everyone was in the highest spirits and the best of tempers. It was like a race luncheon before the Derby.
>
> "Is there really going to be a battle?" I asked.
>
> "In an hour or two," replied the General.

Churchill thought it a "good moment to live" and determinedly set about the meal. "Of course we should win. Of course we should mow them down."

But there was no encounter that day. Instead they all concentrated

"They crept up to him on all fours." The Submission of King Prempeh. *Illustrated London News*, February 26, 1896

on the preparations for dinner. A gunboat approached, and the officers, "spotlessly attired in white uniforms," flung ashore a large bottle of champagne. Churchill waded out into the water up to his knees and grabbed the precious gift, then bore it in triumph back to the mess.

> This kind of war was full of fascinating thrills. It was not like the Great War. Nobody expected to be killed. . . . To the great mass of those who took part in the little wars of Britain in those vanished light-hearted days, this was only a sporting element in a splendid game.

51

Unfortunately the British often missed out on their splendid game. Their opponents learned all too quickly that it was pointless to fight against modern weapons. They gave up before the British had the pleasure of wiping them out.

Lord Garnet Wolseley, commander of the British troops in the first Ashanti war in 1874–76, met resistance and really enjoyed himself. "It is only through experience of the sensation that we learn how intense, even in anticipation, is the rapture-giving delight which the attack upon an enemy affords. . . . All other sensations are but as the tinkling of a doorbell in comparison with the throbbing of Big Ben." [27]

The second Ashanti war in 1896 provided no opportunity for experiences of that kind. Two days' march away from the capital, Kumasi, Robert Baden-Powell, the commander of the advance troop, later to found the Boy Scouts, received an envoy offering unconditional surrender.

To his disappointment, Baden-Powell did not fire a single shot at the natives. To get hostilities going, the British planned extreme provocations. The king of Ashanti was arrested together with his whole family. The king and his mother were forced to crawl on all fours up to the British officers sitting on crates of biscuit tins, receiving their subjugation.

The Submission of King Prempeh. The final
humiliation. *The Graphic*, February 29, 1896

In *Heart of Darkness*, Harlequin describes how the natives used
to approach their idol, Kurtz, crawling on all fours. Marlow reacts
violently. He starts back and shouts that he does not want to know
anything about the ceremonies used when approaching Mr. Kurtz.
The thought of the crawling chieftains seems to him even more unbearable than seeing the heads of murdered people drying on poles
around Kurtz's house.

The reaction becomes comprehensible when you see the drawings of the ceremony in Kumasi two years earlier. These drawings
were all over the illustrated press and are an expression of a racist
arrogance that does not flinch from the extreme degradation of its
opponents.

This time the British found no use for their weapons. They re-
turned sadly to the coast. "I thoroughly enjoyed the outing," Baden-
Powell writes to his mother, "except for the want of a fight, which
I fear will preclude our getting any medals or decoration."[28]

"Unspeakable rites." Golgotha, Benin. *Illustrated London News*, March 27, 1897

Crucified human sacrifice from *Benin—The City of Blood* (1897) by R.H. Bacon.

52

Sometimes, however, provocation did succeed.[29]

British consuls at the mouth of the Benin River had for years suggested that the kingdom of Benin should be taken. Trade demanded it, and the expedition would pay for itself by plundering the king of Benin's store of ivory. But the Foreign Office nevertheless regarded it as too expensive.

In November 1896, the suggestion was made again by the temporary consul, Lieutenant Phillips. Provisions and ammunition were ready for the assault scheduled for February–March 1897. On January 7, 1897, the Foreign Office reply arrived. As usual, it was negative.

But to be on the safe side, on January 2, Lieutenant Phillips had already set off with nine other white men and two hundred African bearers on a courtesy visit to the king of Benin.

That first evening he was met by a messenger from Benin who asked him to postpone his visit for a month as the king was occupied with ceremonies before their annual religious festival.

Phillips went on.

The following evening more representatives from Benin came and pleaded with the white men to turn back. Phillips sent the king his stick, a deliberate insult, and went on.

The next day, January 4, eight white men—including Phillips—and their bearers were killed in an ambush. On January 11, the news of "the Benin Disaster" reached London. The press raged and demanded revenge. The attack on Benin that Lieutenant Phillips had planned in November, but had been turned down in January, was now put into action as a punitive expedition in revenge for his death.

Despite stiff resistance, the British captured Benin City on February 18. The town was plundered and burned to the ground.

How many Benin inhabitants were killed by the British troops was never investigated. Instead, the human sacrifices by the Benin king were sensationally exaggerated in the illustrated magazines. Skulls glowing like wood anemones on the ground were clearly evidence that no inhabitant of Benin ever died a natural death. In Captain R.H. Bacon's book, *Benin—The City of Blood* (1897), the crucified who hung with ripped-open bellies were the real reason for civilization conquering Benin.

What is certain is that, when the first readers of Joseph Conrad's *Heart of Darkness* read two years later that Kurtz had allowed himself to be worshipped as a god and participated in "unspeakable rites," it was the pictures from Benin that readers saw in their mind's eye; then they remembered descriptions of the stench of mass graves into which the dead and living were thrown together and of the idols covered with dried blood.

These "idols" are today reckoned to be outstanding masterpieces of world art. But the press accounts of Benin as the special hell of the dark races were so powerful, the British could not see the artistic value of the sculptures. They were sold in London as curios to pay for the cost of the punitive expedition. German museums bought them cheaply.

53

What did the king of Benin feel as he was hunted like a wild animal in the forests while his capital was going up in flames? What did the king of Ashanti feel as he crawled up to kiss the boots of his British overlords?

No one asked them. No one listened to those whom the weapons of the gods subjugated. Only very rarely do we hear them speak.

At the end of the 1880s, the British South Africa Company advanced from the south into Matabeleland in today's Zimbabwe. In 1894, the Matabelele people were conquered. The company shared their grazing lands out to white agents and adventurers, reduced their herds of cattle from two hundred thousand head to fourteen thousand and prohibited all arms. White death patrols ruled with martial law, labor was forcibly recruited, and anyone who protested was immediately shot.

The rebellion comes in 1896. The company calls in British

troops. Baden-Powell is with them, pleased "to have a go" at last against an enemy "without much capacity to inflict damage on trained soldiers." In the very first battle, he and his troops kill two hundred "natives" at the cost of one dead European.[30]

It had become easy and amusing to kill, but in this case still too expensive. The army was there at the request of the company and received payment for their military services. After a few months of fighting, the company was on the verge of bankruptcy. In order to bring about peace, on August 21, Cecil Rhodes and other white leaders were for the first time forced to listen to the black Africans.

54

"I once visited Bulawayo," said Somabulano.

> I came to pay my respects to the Chief Magistrate. I brought my indunas with me, and my servants. I am a chief. I am expected to travel with attendants and advisers. I came to Bulawayo early in the morning, before the sun had dried the dew and I sat down before the Court House, sending messages to the Chief Magistrate that I waited to pay my respects to him. And so I sat until the evening shadows were long. And then . . . I sent again to the Chief Magistrate and told him that I did not wish to hurry him in any unmannerly way; I would wait his pleasure; but my people were hungry; and when white men came to see me it was my custom to kill that they might eat. The answer that came from the Chief Magistrate . . . was that the town was full of stray dogs; dog to dog; we might kill those and eat if we could catch them.

Lord Grey's priest, Father Bihler, was convinced that the blacks had to be exterminated. "He states that the only chance for the future of the race is to exterminate the whole people, both male and female over the age of fourteen," Grey writes to his wife on January 23, 1897.

He himself did not wish to accept such a pessimistic conclusion. But the idea of extermination was near to hand, produced again and again in the white man's press.

African leaders were quite aware of the risk of their people being exterminated. Somabulano himself took up the threat of extermination in his speech at the peace negotiations: "You came, you conquered. The strongest takes the land. We accepted your rule. We lived under you. But not as dogs! If we are to be dogs it is better to be dead. You can never make the Amandabele dogs. You may wipe them out. But the Children of the Stars can never be dogs."[31]

55

At Omdurman, the strongest African military resistance was crushed. The battle can best be followed in the book Churchill wrote immediately after the experience, *The River War* (1899). The morning of September 2, 1898, the following occurred:

> The white flags were nearly over the crest. In another minute they would become visible to the batteries. Did they realise what would come to meet them? They were in a dense mass, 2,800 yards from the 32nd Field Battery and the gunboats. The ranges were known. It was a matter of machinery. . . .
>
> The mind was fascinated by the impending horror. I could see it coming. In a few seconds swift destruction would rush on these brave men. They topped the crest and drew out into full view of the whole army. Their white banners made them conspicuous above all. As they saw the camp of their enemies, they discharged their rifles with a great roar of musketry and quickened their pace. . . . For a moment the white flags advanced in regular order, and the whole division crossed the crest and were exposed.
>
> About twenty shells struck them in the first minute. Some burst high in the air, others exactly in their faces. Others, again, plunged into the sand, and, exploding, dashed clouds of red dust, splinters, and bullets amid the ranks. The

The Battle of Omdurman. "The maxims and infantry annihilated them. Whole battalions vanished under the withering fire." *The Graphic*, September 24, 1898

white flags toppled over in all directions. Yet they rose again immediately, as other men pressed forward to die for the Mahdis' sacred cause and in defence of the successor of the True Prophet of the Only God. It was a terrible sight, for as yet they had not hurt us at all, and it seemed an unfair advantage to strike thus cruelly when they could not reply.

The outmoded character of this description is particularly evident in the last sentence. An old-fashioned concept of honor and fair play, an admiration for such pointless bravery, had still not been superseded by the modern understanding that technical superiority provides a natural right to annihilate the enemy even when he is defenseless.

56

Eight hundred yards away a ragged line of men was coming on desperately in the face of the pitiless fire, Churchill goes on. White banners tossing and collapsing, white figures subsiding in dozens . . .

The infantrymen fired steadily and stolidly, without hurry or excitement, for the enemy were far away . . . Besides, the soldiers were interested in the work and took great pains. But presently the mere physical act became tedious.

The rifles grew hot—so hot they had to be exchanged for those of the reserve companies. The Maxim guns exhausted all the water in their jackets. . . . The empty cartridge cases, tinkling to the ground, soon formed small but growing heaps round each man.

And all the time out on the plain on the other side the bullets were shearing through flesh, smashing and splintering bone; blood spouted from terrible wounds; valiant men were struggling on through a hell of whistling metal, exploding shells and spurting dust—suffering, despairing, dying.

Churchill's empathy with the opponents' situation was not concerned with an enemy in wild flight away from there. This concerned a still attacking enemy who, if not stopped, in a short while would have shown themselves to be superior. The Caliph had put fifteen thousand men into this frontal assault. Churchill finds the plan of attack wise and well thought-out except on one vital point; it was based on a fatal underestimation of the effectiveness of modern weapons.

Meanwhile the great Dervish army, which had advanced at sunrise in hope and courage, fled in utter rout, pursued by the 21st Lancers, and leaving more than 9,000 warriors dead and even greater numbers of wounded behind them.

Thus ended the battle of Omdurman—the most signal triumph ever gained by the arms of science over barbarians.

The Battle of Omdurman. The picture portrays the battle
as man-to-man combat—but no Sudanese got closer than
three hundred yards from the British positions.

Within the space of five hours, the strongest and best-armed savage army yet arrayed against a modern European Power had been destroyed and dispersed, with hardly any difficulty, comparatively small risk and insignificant loss to the victors.

57

For a few weeks in October, 1898, it looked as if the victory at Omdurman would lead to a major European war.[32] The French had dug in at the little outpost of Fashoda south of Omdurman and demanded a share of the booty Kitchener had gained. Day after day the patriotic press in both countries showed off their biggest guns, while Europe slid nearer and nearer to the precipice.

But finally, on November 4, at a major gala dinner in London at which Kitchener received the signia of victory (a gold sword in monstrous bad taste), the news came that the French had given way. The Fashoda crisis was over. Great Britain remained the undisputed superpower, and the great poet of imperialism, Rudyard Kipling, wrote

> Take up the white man's burden
> Send forth the best ye breed
> Go bind your sons to exile
> To serve your captives' need[33]

58

While Kipling was writing "The White Man's Burden," Joseph Conrad was writing *Heart of Darkness*. That leading expression of imperialist ideology appeared at the same time as its opposite pole in the world of writing. Both works were created under the influence of the battle of Omdurman.

Already in *An Outcast of the Islands* (1896), Conrad had described what it felt like to be shot at by naval guns. Around Babalatchi, the ground is slippery with blood, the houses in flames, women screaming, children crying, the dying gasping for breath. They die helpless, "stricken down before they could see their enemy." Their courage is in vain against an invisible and unreachable opponent.

The invisibility of the attackers is remembered far later in the novel by one of the survivors: "First they came, the invisible whites, and dealt death from afar. . . ."

Few Western writers have described with greater empathy the helpless rage when faced with superior forces killing without having to go ashore, victorious without even being present.

That novel had just been published when the battle of Omdurman was taking place. In *Heart of Darkness*, written during the patriotic delirium after Kitchener's homecoming, Conrad opens the imperial toolbox and one after another examines what the historian Daniel R. Headrick calls "the tools of imperialism": The ship's guns that fire on a continent. The railway that is to ease the plundering of the continent. The river steamer that carries Europeans and their arms into the heart of the continent. "Thunderbolts of Jupiter" carried in procession behind Kurtz's stretcher: two shotguns, a heavy rifle, and a light revolver-carbine. Winchester and Martini-Henry rifles spurting metal at the Africans on the shore.

"Say! We must have made a glorious slaughter of them in the bush. Eh? What d'you think? Say?" Marlow hears the whites saying.

"We approach them with the might as of a deity," Kurtz writes in his report to the International Society for the Suppression of Savage Customs. He means the weapons. They provided divine power.

In Kipling's verse, the imperial task is an ethical imperative. That is also how it is depicted by Kurtz, who surrounds himself in a cloud of Kiplingesque rhetoric. Only in a footnote to his torrent do we see what the task truly is, for Kurtz as well as for Kitchener, at the Inner Station as well as at Omdurman: "Exterminate all the brutes."

To Tam

59

The buses that ply the four hundred miles between In Salah and Tamanrasset are rebuilt Mercedes trucks painted orange, to be visible in the swirl of sand. The passenger compartment on the back is like a diving bell with small peepholes instead of windows. It is hideously hot and cramped inside, and there is no question of anything like springs—you have to bring them with you in your own body.

I am frightened, as usual. But when departure finally cannot be postponed any longer, as I stand there at dawn with my heavy pack, crouching before the leap—then I am again elated at being where I am.

The Sahara lies spread out before me like a fireman's canvas sheet. All I have to do is to jump.

The day starts among white dunes, exquisite and conical like whipped cream. Sand-worn roadsigns with almost eradicated symbols. As the road changes direction, the sand also changes color—white dunes become ash gray, yellow, red, brown, even black when the light comes from another quarter.

Then the first mountains appear, coal black, purple, scorched. They are badly weathered, surrounded by masses of fallen rock resembling slag raked out of some immense forge. Occasional tamarisks, mostly withered and dead. The driver gets down and collects them for the fire that night.

The bus stops for the night in Arrak, where there is a small café calling itself a restaurant and hotel. You sleep two by two in straw huts on mattresses directly on the sand.

60

On the map it looks as if the road would improve after Arrak, but it is the same turgid grinding in first gear, second, or four-wheel drive. You drive straight into the desert within a track area about a kilometer wide, all the time searching for the most navigable in a tangle of tracks.

Now and again huge plumes of smoke from other vehicles appear on the horizon. Toward midday the smoke mixes with the clouds of sand the evening wind blows up. They surround the setting sun with a thick mist through which occasional mountains and tamarisks can be seen outlined.

The rocks are ancient, their shapes often like vertebrae fallen from the spine of a mountain. Nearer to Tam, inside the Ahaggar massif, the peaks are higher, the core of the mountains offering greater resistance—but even there the landscape testifies most of all to the terrible power of the forces of erosion.

You travel for miles through a desert of shards, searching for a reality that has been irretrievably shattered.

I start back when I catch sight of my face in the mirror. Even I have been exposed to eroding forces, sun and wind, heat and cold, those that make the mountains fall to pieces.

61

Tam is the focal point of southern Algeria, an international town in close contact with neighboring Niger and Mali owing to transit traffic, streams of refugees, and smuggled goods.

European desert expeditions and tourists—all come to Tam sooner or later; and all get lost in the corridors of Hotel Tahat.

Its architect had an exaggerated preference for symmetry. The hotel has sixteen precisely identical points at which precisely identical corridors radiate out to the four points of the compass.

When Reception shouts that they have La Suède on the phone, I rush round in the labyrinth like an overstimulated lab rat until I finally come out at the right place, panting for breath; on the telephone I can hear my own gasps, vastly exaggerated, being thrown between relay stations in Ouargla, Algiers, and Paris. Wiped out by these huge reverberations, my daughter's voice disappears and grows fainter than a whisper. I finally have to give up, overpowered by my own echo.

One of the cleaners has a small child with her, and she puts it down on the stone floor in the broom cupboard, then goes to work. The child cries ceaselessly from eight in the morning until late afternoon, by which time it is so exhausted it can manage only a few pitiful whimpers.

If an adult lay crying so tortured as that, how long would it be before anyone reacted? But children—children cry, everyone knows that. Everyone seems to think it perfectly natural.

62

It is on your back you feel the loss.

Your front can keep up appearances. If nothing else, your face can face itself in the mirror. It's the nape of your neck that is lonely.

You can embrace your stomach and roll yourself round it. But your back remains, alone.

That is why sirens and djinns are portrayed with hollowed-out backs—no one ever presses a warm stomach from behind against them. The carving chisel of loneliness works there instead.

You don't meet loneliness. It comes from behind and catches up with us.

63

Conrad lost his mother when he was seven and his father when he was eleven. He emigrated from Poland to France, from France to England. He served on sixteen different ships. Every time he changed country or ship, he had to find new friends or remain lonely.

Then he exchanged the loneliness of the seaman for that of the writer. His wife was his housekeeper. It was in his friends he sought sympathy and confirmation.

One of Conrad's oldest English friends was called Hope and lived in a small village called Stanford-le-Hope. After his marriage, Conrad moved with his wife to Stanford-le-Hope to be near his friend.

Marlow tells the story about Kurtz to a small circle of four friends. That kind of circle was just what Conrad longed for all his life. In 1898, he thought he had at last found it.

As he sat down to write *Heart of Darkness*, he had just left Stanford-le-Hope and moved to Pent Farm in Kent. With that, he also moved into a circle of writer friends who lived quite near to each other. They are all there as invisible listeners to Marlow's story.

64

I have rigged up a table to start work, but am having great problems with the dust invading the disks. Tamanrasset is as dry as an early spring day in Peking. Swirling dry and windy, the town is constantly shrouded in a cloud of its own dust.

Just as the Peking wind brings with it the Gobi, this wind brings with it the Sahara—the same desert that runs on through Libya and Egypt, through the Middle East and Iran, Baluchistan and Afghanistan up to Sinkiang and on from there to the Gobi. All those millions of square miles of dust show a definite inclination to make their way to Tamanrasset and collect right there on my disks.

Clusters of animals and people are incessantly on their way across the dried-out riverbed that is Tam's equivalent of Hyde Park. Weary camels lower their heads and blow at the dust to see if it conceals anything edible, and patient goats graze pieces of paper. Women come with their burdens, not on their hips as in In Salah, but on their heads. Groups of boys drift around, every step tearing up a cloud.

But Tam has a specialty. It has a road—indeed, a motorway—on which if necessary you would be able to make your way across the riverbed with polished shoes. It is reserved for the army.

An officer comes across this bridge on his way to the post office, four men with him in white lace-up boots and white helmets, the chinstraps under their noses. Outside the post office they march on the spot while he walks past the queue, demands a stamp, and sticks it on. Then six steps forward and another spell in neutral as he mails the letter—at which they all march on with the same solemn expression of satisfaction.

65

The barber's in Tam has a poster of Elvis in its window and another of the Algerian national football team. I read Wells and listen to Algerian radio while I wait my turn.

Afterward, I slowly return to the hotel, zigzagging between the shadows. I think I know how I shall go on.

When Conrad was writing *Heart of Darkness*, he was not only influenced by the Congo debate, Kitchener's return, and other events of the day. He was also influenced by a literary world, a world of words, in which Kipling was the rival and the opposite pole, but several other writers meant more to him: Henry James, Stephen Crane, Ford Madox Ford, and, most of all H.G. Wells and R.B. Cunningham Graham.[34]

The Friends

66

The time traveler in H.G. Wells's *The Time Machine* (1895) takes us with him into a future world in which the human family has divided itself into two species: the weak flower children of the upper world and the dark creatures of the underworld, the "morlocks."

It is as if Dr. Jekyll and Mr. Hyde had bred and created two different families, each of which populates the future. As if superego and alter ego had been separated and each created a people of his own. As if the working classes of "darkest England" had been forced down below the earth and had created another race there. As if the inhabitants of "darkest Africa" had lived an underground life in the actual heart of the empire.

Of these potential interpretations, the last-mentioned is the one to carry the story on: the morlocks turn out to be cannibals, and they have the power. The beautiful people on the surface are simply fattened cattle the cannibals capture, slaughter, and eat.

Hatred and fear seize the traveler. He longs to kill morlocks. He wants to go straight into the darkness, "killing the brutes."

This killing in Wells is both horrific and voluptuous. The time traveler falls asleep as he sits there in the darkness, and when he wakes the morlocks are onto him, soft and repugnant. He shakes "the human rats" off him and starts striking out. He enjoys the feeling of a swishing iron pipe smashing into juicy flesh and crushing bones . . .

67

The leading philosopher of the day was Herbert Spencer. As a child, he had been very strictly brought up. The principle of this upbringing became for Spencer the innermost secret of life. All living things are forced to progress through punishment. Nature appears to be an immense reformatory in which ignorance and incompetence are punished with poverty, illness, and death.

The time machine is an experiment with Spencer's theory of evolution. The novel shows how mankind, as the time traveler puts it, "commits suicide" by minimizing the pain that is the mother of intelligence and evolution.

Wells's next book, which we know Conrad also read, was called *The Island of Dr. Moreau* (1896). In this, the opposite possibility is investigated: maximizing the pain and thereby hastening evolution.

Dr. Moreau uses his surgical skill to create a kind of human being out of animals. He tortures the animals so that pain will increase the pace of their evolutionary progress: "Each time I dip a living creature into the bath of burning pain, I say, this time I will burn out all the animal, this time I will make a rational creature of my own. After all, what is ten years? Man has been a hundred thousand in the making."

Dr. Moreau has created one hundred and twenty creatures, of which half are dead, but he has not succeeded in creating a real human being. As soon as the doctor takes his hand off the creatures, they revert to bestiality. The animal in them is strongest at night, in the dark. One night, the puma tears itself free and kills its torturer. The monsters rebel and take over power on the island. The narrator sees, day by day, the way they become hairier, their foreheads lower, and they growl instead of speaking.

When he has saved himself and returned back to civilization, he sees the same there. Human beings seem to him to be tormented; animals soon to revert to all fours. He chooses solitude beneath the stars. "It is out there in the starry sky that whatever is more than animal within us must find its solace and its hope. And so, in hope and solitude, my story ends."

The Island of Dr. Moreau can be read as a story of colonialism. Just as the colonizer civilizes the lower, more animal races with the whip, Dr. Moreau civilizes the animals with torture. Just as the colonizer tries to create a new kind of creature, the civilized savage, Dr. Moreau tries to create the humanized animal. In both cases the means is terror. Just like Kurtz, he teaches his created creatures to worship him as a god.

68

In *An Outcast of the Islands*, which Wells reviewed in May 1896, Conrad assembles the criticisms of the colonialists in the image of "the invisible whites," who kill without even being present. Perhaps it was Conrad who inspired Wells to write another story of colonialism, *The Invisible Man* (1897).

This is the story of Kemp, a man who, owing to a much too successful scientific experiment, has made himself invisible and does not know how to get his visibility back again. At first he is desperate about his position, but he soon realizes it can be exploited. As no one can see him, he can commit any outrage he likes without being punished. No one can stop him from killing anyone who resists his reign of terror. Invisibility has made him inhuman.

"He is mad," said Kemp. "Inhuman. He is pure selfishness."

"Pure selfishness" were also the words Conrad chose when he described to his publisher the main theme of *Heart of Darkness*.

The men representing civilization out in the colonies were "invisible" not only in the sense that their guns killed at a distance, but also in that no one at home really knew what they were doing. Cut off from their native country by enormous distances, poor communications, and impenetrable jungles, they exercised imperial power without any control from home.

Charles Dilke had taken up these questions in "Civilisation in Africa" in the summer of 1896. They were discussed in 1897 in connection with some articles in *The Times* by Benjamin Kidd and again in 1898 when the articles came out in book form under the title *Control of the Tropics*. Wells was topical as usual.

Conrad had already taken up this theme when he found it in Dilke and wrote "An Outpost of Progress," about the two rogues who become more and more inhuman when no one can see them. On November 17, 1898, he asked Wells if he would send him *The*

Invisible Man because he had mislaid his own copy. On December 4, he praised it enthusiastically in a letter to Wells, and, at Christmas, Conrad wrote to his young relative Aniela Zagórska and urged her to read it. *The Invisible Man* was one of the books Conrad had just read when he was writing the story of Kurtz.

69

The letter to Zagórska also recommends Wells's most recent book, *The War of the Worlds* (1898). Criticism of colonialism in this book is even more pronounced, perhaps because it was written in the 1897 jubilee year, during the orgy of self-satisfaction the British Empire was indulging in at the time.

In Wells's novel, London is attacked by an extraterrestrial master race. The Martians have lived in perpetual cold, which has sharpened their brains and enabled them to invent spaceships and death rays. They envelop London bit by bit in a cloud of black gas, an impenetrable, irresistible killing darkness.

The story seethes with words that also have a signaling function in *Heart of Darkness*: "darkness," "blackness," "extermination," "brutes," "horror."

The Martians' weapons kill "like an invisible hand." They are as superior to those of the British as the British's are superior to those of the colored peoples. And just as the British consider themselves to have the right to conquer the lands of the lower races, the Martians think they have the right to conquer the Earth, taking it from people they regard as a lower species of animal. As Wells wrote:

> [B]efore we judge of them too harshly, we must remember what ruthless and utter destruction our own species has wrought, not only upon animals, such as the vanished bison and the dodo, but upon its own inferior races.
>
> The Tasmanians, in spite of their human likeness, were entirely swept out of existence in a war waged by European immigrants, in the space of fifty years. Are we such apostles

of mercy as to complain if the Martians warred in the same spirit?

In the London area, humanity is soon exterminated, down to about a few stragglers. The narrator meets one of them on Putney Hill. He suggests future life and resistance in the sewers. The risk is that the humans "will go savage," degenerate into a kind of large wild rat. The extreme situation justifies extreme solutions: "We can't have any weak and silly. Life is real again, and the useless, the cumbersome and mischievous have to die. They ought to die. They ought to be willing to die. It's a sort of disloyalty after all, to live and taint the race."

When that was written, Adolf Hitler was just eight years old.

The riddle of malaria was solved in 1897, when Wells wrote his novel. Just as malaria had long been the natives' best protection against the white conquerors, the bacteria in the novel become man's protection against the Martians. It is the bacteria that save humanity. The Martians have conquered the whole earth only to fall victim to its smallest and most insignificant inhabitants.

Just because we have been successful at one time, we should not think the future belongs to us, Wells warns. "In the case of every other predominant animal the world has ever seen, I repeat, the hour of its complete ascendancy has been the eve of its complete overthrow."

70

Wells had studied biology and paleontology under Thomas Huxley, and his popular science articles demonstrate a special interest in extinction. "On Extinction" (1893), for example, deals with the "saddest chapter" in biological science, describing the slow and inexorable extinction of struggling life. [35]

In the long galleries of the geological museum are the records of judgments that have been engraved on the rocks. Example: *Atlantosaurus*. Whether it was through some change of climate, some subtle disease, or some subtle enemy, these titanic reptiles dwindled in numbers and faded at last altogether. Save for the riddle of their scattered bones, it is as if they had never been.

The long roll of paleontology is half-filled with the records of extermination; whole orders, families, groups, and classes have passed away and left no mark and no tradition upon the living fauna of the world. Many fossils of the older rocks are labeled "of doubtful affinity." Nothing living has any part like them. They hint merely at shadowy dead subkingdoms, of which the form eludes the zoologist. They are index fingers, pointing into unfathomable darkness and saying only one thing clearly, the word *extinction*.

Even in the world today, the forces of extinction are at work. In the last hundred years, human beings have swarmed all over the globe and shoved one species of animal after another over the edge of the precipice. Not just the dodo, but hundreds of families and species.

The annihilation of the bison was swift and complete. Seals, Greenland whales, and many other animals are faced with the same cruel destiny. Their situation is almost beyond our ability to comprehend, Wells writes. Our earth is still warm from human beings, our future apparently full of human life. The most terrible thing we can imagine is a desolated earth in which the last human being, utterly alone, stares extinction in the face.

71

The air in the big department store is dry, and I find it more and more difficult to breathe. They take me to the inhalation room, where the air is as moist as in a greenhouse, soft and pleasant to the lungs. After a minute or so in there, I feel quite recovered. But as soon as I come out into the dry air of the store, I am again breathless and hurry back into the inhalation room. In a few moments, it has been totally changed. It is empty. There is not a human being there, no equipment, nothing.

"I want the inhalation room," I say.

"You've gone astray," replies an invisible loudspeaker. "This is the annihilation room."

"I don't understand."

"There's a great difference," the matter-of-fact voice explains. "You're annihilated here."

"And that means?"

"This is the destruction chamber. All life ceases here. It ends."

The words explode in slow motion within me, their meaning unfolding like parachutes and slowly sinking down through the mind to the sudden realization: I don't exist any longer. The end has come.

72

In April 1897, while Wells was writing *The War of the Worlds*, the English newspaper *Social-Democrat* published a story marked with the same biting irony, the same rebellious pessimism. The piece was called "Bloody Niggers."

Why did God create man? Was it out of carelessness or ill will? We don't know. But in all events, man exists, black, white, red, and yellow.

Far back in history, Assyrians, Babylonians, and Egyptians lived and fought, but God was aiming all the time at something different and better. He let Greeks and Romans appear out of the darkness of barbarity to prepare the way for the race that from the start was chosen to rule over mankind, namely the British race—"limited islanders, baptised with mist, narrowed by insularity, swollen with good fortune and wealth."

Lower races live in Africa, Australia, and America and on all the thousands of islands in the South Seas. They perhaps have different names and petty differences between them, but all of them are essentially "niggers," "bloody niggers." Nor are Finns or Basques or whatever they are called anything to be reckoned with. They are just a kind of European nigger, "destined to disappear."

Niggers remain niggers whatever color they are, but the archetype is found in Africa. Oh, Africa! God must have been in a bad mood when He created that continent. Why otherwise fill it with people who are doomed to be replaced by other races coming from outside? Would it not have been better to make the niggers white, so that in all good time they could become Englishmen, instead of giving us all the trouble of exterminating them?

Niggers have no guns, so no rights. Their land is ours. Their cattle and fields, their wretched household utensils and all they possess is ours—just as their women are ours to have as concubines, to thrash or exchange, ours to infect with syphilis, leave with child, outrage, torment, and make by contact with "the vilest of our vile, more vile than beasts."

Our bishops scream to high heaven when the Armenians are violated by Turks, but say nothing about the much worse crimes committed by their own countrymen. The hypocritical British heart beats for all except those their own empire drowns in blood. The God who has created people like us—must not he have been a fool?

73

The author of this screed was the Scottish aristocrat and socialist R.B. Cunningham Graham. After an adventurous life in South America, he had returned to his native country and begun a new career as politician and writer.

A few months after "Bloody Niggers" was printed, Graham read "An Outpost of Progress" and recognized a soulmate in the criticism of imperialism and hatred of hypocrisy. He wrote to Conrad, and with that begins a correspondence remarkable in its seriousness, intimacy, and intensity. Graham became Conrad's closest friend.

The two friends always loyally praise each other's stories and articles, but in one case Conrad's reaction is much stronger than usual. That is when in June 1898 he read "Bloody Niggers," by then over a year old.

It is good, he writes. Very good, but . . . (here he switches into French) but, my dear friend, you spread yourself too thin, your thoughts drift around like wandering knights when they ought to be kept gathered together in firm and penetrating battle array.

"And why preach to the already converted?" Conrad continues. "I am being stupid. Honour, justice, compassion and freedom are ideas that have no converts. There are only people, without knowing, understanding or feeling, who intoxicate themselves with words, repeat words, shout them out, imagining they believe them without believing in anything else but profit, personal advantage and their own satisfaction."

The criticism of language Conrad made in the summer of 1896—great words are nothing but sounds—is repeated here, sharpened to extreme despair: "Words fly away—and nothing remains, do you see? Absolutely nothing, you man of good faith! Nothing at all. One moment, and nothing remains—except a lump of dirt, a cold, dead lump of dirt thrown out into black space, spinning round an extinguished sun. Nothing. Neither thought, sound nor soul. Nothing."

74

Conrad calls Graham an "*homme de foi*," a man of good faith.

Conrad neither wanted nor was able to have anything to do with Graham's socialism (or with politics in general). He was his father's son and knew what politics led to. Politics had killed his mother, broken his father, made him an orphan, and driven him into exile.

Graham, with his secure national identity, could perhaps afford politics. Conrad, writer in exile, could not. He could love and admire his father's politics in Graham, but he also hated them and could never forgive what they had done to his father.

Who today could be called an *homme de foi*? The species seems to have died out. Graham's problems, however, remain, utterly recognizable, his despair as well. It is only his faith and his hope that have been taken away from us.

75

On December 1, 1898, Conrad read Graham's newly published travel book *Mogreb-el-Acksa*. He wrote to Graham's mother on December 4: "It is *the* book of travel of the century. Nothing approaching it has appeared since Burton's *Mecca*."

And on December 9, Conrad wrote to Graham himself: "The individuality of the work imposes itself on the reader—from the first. And then come other things: skill, pathos, humour, wit, indignation. . . . This should work for material success. Yet who knows! No doubt it is too good."

Graham's book was one of the most recent Conrad had read when on December 18 he started writing *Heart of Darkness*.

The narrator in *Mogreb-el-Acksa* turns to a small circle of men lying around the evening fire, their pipes lit and staying their tin mugs on the way to their mouths when they hear the horses sneezing. He is a mounted equivalent of the seaman Marlow in his circle of sailors.

He tells, he says, only of what he has seen, with no flag-waving, no pretence of fulfilling some great moral mission. He has no theories on empires, the destiny of the Anglo-Saxon race, the spread of Christian faith, or the expansion of trade. He is as guarded and distanced as Marlow.

He is on his way to Taroudant. At first, like Marlow, he is taken by boat along the coast of Africa. He thinks about "the Orient," "the East," a concept which at that time covered almost the whole of the non-European world.

"As I see the matter, Europeans are a curse throughout the East. What do they bring worth bringing, as a general rule? Guns, gin, powder, and shoddy cloths, dishonest dealing only too frequently, and flimsy manufactures which displace the fabrics woven by the women, new wants, new ways and discontent with what they know . . . these are the blessings Europeans take to Eastern lands."

The ruling classes in Morocco "understand entirely the protestations about better government, progress, morality and all the usual 'boniment' which Christian powers address to weaker nations when they can contemplate the annexation of their territory." Some areas are already in foreign hands, and "the Moroccans like the fact as much as we should like the Russians in the Isle of Wight," Graham writes. [36]

Even these modest attempts to see Europe from the point of view of the threatened were in the 1890s so rare and challenging that they gave Graham a profile as a writer entirely his own. It is the same narrative attitude Conrad had taken in "An Outpost of Progress" and that he again lets Marlow take at the beginning of *Heart of Darkness*.

When Conrad read Graham's story of a Westerner traveling farther and farther into an unknown and dangerous Africa, he read not only what was in the book. Alongside or behind his friend's experiences, he saw his own. Behind his friend's words, he saw his own words, the story he himself would be able to write on the same theme, in the same spirit, with his friend as a secret addressee.

76

Earlier in the autumn, Graham had worded his criticism of European influence in "the Orient" even more sharply in his story "Higginson's Dream," which Conrad proofread for his friend, in September 1898.

"It is super-excellent," wrote Conrad to Graham's mother on October 16. "It is much too good to remind me of any of my work, but I am immensely flattered to learn you discern some points of similitude. Of course I am in complete sympathy with the point of view."

During the final battles over Tenerife, it says in "Higginson's Dream," the Guanches were afflicted by a strange disease which killed more than those who fell in battle. The whole country was covered with the dead, and Alfonso de Lugo met a woman who said: "Where are you going, Christian? Why do you hesitate to take the land? The Guanches are all dead."

The disease was called *modorra*. But in fact it only required the white man's presence—with his rifle and Bible, with his gin and cotton and his heart full of charity—to exterminate the people he wished to save from barbarism.

It is "apparently inevitable that our customs seem designed to carry death to all the so-called inferior races, whom at a bound we force to bridge a period it has taken us a thousand years to pass," writes Graham.[37]

It is worth noting that in contrast to most other intellectuals of the day, Graham writes "the so-called inferior races." According to him, the fact that colored peoples died out was not due to any biological inferiority but to what we today would call culture shock, the demand for immediate adaptation to a strange variant of Western culture (gin, Bible, and firearms).

77

In the autumn of 1898, Conrad was working on his novel *The Rescue*, about a noble and chivalrous imperialist who puts his whole existence at risk to help a Malayan friend who had once saved his life. The theme is the exact opposite of that in *Heart of Darkness*. The novel caused Conrad endless torment and brought him several times to the brink of suicide.

It is also very bad. I have only one reason to concern myself with it, and that is a passage in which Mr. Travers "with some force" utters the following words: "And if the inferior race must perish, it is a gain, a step towards the perfecting of society which is the aim of progress."

These words appear in part three of the book, which means Conrad must have written them at about the time when he proofread "Higginson's Dream." Both texts allude to the same widely known concept—that the "inferior" races must be sacrificed for "progress."

It is worth noting that the character in the novel pronouncing these words is Mr. Travers, and that his words immediately are associated with "the coming of utter darkness."

78

Things had gone well for Higginson. At this time he was already wealthy and lived in Nouméa, the group of islands he had "rescued from barbarism."

Higginson had spent his youth on the islands, loved their women, hunted with their youths, learned their language, lived their lives and considered it the best of lives. Tired of his wealth, he now often dreamed of returning to the little bay not far from Nouméa, where in his youth he had had a friend called Tean.

One day when the champagne seems flat and the demimonde particularly vulgar, he does return. The place is oddly changed. It seems deserted. He slashes his way through the undergrowth, finds a hut and a man digging yams. He asks:

"Where black man?"

The man leans on his hoe and replies, "All dead."

"Where Chief?"

"Chief, he dead."

Conrad read—not only read, but proofread—these words in his best friend's story a month or two before he himself wrote the words that would one day be the epigraph to T.S. Eliot's "The Hollow Men" (1925):

"Mistah Kurtz, he dead."

79

Inside the hut he finds Tean, the friend of his youth, dying. A strange conversation ensues in which Tean tries with metaphors—bird, mouse, rain—to explain what is happening within him, and Higginson replies as if the metaphors were an external reality in which the bird can be shot and the cat set on the mouse.

"It's no use," says Tean. "I die, John, black man all die, black women no catch baby, tribe only fifty 'stead of five hundred. We all go out, all same smoke, we vanish, go up somewhere into the clouds. Black men and white men, he no can live."

Having got that far in his story, Higginson starts blaspheming the gods, cursing progress, and railing at civilization (just as Graham had in "Bloody Niggers") in a torrent of half-French and half-English (just as Conrad had when he read "Bloody Niggers")—and then in confusion reminds himself that he made the roads, started up the mines, built the pier, that he and no one else had opened up the island to civilization . . .

Higginson is, as Kurtz is, a cosmopolitan, "half French, half English." In short, he is European. Just as Kurtz does, he represents a Progress that presupposes genocide.

PART III

To Arlit

80

How do I go on? The bus south from Tamanrasset stops at the Algerian border. The Niger State buses stop in Arlit, 170 miles from the border. You have to hitchhike those 170 miles, and if you don't want to find yourself stuck on the actual border, it is wise to start hitching as early as in Tam.

I purchase a place on a truck full of young Australians on their way to Nairobi. We start at dawn. The police let us through, but Customs refuses to.

At midday, the customs officials go for lunch without having let us through. The sun is oppressive, the strong light throbbing in your head. The queue of vehicles grows the longer the customs men's lunch lasts. Flies buzz and irritation increases. At half past two, the customs men come back, and suddenly, with no explanation, they let the whole queue through at once.

Ahead of us lies 240 roadless miles of desert. We cover seventy-two before darkness falls. The night is still and starlit, with no wind or moon.

81

When we crawl out of our sleeping bags in the dawn light, we find ourselves in a seldom used piste with no fresh wheel tracks. That can be an advantage, as the sand is not so churned up. But it can also be fatal if you have engine failure a long way from any other traffic.

Sure enough, we have trouble with the dynamo and have to continue on the batteries without recharging them.

Groups of white stones like bird droppings lie in the dark sand. That goes against the main rule of the desert: the brighter the lighter, the darker the heavier.

At about eleven, we meet a Tuareg in a Land Rover who warns us not to continue. Ahead are dunes that are impassable for a heavy truck such as ours. We change direction and by lunchtime we are back on the "main road" in deeper and more churned-up tracks.

We eat beneath some thin tamarisks before setting off into the ill-reputed Lion dunes.

There are plenty of wrecked vehicles in the desert, there forever, as there is no damp to rust them away. But the Lion dunes are the true cemetery for cars. For many people, it is a sport trying to get through the desert in ordinary sedans, and such attempts often end just here.

Wind and sand soon blast away all the paint, and in the end the actual metal would be worn away had the wandering dunes not buried the skeletons of the cars, just as they previously buried the bones of dead camels.

We drive through this landscape to the notes of Vivaldi's constantly interrupted *Four Seasons* on a tape on which they have superimposed recordings of third-rate cheap comedians—the kind who delight the audience by telling them of their poverty-stricken childhood and never having had a hot meal except when some rich bastard farted. Their anal comedy is oddly integrated with fear and contempt of women, and anti-intellectualism.

The dancers on board turn the music up as high as possible and add their own bouncing and swaying to the truck's movements in the sandy hollows. The photographers keep their cameras constantly at the ready and experience the desert only through the lens.

The afternoon is flat and eventless. We strike camp at Gra-Ekar, a collection of strange, probably volcanic rock formations that remind me of the stelae of Gotland. They are deeply furrowed, cracked and porous like sponges, but at the same time as hard as metal and clearly much more resistant than anything that had once existed around them.

82

The In Guezzam border station has a bad reputation. There are innumerable stories of the way police and customs men with dictatorial powers constantly manage to find new reasons for sending people back to Tam or preferably even Algiers. Others are said to have been made to stand waiting in the scorching sun from ten o'clock, when the policeman goes for his lunch, until half past four, when the same man comes back after his siesta.

So we are prepared for the worst. I put on a dark suit, clean white shirt, and tie, and as the only French speaker on the truck, I have been given the task of finding an appropriate topic of conversation.

So I say it couldn't be much fun sitting isolated out here down in In Guezzam, exposed to the heat, the dust, and the risk of infection from the refugee camps, for only a 31.5 percent bonus, when you know those who work in the comparatively centrally placed In Salah, 660 miles nearer to Algiers get a 35 percent bonus—just because they are at a greater distance from the provincial capital, Tam. The injustice of these wage differentials, I say, cry up to the skies.

After that, we had no difficulties with the customs or police. They worked overtime to clear us before lunch.

83

After journeying for an hour or two, great trees appear on the horizon. This is Assamaka.

You long for trees in the desert, not just for the shade they provide, but also because they stretch up toward space. When the ground is flat, the sky sinks. Trees raise the sky by being so big and yet having so much farther to go. Trees create room.

The border policeman sits in a clay hut crammed like a junk dealer's shed with things left behind: tires worn smooth, broken radios, dusty rags, yellowing printed matter, cracked cups, half a lampshade, and a baton. In the middle of this confusion is a bed on which he sleeps, a table at which he works, and a transistor radio to which he listens.

His job consists of checking that those entering have either the equivalent of three thousand French francs or a valid air ticket for their return home. It is a delicate task to have to say to people that they are too poor to be allowed to travel in one of the poorest countries in the world. But he does this with good humor and good judgment, swiftly and in a friendly way, although he has no calculator and has to convert all currencies into francs in his head.

A stone's throw from there is a bar, the first since Tam. A Nigerian beer turns out to cost about half as much as an Algerian beer. The bottle is also twice the size and the supply of bottles apparently unlimited. Someone starts by ordering two beers each for the whole gang—then the party starts, communal singing, a babble of talk, great guffaws of laughter, tussles, drinking songs, and rhythmical hand clapping.

When the bar closes at midnight, eighteen whooping beery maniacs rush for the truck and set off with a bottle in each hand, yelling and laughing, straight out into the darkness, six miles, twelve miles, perhaps eighteen, then stop the truck somewhere in the sand and go on celebrating—chasing each other in the dark, rolling round, drinking, fighting, fucking, giggling, hiccoughing, and spewing until the small hours, when they all fall asleep scattered about in the sand.

84

I am woken by the tent flapping like a whiplash. The wind has risen. It is four o'clock. Everything is covered with sand, my sleeping bag, my notebook, my suitcase, even my body. My eyelids are like sandpaper against my eyeballs. The air is too thick to breathe.

I am scared. I daren't stay lying there in my sleeping bag, frightened of being buried in sand if I fall asleep again. I crawl over and try to look out. The tent fills like a balloon and almost lifts off the ground. The truck is no longer visible. Everything has disappeared. The beam from my torch is useless against the flying sand.

I get dressed and wrap the sleeping bag around me like a quilt. The hours pass. The sand rustles over the tent canvas. Foolish strings of words run through my head. East, West, home's best. Be not afraid, young man. Hear the palm tree rustling, at your feet your date doth fall.

Sometimes I persuade myself the wind is dropping, sometimes that it is rising. Dawn makes no difference; the air is equally impenetrable. I am sitting as if walled inside it. Terror comes creeping up on me.

I rinse the sand out of my mouth with water from my flask and dip my fingers in so that I can wash out my nostrils and breathe a little more easily. I can consider myself lucky to have water. Don't you see the water is running low? What wouldn't I do for a glass of mineral water!

It is nine o'clock. I try to remember exactly where the vanished truck was. Anyone who has studied sandstorms will agree they are most dangerous close to the ground, where the heavy sand glides along like a flying carpet. Lighter grains of sand bounce on. Only the dust really lifts.

When this dust has blown away, the sand goes on moving over the ground like a thick, low-flying cloud with a clearly marked upper surface. You can often see people's heads and shoulders sticking up above the cloud of sand as if out of a bath, Bagnold says. When the ground consists of coarse gravel or stones, the cloud can be as high as six feet, but when the ground is loose sand as it is here, the cloud is usually considerably thinner.

So the high truck might be my salvation. If I remember rightly, it cannot be more than ten yards away. Or at the most twenty. Once up in the truck, I could perhaps get my head above the sand and be able to breathe again. The others are probably there already.

But what if I miss it? If I don't find my way back? All authorities say you should never move in a sandstorm, but stay where you are. I stay. Suddenly, I realize this is my very last moment. That this is where I have come to die.

Dying of an overdose of heroin in a public convenience in Stockholm or of an overdose of desert romanticism in a sandstorm in the Sahara—the one is as stupid as the other.

85

"L'homme est entré sans bruit," says Teilhard de Chardin on the birth of history. Man entered with no fuss. Came unannounced. Arose with no commotion. Arrived soundlessly.

And how does he depart? Just as soundlessly?

86

Death was not included in my education. In twelve years of schooling and fifteen at various universities, I was never given any education in the art of dying. I don't even think death was ever mentioned.

Even now, afterward, after arriving in Arlit and having slept it all
off and showered and filled my body's reservoirs with water—even
now when terror has slackened its grip, I think it peculiar that death
was never even mentioned.

The Norwegian philosopher Tönnesen said that to think about
anything except death is evasion. Society, art, culture, the whole of
human civilization is nothing but evasion, one great collective self-
delusion, the intention of which is to make us forget that all the time
we are falling through the air, at every moment getting closer to
death.

Some of us get there in a few seconds, others in a few days, others in a few years—but that is a matter of indifference. The point
in time is a matter of indifference; what is decisive is that the end
awaits us all.

What should I do during my remaining time? Tönnesen would
have answered, "Nothing." He believed that to be born is to jump
off a skyscraper. But life is not like jumping off a skyscraper. It's not
seven seconds you have, but seven decades. That is enough to experience and achieve a good deal.

The shortness of life should not paralyze us, but stop us from
diluted, unconcentrated living. The task of death is to force man into
essentials.

That was how I felt when I was still not yet thirty and had a long
way to go down to the paving stones below. I did not even see them.
Now I can see them rushing up toward me and feel myself falling
headlong.

Then I realize something was missing in my education. Why
have I never learned how to die?

Cuvier's Discovery

"the less intellectual races being exterminated"

87

On January 27, 1796, the ambitious young Georges Cuvier, then aged twenty-six, had just arrived in Paris and held his first lecture at the newly opened Institut National de France.

Cuvier was a lively and captivating speaker. There and then, he had his great chance of making his name in the scientific world, and not least in Parisian society, which flocked to scientific lectures—if they were sufficiently sensational.

Cuvier was sensational. He spoke of the mammoth and the mastodon. Remnants of these huge elephantine animals had recently been found in Siberia and North America. Cuvier demonstrated that they did not belong to the same species as either the Indian or the African elephant, but constituted species of their own, now extinct.[38]

88

Now extinct—that was what horrified the listeners. In the eighteenth century, people still believed in a ready-made universe to which nothing could be added. Perhaps even more important to mankind's peace of mind, nothing could be subtracted from it. All the creatures God had once created still remained in his creation and could not disappear from it.

What then was the explanation for these gigantic bones and strange animal-like stones that had puzzled man since antiquity? For a long time scientists evaded the thought, so charged with anguish, that they could be the remnants of extinct animals. "If one link in Nature's chain be lost," wrote the vice president of the United

States, Thomas Jefferson, in 1799, "another and another might be lost, till this whole system of things should vanish by piecemeal."[39]

89

The idea that there could be species that had died out gave rise to such resistance, it took over a hundred years to become accepted.

Fontenelle had begun cautiously in 1700 with an indication that there perhaps were species that had been "lost." As if Mother Nature had gone and dropped them. Half a century later, Buffon spoke in his *Theory of the Earth* of a "vanished" species. Perhaps it had gone astray and never found its way home again.[40]

Cuvier did not speak as if nature had been neglectful. He talked of a crime, a massacre. His dying species had not been lost nor had they vanished; they were creatures that had been destroyed, died, been killed, not one by one but en masse, by vast repeated catastrophes, which, what is more, Cuvier called "the earth's revolutions." This could not help but make an impression on an audience that had just experienced the French Revolution.

What Citizen Cuvier really showed that day was that the reign of terror of the French Revolution, which his audience had only just survived, while many other grand old families had been wiped out— this reign of terror had in the far distant past a geological equivalent that had eradicated forever some of the largest of the animal species extant at the time.

Not only that. Cuvier ended with the prediction that the new creatures that had taken the place of the extinct species would one day be annihilated themselves and replaced by others.

90

Cuvier advanced rapidly. He became the Napoleon of French science, but for a man of such power, he was unusually skeptical of hierarchies. To him, the belief in a "ladder" of creatures was the greatest of all scientific mistakes. In his lectures in comparative anatomy, he writes:

The circumstance that we put one species or family before another does not entail that we consider it more perfect or superior to others in the system of nature. Only someone who thinks he can arrange all organisms into one long series can entertain such pretensions. The further I have progressed in the study of nature, the more convinced I have become that this is the most untruthful concept ever brought into natural history. It is necessary to regard every organism and every group of organisms separately. . . .

By selecting out a certain organ, one could indeed construct long series from simpler to more complicated, more perfect forms. But one acquired different hierarchies depending on which organ one selected. Instead of one single "ladder," Cuvier found a "network" of connections between creatures, all of which had a feature or some features in common. Only through arbitrary choice could a scientist set up an apparent hierarchical order in this network.

Cuvier knew that. And yet apparent hierarchical orders of that kind had an invisible power over his mind. When in his great sixteen-volume work *The Animal Kingdom* (1827–1835) he divided human beings into three races, he had forgotten that no hierarchies existed.

On the negroid races, he wrote that with their protruding jaws and thick lips, they approached the primates. "The hordes belonging to this variant of human being have always remained in a state of total barbarism."[41]

91

In the medieval hierarchy, the human being had been one and indivisible, created by God in His image and by Him placed on the top rung of the ladder of Creation.[42]

The first person to divide the abstract human being of medieval theology into several species, of which some were considered to be closer to animals, was William Petty. "There seem to be several species even of human beings," he wrote in *The Scale of Creatures*

(1676). "I say that the Europeans do not only differ from the afore-mentioned Africans in colour . . . but also . . . in natural manners and in the internal qualities of their minds." Here human beings are divided up not only into nations or peoples, but also biologically separate species. This occurred in passing and aroused no particular attention.

At the beginning of the 1700s, the anatomist William Tyson set off on a search for the missing link in the hierarchy of creation. In his book *Orang-Outang, or The Anatomy of a Pygmie* (1708), Tyson demonstrated that in its build, this primate is more like humans than other animals and the pygmy more like primates than other people. Tyson classified the pygmy as an animal, "wholly a brute," but so close to humans that "in this chain of creation for an intermediate link between ape and man I would place our pygmy."

Nor did Tyson cause any commotion. Not until the end of the eighteenth century, when Europeans were well on their way to conquering the world, did the idea of a hierarchy of the races seriously strike root.

The same year as the publication of Cuvier's first lecture, 1799, a doctor from Manchester, Charles White, produced the first extensively motivated and illustrated hierarchy of race, entitled *An Account of the Regular Graduations in Man*. In it he "proves" that the European stands above all other races: "Where shall we find unless in the European that nobly arched head, containing such a quantity of brain . . . ? Where that perpendicular face, the prominent nose and round, projecting chin? Where that variety of features and fulness of expression . . . those rosy cheeks and coral lips?"[43]

White's illustrations to his thesis—a series of profiles with primate and native halfway between ostrich and European—had enormous power and were still common in my childhood. At the moment of publication, White's thesis seemed to have an almost irresistible authority that continued to increase throughout the nineteenth century, in pace with the development of European arms technology.

92

I am called up for military service. The orders are in soft pastel colors, delicious, as if illustrating a fish recipe from Wedholm's restaurant in Stockholm. The background is mildly sand-colored like a desert dune and decorated with dark mussel shells. The actual dish is bluish with a touch of lilac. I look more closely at it and see that it is a corpse. It is myself who is dead, hideously swollen and distorted.

93

According to Cuvier there is one, and only one, state that hinders chemical and physical forces in their constant striving for the dissolution of the human body. That state is called "life."

For Cuvier, the state called life ceased in 1832 in the first great cholera epidemic that afflicted Europe. All his children died before he did. The species Cuvier was extinct.

Balzac paid tribute to him in *La peau de chagrin* (1831). Have you ever let Cuvier's geological works throw you out into the infinity of space and time? Balzac asks. Is Cuvier not the greatest poet of our century? He calls forth destruction, death becomes alive; in a kind of retrospective apocalypse we experience the terrifying resurrection of dead worlds, "and the little scrap of life vouchsafed us in the nameless eternity of time can no longer inspire anything but compassion."

Thus Cuvier captured the imagination of his day. He performed a postmortem on death and showed that it is not only of a personal nature, but wipes out whole species. He took the Parisians to the limestone quarry, where they could see that their city was an immense mass grave of long-since annihilated creatures. As they had gone under, so would we ourselves, their descendants, go under. Our future destiny could be read in the ground we were treading on.

It was a major scientific contribution. Cuvier cannot be blamed for the fact that, after his death, it all became associated with the hierarchical thinking he had seen through and loathed, but nevertheless yielded to.

94

On February 23, 1829, the young British geologist Charles Lyell describes in a letter his visit to Cuvier. He is full of admiration for the perfect order in Cuvier's study. In actual fact, this mania for order was probably Cuvier's great weakness.

Cuvier had been very strictly brought up both at home and at school. The chaos of the years of revolution reinforced the need for order he brought from home. All his life, he studied in fossils the results of the annihilating catastrophes. All his life, he sought calm and stability. Nature, like society, must obey inexorable laws. Metamorphosis frightened him. It was in his very nature to prefer destruction to transformation.

The French Revolution was the decisive experience of Cuvier's youth, while Lyell was instead marked by the Industrial Revolution in England. He had seen society fundamentally changed, not through one single violent catastrophe, but through thousands of small changes, each one scarcely perceptible.

Lyell wrote the classic work of nineteenth-century British geology, *Principles of Geology* (1832). In it he transfers his image of society to the geological history of the earth. No catastrophes have ever happened. All geological phenomena can be explained as the result of the same slow processes we see around us today: erosion, decomposition, stratification, rising land, sinking land.

What about mass destructions, then?

Extinct species, according to Lyell, have gone under in the same way, through slow changes in conditions of life: floods and droughts, diminishing access to food, the spread of competing species. The empty places have been filled by the immigration of species better adapted to the changed circumstances.

The ultimate cause of extinction was lack of flexibility and ability to adapt when unfavorable changes occur. Lyell had seen that in the markets during the Industrial Revolution: he now saw it in nature as well.

95

In Arlit, where I am sitting in my hotel room writing this, I suddenly catch sight of a man carrying an empty picture frame.

I usually see quite different things through my window—the woman on the corner making small pancakes in green oil on a black metal plate with circular hollows, the tea vendor swinging his glowing metal basket to get the water to boil, some boys playing at being a band with wooden sticks and empty cans. The rhythm is clearly different in Arlit than in Tam: at the same time more indolent and more active, as it is less tense.

That is the kind of thing I usually see from my window. But then a white-cloaked black man suddenly comes along carrying a heavy gold frame.

It frames his own person as he carries it, only his head and feet outside it. It is strange to see the way the frame separates him, brings him out, yes, even elevates him. When he stops for a moment to move it from one shoulder to the other, he seems to step out of the frame. It looks as if that were the simplest thing in the world.

96

Even in the most authentic documentary there is always a fictional person—the person telling the story. I have never created a more fictional character than the researching "I" in my doctorate, a self that begins in pretended ignorance and then slowly arrives at knowledge, not at all in the fitful, chancy way I myself arrived at it, but step by step, proof by proof, according to the rules.

Cuvier, Lyell, Darwin—they are all, in their work, fictional characters. The story of how they made their discoveries is nothing but a story, as it says nothing about them themselves. The omission of all that is personal makes the scientific "self" into a fiction lacking any equivalent in reality.

The reality "I" experience in the desert is authentic, however condensed. I really am in Arlit. I can see the black man with the gold frame. But I can never, by the very nature of things, step out of the frame.

As a reader, as soon as I see the word I used (or avoided, for even avoidance is a way of using it) I know I have a fictional character in front of me.

97

Darwin took Lyell's *Principles* with him on his voyage on the *Beagle*.[45]

In the spring of 1834, he was in Patagonia and found the remains of gigantic animals that had lived in late geological periods. No great land risings or sinkings had occurred since then. What then had exterminated so many species, yes, even whole families?

"The mind at first is irresistibly hastened into the belief of some great catastrophe," Darwin writes, clearly alluding to Cuvier's disaster theory. "But thus to destroy animals from southern Patagonia up to the Behring's Straits, we must shake the entire framework of the globe."

A geological investigation shows no sign of such shakings.

Well, what about the temperature? Darwin replies with a counterquestion: What change of temperature would exterminate the animal world on both sides of the equator, in tropical, temperate, and arctic areas?

"Certainly, no fact in the long history of the world is so startling," Darwin observes, "as the wide and repeated extermination of its inhabitants."

But looked at from another direction, this extermination is less amazing, Darwin goes on. In cases in which man exterminates a certain species in a certain district, we know that the species at first becomes increasingly rare and then dies out. That a certain species in nature is already rare does not surprise us, nor that it gradually becomes rarer and rarer; why then should we be surprised that it finally dies out?

98

The study of fossils, Darwin says, will throw light not only on the destruction of living creatures but also on their origins.

He already knew enough. His problem was now to understand it and draw conclusions.

In Cuvier's world there is in the beginning an act of creation, when life occurs, and in the end an act of destruction, when it is wiped out. Lyell destroyed this happy symmetry by replacing the destructive disaster with a number of small causes working slowly.

But if it were admitted that old species slowly and naturally could die out, then why could not new species arise in the same way, for the same natural reasons that had destroyed their predecessors? If dying out did not require a catastrophe, why should genesis require a creation?[46]

This was the logic that led Darwin step by step to *The Origin of Species* (1859).

99

Cuvier fought all his life with his colleague Lamarck. The question was: Can species evolve? Lamarck believed in evolution without having discovered its mechanism, natural selection. Cuvier, on the other hand, faithful to his nature, maintained that species were unalterable.

To this standpoint he brought very powerful scientific reasoning: if animal species had evolved from each other, then somewhere one ought to have come across intermediate forms between the extinct and the present living animal species. As such intermediate forms were absent, the hypothesis of evolution was faulty, Cuvier says.[47]

Darwin took Cuvier's objection very seriously. If it could not be refuted, the whole theory of evolution would have to be rejected, he wrote.[48]

But Darwin thought he had an explanation. The intermediate forms had existed, but they had been forced out by new, better adapted species, so quickly that they had had no time to leave any traces behind them in the geological record before they had gone under in the struggle for existence.

Darwin considered the struggle hardest between the forms that most resemble each other. "Hence the improved and modified descendants of a species will generally cause the extinction of the parent-species."

So according to Darwin, the explanation for the lack of intermediate forms is a kind of biological patricide. Evolution does not eat its children as revolutions do: it is the parents evolution wipes out.

100

In a letter to Lyell in 1859, Darwin considers the idea that this process perhaps also occurs between the human races, "the less intellectual races being exterminated."[49]

In *The Descent of Man* (1871), Darwin made public his conviction. Today between the primates and civilized man are intermediate forms such as gorillas and savages, he says in chapter 6. But both these intermediate forms are dying out. "At some future period not very distant as measured in centuries, the civilised races of man will almost certainly exterminate and replace throughout the world the savage races."

Similarly, the gorillas will die out. An even larger gap than that now found between the gorilla and Australian aborigine will in the future widen between the lower apes and the coming, even more civilized man. Namely, the gap left behind by those who have been exterminated.

To Agadez

"dashing out their brains"

At the bus station in Arlit I turn to the veiled man in the entrance and ask, "Is the office open?"

"Let us first say good-day to each other," replies the native, correcting me mildly. For a moment we devote ourselves to mutual and repeated "Ça va? Ça va bien. Ça va?" Then he tells me that unfortunately the office is closed. Better luck next time.

The next time I actually succeed in buying a ticket. Then I have to leave my luggage on the ground, go to the police at the other end of town to show the ticket, get my passport, go back to the station, where my luggage is now being stowed onto the roof of the minibus together with some oily barrels, several sacks of grain, and a whole market stall, including stands to support the roof, a counter to spread the goods out on, and a whole assortment of bundles. Plus a dried camel head with empty eye sockets.

Then the passengers are packed in. There are three benches, one for women, one for black men, and one for Tuaregs. I am placed among the Tuaregs. Thirty-two people are squeezed in. It is not cramped as long as you can lick your lips. The two conductors push the bus to start it, run alongside, then throw themselves inside, and slam the door shut behind them.

It is a good 150 miles to Agadez. The ground consists of great floes of stone. The desert is flaking off like the dry skin on an arm. Then the first thin, pale steppe grass appears, salt to the tongue, accumulated in the depressions, blond, straw white, glowing like the down on your arm.

I recognize it from the abandoned limestone quarries in

Gotland. There is a light in this short white grass, which makes me intensely happy.

In the middle of all this desolation, we sit pressed close together, body to body, breath to breath. Slim Tuareg youths in copper-purple veils, with long, dark eyelashes, enveloped in inviolable silence, embraced by the people of great laughter and beaming smiles, with their swelling backsides and noisy, colorful women.

Are these the savages Darwin had thought we civilized white men should exterminate? That is hard to imagine when you are sitting in the same minibus.

102

Hotel de l'Air in Agadez was once the Sultan's palace. It is famous for its dining room with four thick pillars that two men can hardly embrace, and for its rooms perpetually sunk in darkness, each with its own way up to the evening cool on the roof terrace.

From up there I look out over the market square, where a brand-new Peugot 504 has just stopped. Two young men in shiny suits jump out and go up to an old man by a small metal-covered desk decorated with two crossed letters. They squat down on their heels in the dust and have their letter written by the old man.

Who is it who is condemned to go under? Those glossy young illiterates, or the literate old man?

He is leaning against the minaret, seventeen floors high with protruding beams splaying out like a prickly fruit. It contains a spiral staircase that, toward the end, is so narrow you can no longer turn round. Everyone has to go up before anyone can come down.

The sun sparkles in the small round pieces of mirror decorating the bedposts of the furniture dealer. Some salt-bitten tamarisks spread thin shade.

The first evening wind brings with it the sound of clunking charcoal and the clatter from the mill that has started grinding the wheat for the evening meal. Chez Nous down on the corner has already thrown open its doors; Au Bon Coin and Bonjour Afrique will soon be open.

103

Cuvier filled his day with horror when he demonstrated that a biological species can go under. Seventy-five years later, few people even raised an eyebrow when Darwin confirmed that whole human races are condemned to extermination. What happened? What were the "Tasmanians" Wells talked about? Who were the "Guanches"?

The Guanches were an advanced, Berber-speaking Stone Age people, the first people to be destroyed by European expansion.[50] They were of African origin but had lived for a long time in "the fortunate isles," what are now the Canary Islands, and had lost contact with the mainland. Their numbers have been estimated at about eighty thousand—before the Europeans arrived.

In 1478, Ferdinand and Isabella sent an expedition with guns and horses to Grand Canary. The plains were quickly captured by the Spaniards, but in the mountains the Guanches continued a stubborn guerilla warfare. Finally, in 1483, six hundred warriors and one thousand five hundred women, children, and old people capitulated—all that remained of a once numerous population.

Las Palmas surrendered in 1494. Tenerife held out until 1496. Finally, one lone native woman signed to the Spaniards to come closer. "There was no one left to fight, no one to fear—all were dead."

Neither horses nor guns decided the outcome of the war. Bacteria were victorious. The natives called the unknown disease *modorra*. Of Tenerife's fifteen thousand inhabitants, only a handful survived.

The forest was cleared, the flora and fauna Europeanized, the Guanches lost their land and thus their living. The *modorra* returned several times, and dysentery, pneumonia, and venereal disease ravaged.

Those who survived the diseases instead died of actual subjugation—loss of relatives, friends, language, and lifestyle. When Girolamo Benzoni visited Las Palmas in 1541, there was one single Guanche left, eighty-one years old and permanently drunk. The Guanches had gone under.

This group of islands in the eastern Atlantic was the

kindergarten for European imperialism. Beginners learned there that European people, plants, and animals manage very well even in areas where they did not exist by nature. They also learned that although the indigenous inhabitants are superior in numbers and put up bitter resistance, they are conquered, yes, exterminated— without anyone really knowing how it happened.

104

When Europeans went east as Crusaders in the twelfth and thirteenth centuries, they came across people who were superior to them in culture, diplomatic cunning, technical knowledge, and not least in experience of epidemics. Thousands of Crusaders died because of their inferior resistance to bacteria. When Europeans went west in the fifteenth century, they themselves were the bearers of those superior bacteria. People died everywhere the Europeans went.

In 1492, Columbus arrived in America. The extent of the so-called demographic catastrophe that followed has been estimated differently by different scholars. Certainly it was without equivalent in world history.[51]

Many scholars today believe that there were roughly equal numbers of people in America as in Europe—over seventy million. During the following three hundred years, the population of the world increased by 250 percent. Europe increased fastest, by between 400 percent and 500 percent. The original population of America on the other hand *fell* by 90 or 95 percent.

Swiftest and most thorough was the demographic catastrophe in the heavily populated parts of Latin America that had first come into contact with Europeans: the West Indies, Mexico, Central America, and the Andes. In Mexico alone there may have been 25 million people when the Europeans arrived in 1519. Fifty years later, the number had fallen to 2.7 million. Fifty more years later there were 1.5 million Indians left. Over 90 percent of the original population had been wiped out in a hundred years.

The great majority of those people did not die in battle. They died quite peacefully of disease, hunger, and inhuman labor conditions. The social organization of the Indians had been wrecked by the white conquerors, and in the new society only a small fraction of the Indians was as yet usable, for, as a labor force for the whites, the Indians were of low quality. And there were many more Indians than the few whites could exploit with existing methods.

The direct cause of death was usually disease, but the underlying cause was this: the Indians were far too numerous to be of any economic value within the framework of the conquerors' society.

Was it defensible to continue a conquest with such disastrous results? That question became a major subject of discussion among Spanish intellectuals of the sixteenth century. This went so far that on April 16, 1550, Carlos V prohibited any further conquests pending a debate on their justification—"a measure with no equivalent in the annals of Western expansion," writes the historian Magnus Mörner.

The debate was held in Valladolid in August 1550 before a court of senior lawyers, who could not agree on any judgment.

And what purpose would that have served? No judgment in the world would have persuaded the Spanish conquerors to carry out what they considered Indian's work. No judgment had stopped them treating the Indians as inferior beings, making them submit to their natural masters. The fact that the Indians also died in the process was unfortunate, but apparently inevitable.

105

Adam Smith framed the law said to regulate the supply of labor: "The demand for men, like that of any other commodity, necessarily regulates the production of men: quickens it when it goes too slowly, and stops it when it advances too fast."[52]

That law also applies, of course, to Indians. They went on dying until there was a shortage of Indian labor in Latin America. Then they became valuable. A series of social reforms were carried out to safeguard the remaining Indians, binding them to economic units where they were needed and rationally exploiting their labor. During the seventeenth century the Indian population slowly began to rise.

By the middle of the nineteenth century, Latin America was affected by economic and technical renewal stemming from western Europe. This entailed increased demand for raw materials and foodstuffs from Latin America. The population increased even more quickly than before, and available labor was exploited even more.

The population continued to increase at a swift pace. At the same time, technical and economic renewal in Europe, which had for a while created an increased demand for labor in Latin America, during later decades, on the contrary, tended to reduce the demand. There can be no doubt that this tendency is continuing.

Industry keeps up with automation in order to be competitive in international markets. Large agricultural holdings are mechanized or go over to ranching. A growing share of the swiftly growing population becomes unsuitable or superfluous from the point of view of employers.

106

Does not Adam Smith's law still apply today? In the long run, will a society that is unable to maintain the right to work be able to maintain the right to live?

To me it seems clear that some of the decisive conditions for the sixteenth-century demographic catastrophe exist again today in Latin America, as in several other parts of the world.

The pressure of the hungry and desperate billions has not yet become so great that world leaders see Kurtz's solution as the only humane, the only possible, the fundamentally sound one. But that day is not far off. I see it coming. That is why I read history.

107

I am in a tunnel or a cellar passage together with many other people. We move on at an excruciatingly slow pace in the darkness. They say we can get out somewhere far ahead, but only one by one up a narrow spiral staircase. The intake is far greater than the discharge and so it becomes insufferably cramped in the tunnel. Some have been standing there for several days and have moved only a few steps. Malthus himself has climbed up the pipes under the roof to get away from the crush on the floor. Irritation goes over into apathy and desperation. Beneath the surface, panic is already trembling.

108

About five million of the indigenous American population lived in what is now the United States. At the beginning of the nineteenth century, half a million still remained. In 1891, at the time of Wounded Knee—the last great massacre of Indians in the United States—the native population reached rock bottom: a quarter of a million, or 5 percent of the original number of Indians.

The fact that the Indians died out in the Spanish occupation was explained in the Anglo-Saxon world by the well-known cruelty and bloodthirstiness of the Spaniards. When the same phenomenon occurred as a result of Anglo-Saxon occupation of North America, other explanations were required. At first it was thought to be divine intervention. "Where the English come to settle, a Divine Hand makes way for them by removing or cutting off the Indians, either by Wars one with the other or by some raging, mortal Disease," Daniel Denton wrote in 1670.

During the nineteenth century, religious explanations were replaced by biological ones. The exterminated peoples were colored, the exterminators white. It seemed obvious that some racial natural law was at work and that the extermination of non-Europeans was simply a stage in the natural development of the world. [53]

The fact that natives died proved that they belonged to a lower race. Let them die as the laws of progress demand, some people said. Others thought that for humanitarian reasons the natives ought to be protected by moving them to some distant place—and then, as if by sheer coincidence, Europeans were able to take over their good arable lands and use them for their own purposes.

Thus, from the 1830s a number of tribes and peoples in North America, South America, Africa, and Australia were displaced, exterminated, or moved away. When Darwin wrote that certain human races are doomed to be exterminated, he built his prediction on generally known historical events. Occasionally, he had himself been an eyewitness.

109

In the backward southwestern parts of South America, the European conquests had not yet been completed when Darwin arrived in August 1832. The Argentine government had just decided to exterminate the Indians who still ruled the Pampas.

The assignment was given to General Rosas. Darwin met him and his troops by the Colorado River and thought he had never seen a more loathsome army of bandits.

In Bahía Blanca, he saw more forces, drunken and covered with blood, filth, and vomit. He interviewed a Spanish commander who told him how they had forced information out of captured Indians about where their kinfolk were. In this way, he and his soldiers had recently found 110 Indians who had all been captured or killed, "for the soldiers saber every man."

> The Indians are now so terrified that they offer no resistance in a body, but each flies, neglecting even his wife and children; but when overtaken, like wild animals they fight, against any number to the last moment. One dying Indian seized with his teeth the thumb of his adversary, and allowed his own eye to be forced out sooner than relinquish his hold.

This is a dark picture, but how much more shocking is the undeniable fact that all the women who appear above twenty years old are massacred in cold blood! When I exclaimed that this appeared rather inhuman, he answered "Why, what can be done? They breed so!"

Everyone here is fully convinced that this is the most just war, because it is against barbarians. Who would believe in this age such atrocities could be committed in a Christian civilised country.

General Rosas' plan is to kill all stragglers and having driven the remainder to a common point, to attack them in a body in the summer, with the assistance of the Chilenos. The operation is to be repeated for three successive years. [54]

When Darwin published *The Descent of Man* in 1871, the hunting down of Indians was still going on in Argentina, financed by a bond loan. When the land was cleared of Indians, it was shared out among the bondholders, each bond giving a right to twenty-five hundred hectares. [55]

110

All night I search for flowers in a dark dirty city landscape. All round me is deserted, ruined, urinated. In a stinking tunnel, two men are coming toward me. Flowers? They don't understand what I am talking about. I sign "bouquet" by gripping the stalks in my hand. They take it as a sign for "knife" and understand exactly what I mean.

111

Darwin was disturbed by the brutality of the Argentinian hunt for human beings. His teacher, Charles Lyell, helped him to place what he had seen into a larger context. Man was a part of nature and in nature even destruction is natural.

We human beings, Lyell says in his *Principles of Geology* (the chapter headed "Extirpation of Species by Man"), have no reason to feel guilty because our progress exterminates animals and plants. In our defense, we can state that when we conquer the earth and defend our occupations by force, we are only doing what all species in nature do. Every species that has spread over a large area has in a similar way reduced or wholly eradicated other species and has to defend itself by fighting against intruding plants and animals. If "the most insignificant and diminutive species . . . have each slaughtered their thousands, why should not we, the lords of creation, do the same?"

The gentle Lyell had as little desire as the gentle Darwin to do the Indians any harm. But the right to eradicate other species that Lyell so thoughtlessly ascribed to man had already long been used even to exterminate humans.

112

The Tasmanians were the most well known of the exterminated peoples and were often held up as symbols for them all.[56]

Tasmania is an island the size of Ireland and lies southeast of the Australian continent. The first colonists—twenty-four prisoners, eight soldiers, and a dozen volunteers, of whom six were women—arrived in 1803. The following year, the first massacre of the natives occurred. The "bushrangers," escaped prisoners, had a free hand, killing kangaroos and natives. They took their women. They threw native bodies to the dogs or roasted them alive.

A man called Carrots became renowned for having murdered a Tasmanian; he then forced the man's wife to carry her dead husband's head hanging round her neck. The natives did not have to be treated like humans, they were "brutes" or "brute beasts."

In the 1820s, white immigration increased and with that the pressure on the livelihood of the natives. As they starved, they began to steal from the whites, who set traps for them and shot them from the treetops. The Tasmanians replied by attacking isolated settlers. The natives' leader was captured and executed for murder in 1825.

Van Diemens Land Company exterminated the kangaroos and brought in sheep on half a million acres. The white population doubled every fifth year. The local press demanded more and more loudly that the government should "move" the natives. If not, they should be "hunted down like wild beasts and destroyed."

That was what happened. In 1827, *The Times* (London) reported that sixty Tasmanians had been killed in revenge for the murder of a settler; on another occasion seventy Tasmanians lost their lives. The violence increased until the settlers also hauled women and children out of their caves, "dashing out their brains."

In 1829, the government decided to concentrate the natives in an area on the infertile west coast. Prisoners were sent out to hunt them down and were given five pounds for every native they brought with them to the assembly camp. It is estimated that nine Tasmanians died for every one to arrive alive. The "black war" went on.

In 1830, five thousand soldiers were mobilized for a search party to drive all the natives onto a small headland in the southeast. The operation cost thirty thousand pounds. For several weeks, the chain ran with forty-yard gaps right across the whole island. When it arrived, not a single native had been caught. There were, it turned out later, only three hundred left.

113

A Methodist mason by the name of G.A. Robinson wanted to save them. He went unarmed into the bush, was close to being killed, but was saved by a native woman called Truganina. Together with her, he succeeded in convincing two hundred Tasmanians to join them and go to the safety of Flinder's Island, where no one would hunt them down.

It was at this stage Darwin visited Tasmania. "I fear," he noted in his diary on February 2, 1836, "there is no doubt that this train of evil and its consequences, originated in the infamous conduct of some of our countrymen."

Robinson tried to civilize his protégés by bringing a market economy and Christianity to Flinder's Island. He was soon able to report exceptional progress. The Tasmanians had started working, had bought clothes, and were eating with knives and forks. Nightly orgies had been replaced by hymns. Knowledge of the commandments was progressing fast. There was only one snag: they were dying like flies.

Six months later half of them were dead. When that half in its turn was again halved, the remaining forty-five left the island and moved to a slum outside the capital, Hobart Town, where they quickly died out from alcoholism.

When Darwin's *The Origin of Species* came out in 1859, there were only nine Tasmanian women left, all too old to have children. The last Tasmanian man, William Ianney, died in 1869. His skull was stolen even before his funeral, and afterward the body was dug up from the grave and the remains of his skeleton were taken.

The last Tasmanian was Truganina, the woman who saved Robinson's life. She died in 1876, a few years after Darwin's *The Descent of Man* came out. Her skeleton is in the Tasmanian Museum in Hobart.

114

Nineteenth-century scholars interpreted the fate of the Tasmanians in the light of Cuvier's discovery, now common knowledge. Among the thousands of already extinct species, the Tasmanians had survived owing to their geographical isolation. They were "living fossils," remains of a vanished prehistoric time, which had not coped with sudden contact with the other end of the time scale. The fact that they were exterminated meant only that they had returned to the long since dead world in which they belonged from the viewpoint of evolution.

Nineteenth-century scholars interpreted the fate of the Tasmanians in the light of Darwin's discovery. The "ladder" of creation the Middle Ages had believed in, the zoological hierarchy that William Petty, William Tyson, and Charles White had thought up, with Darwin became an historical process. The "lower" forms in the hierarchy were the predecessors in time of the "higher." And not only that.

"Lower" and "higher" were bound together as cause and effect. The struggle between them created ever "higher" forms.

We Europeans were modified and improved descendants of the Tasmanians. So according to the logic of the Darwinian patricide, we were forced to exterminate our parent species. That included all the "savage races" of the world. They were doomed to share the fate of the Tasmanians.

PART IV

The Birth of Racism

*"Race is everything: literature, science, art,
in a word, civilization, depend on it."*

115

At the beginning of the nineteenth century, eighteenth-century criticism of imperialism still lived on, and for many it was self-evident
to take a stand against genocide.

In his great history of colonialism, *European colonies in various
parts of the world viewed in their social, moral and physical condition*
(1834), John Howison writes:

> The continent of America has already been nearly depopu-
> lated of its aborigines by the introduction of the blessings
> of civilisation. The West Indian archipelago, from the same
> cause, no longer contains a single family of its primitive in-
> habitants. South Africa will soon be in a similar condition,
> and the islanders of the Pacific Ocean are rapidly diminish-
> ing in numbers from the ravages of European diseases and
> the despotism of self-interested and fanatical missionaries.
> It is surely time that the work of destruction should cease;
> and since long and melancholy experience has proved us to
> be invariably unsuccessful in rendering happier, wiser, or
> better, the barbarians whom we have visited or conquered,
> we may now conscientiously let them alone and turn a cor-
> recting hand towards ourselves and seek to repress . . . our
> avarice, our selfishness, and our vices.

This was an attitude with roots in both Christian faith and
Enlightenment ideas of equality. But during nineteenth-century

European expansion, another attitude appeared. Genocide began to be regarded as the inevitable by-product of progress.

To the great anthropologist, J.C. Prichard, it was obvious that "the savage races" could not be saved. What had to be aimed at instead, he said in his lecture "On the Extinction of Human Races" (1838), was to collect in the interests of science as much information as possible on their physical and moral characteristics.[57]

The threat of extermination provided motivation for anthropological research, which in exchange gave the exterminators an alibi by declaring extermination inevitable.

116

That same year, 1838, Herman Merivale gave a series of lectures at Oxford on "Colonization and Colonies." He noted Prichard's theory that "the white is destined to extirpate the savage" was becoming more and more usual. Extermination was not only due to war and epidemics, but had deeper and more secret causes: "the mere contact with Europeans is fatal to him in some unknown manner."

Merivale fiercely rejects this theory. There are no examples of inexplicable mortality. "The waste of human life" is enormous, we know that. But it has natural reasons. The main reason is that "civilization" out there in the wilderness is represented by "the trader, the backwoodsman, the pirate, the bushranger"; to put it briefly, by whites who can do anything they like with no risk of criticism or control.

"The history of European settlements in America, Africa and Australia, presents everywhere the same general features—a wide and sweeping destruction of native races by the uncontrolled violence of individuals, if not of colonial authorities, followed by tardy attempts on the part of governments to repair the acknowledged crime."

A British parliamentary commission set up in 1837 to investigate the causes of the misfortunes that had afflicted the Tasmanians and other native peoples came to the same conclusion. The commission found that Europeans unlawfully took over native territories, reduced their numbers, and undermined their way of life. "Gross cruelty and injustice" were the main causes of the natives dying out. [58]

As a direct consequence of the commission's work, The Aborigenes Protection Society was formed in 1838 with the aim of putting a stop to the extermination of native peoples. For the rest of the century, this organization continued its increasingly uphill battle against genocide.

117

Where am I? In a concentration camp? In the Third World? The naked bodies around me are emaciated and covered with sores. Christmas is approaching. Some well-fed men are putting up a net with coarse, strong meshing. On the other side of the net is the sculpture of a naked giantess painted in red and gold and decorated with an iron, a club, and boots. The net stops us reaching this fat and happy woman.

The men putting up the net are working in a hail of crude jokes. They will soon set their dogs on us. They are already laughing themselves silly when they see us scrambling on the net. In vain we reach out for club and iron. We don't even reach the boots.

118

Prejudice against alien peoples has always existed. But in the middle of the nineteenth century, these prejudices were given organized form and apparent scientific motivation. In the Anglo-Saxon world, the pioneer was Robert Knox. His book, *The Races of Man: A Fragment* (1850) reveals racism at the actual moment of birth, just as it takes the leap from popular prejudice via Knox's conceded ignorance to "scientific" conviction.

Knox had studied comparative anatomy with Cuvier in Paris. Cuvier's great feat was to prove that innumerable animal species had ceased to exist. But how they died out and why, he did not explain, Knox says.

We know equally little about why the dark races go under. "Did we know the law of their origin we should know the law of their extinction; but this we do not know. All is conjecture, uncertainty."

All we know is that since the beginning of history, the dark races have been the slaves of those lighter skinned. What is that due to? "I feel disposed to think that there must be a physical and consequently, a psychological inferiority in the dark races generally."

This is perhaps not due to lack of size in the brain but rather a lack of quality in it. "The texture of the brain is, I think, generally darker, and the white part more strongly fibrous; but I speak from extremely limited experience."

How limited this experience was is clear in another part of the book, where Knox says that he had done an autopsy on only *one* colored person. He maintains he found in this corpse a third fewer nerves in arms and legs than in a white man of corresponding size. The soul, instinct, and reason of both races must therefore, it is obvious, he maintains, be different to a corresponding degree.

From total ignorance, via this single autopsy, Knox takes a giant stride directly to statements such as: "To me, race, or hereditary descent, is everything; it stamps the man," and "Race is everything: literature, science, art, in a word, civilization, depend on it."

There is something almost touching about the childish openness with which Knox exposes the lack of empirical basis for his statements. The sixth chapter of *The Races of Man*, which deals with the dark races, goes on like this: "But now, having considered the physical constitution thus briefly of some of these dark races, and shown you that we really know but little of them; that we have no data whereon to base a physical history of mankind; let me now consider . . ."

Consider what?

Well, on the basis of this established lack of facts, Knox unhesitatingly delivers categorical statements on the inferiority and inevitable destruction of the dark races.

119

Darwin spoke of "the savage races," without clearly stating which he meant. Wallace and several other authors wrote "the lower" or even "the lower and more depraved races," leaving the reader in profound uncertainty. Was it what we in our day call the Fourth World they were talking about? Or was it the entire Third World? Or even more?

Many people considered that *every* race was inferior and more depraved than the white race; and among the white "races," *all* were lower than the Anglo-Saxon race. Under such circumstances, how large a part of mankind was condemned to extinction?

Knox uses the expression "the dark races." Which are they exactly? That question is not easy to answer, says Knox. Are the Jews a dark race? The Gypsies? The Chinese? Dark they certainly are to some extent; and so are the Mongolians, American Indians, and Eskimos, the inhabitants of almost the whole of Africa, the Far East, and Australia. "What a field of extermination lies before the Saxon, Celtic, and Sarmatian races!"

He is indignant over one thing only: hypocrisy. The British in New Zealand have just (1850) carried out the most audacious annexation in the history of aggression. "The Aborigenes are to be protected!" the British say. Thank you very much! says Knox. They may not become British, when their land is taken from them; they are to be "protected"!

The Saxons do not protect the dark races, says Knox, do not mix with them, do not let them keep a single acre of the land in the occupied countries; at least that is the situation in Anglo-Saxon America, and the Saxon conquerors are moving south.

"The fate, then, of the Mexicans, Peruvians and Chileans, is in no shape doubtful. Extinction of the race—sure extinction—it is not even denied."

120

Can the dark races become civilized? "I should say not," says Knox. "Their future history, then, must resemble the past. The Saxon race will never tolerate them—never amalgamate—never be at peace. . . . The hottest actual war ever waged—the bloodiest of Napoleon's campaigns—is not equal to that now waging between our descendants in America and the dark races; it is a war of extermination—inscribed on each banner is a death's head and no surrender; one or other must fall."

"I blame them not," Knox goes on. "I pretend not even to censure: man acts from his impulses, his animal impulses, and he occasionally employs his pure reason to mystify and conceal his motives from others."

The Americans were presumably already on their way to extinction when the Europeans first arrived. "Now, the fate of all these nations must be the same; it results from the nature of their populations, and nothing can arrest it."

Look at South Africa. The Saxon spirit of progress there led to massacres of the natives. "Have we done with the Hottentots and Bosjeman race? I suppose so: they will soon form merely natural curiosities: already there is the skin of one stuffed in England; another in Paris if I mistake not. . . . In a word, they are fast disappearing from the face of the earth."

And Chinese, Mongolians, Tartars, or whatever they are called, how will things go for them? Well, it is known what happened in Tasmania. The Anglo-Saxon swept the natives out of their own country. "No compunctious visitings about the 'fell swoop' which extinguished a race."

The Chinese can expect the same. China appears to be totally at a standstill with neither inventions nor discoveries. The famous Chinese art must belong to another race from which the Chinese borrowed it without really understanding it.

No, the Chinese have probably seen their best days, have lived through their definitive track and period of time, now hastening toward the terminal where all that remains are remnants left by extinct creatures—like the mammals and birds in Cuvier's world of the past—that have long since ceased to exist.

Robert Knox. Contemporary caricature from *Knox,
the Anatomist* by Isobel Rae, Edinburgh, 1964.

121

Who was this man who with such delight wallowed in the destruction of human beings? He was a Scot, had served as an army doctor
in South Africa, and had founded a school of anatomy in Edinburgh.
As a young student, Darwin heard his controversial lectures. [59]

All anatomists at that time bought specimens from grave rob-
bers, but Knox was suspected of having turned to professional as-
sassins to ensure suitable corpses. That was the end of his scientific
career.

He saw himself as a voice crying in the wilderness. He and he
alone had discovered a great truth, the truth of race, which only
numskulls and hypocrites could deny.

Origin of Species meant a turning point for Knox's ideas. Darwin
neither confirmed nor denied them, but his theory of evolution was
clearly useful for the racists.

Knox was restored to favor and shortly before his death he became a member of the Ethnographical Society, in which a new group
of "racially conscious" anthropologists were now setting the tone.

In 1863, Knox's followers broke away and formed the Anthropological Society, which was more markedly racist. The first
lecture—"On the Negro's Place in Nature"—emphasized the Negro's close relationship to the ape. When a rebellion of rural blacks
was ruthlessly crushed in Jamaica, the society held a public meeting.
Captain Gordon Pim stated in his speech that it was a philanthropic
principle to kill natives; there was, he said, "mercy in a massacre."

Time had begun to catch up with Robert Knox. Previously, race
had been seen as one of several factors influencing human culture.
After Darwin, race became the wholly decisive explanation in far
wider circles. Racism was accepted and became a central element in
British imperial ideology.[60]

122

I am in good company, simply following those in front of me and
knowing others are following behind. We are on our way up a narrow staircase. The banister is a thick rope suggesting safety. The
stairs go around and around inside a church tower; or perhaps it is a
minaret? The whorls of the staircase grow narrower and narrower,
but as there are so many people behind, there is no longer any possibility of turning around or even stopping. The pressure from behind
forces me on. The staircase suddenly stops at a garbage chute in the

wall. When I open the hatch and squeeze my way through the hole, I find myself on the outside of the tower. The rope has disappeared. It is totally dark. I cling on to the slippery, icy wall of the tower while vainly trying to find a foothold in the emptiness.

123

After Darwin, it became accepted to shrug your shoulders at genocide. If you were upset, you were just showing your lack of education. Only some old codgers who had not been able to keep up with progress in natural history protested. The Tasmanian became the paradigm, to which one part of the world after another yielded.

W. Winwood Reade, a member of both the Geographical Society and the Anthropological Society in London, and a correspondent member of the Geological Society in Paris, ends his book *Savage Africa* (1864) with a prediction on the future of the black race.

Africa will be shared between England and France, he prophesies. Under European rule, the Africans will dig the ditches and water the deserts. It will be hard work, and the Africans themselves will probably become extinct. "We must learn to look at this result with composure. It illustrates the beneficent law of nature, that the weak must be devoured by the strong."

A grateful posterity will honor the memory of the blacks. One day, young ladies will sit tearfully beneath the palm trees and read *The Last Negro*. And the Niger will be as romantic a river as the Rhine.[61]

124

On January 19, 1864, the Anthropological Society in London arranged a debate on the extinction of the lower races.[62]

In his introductory talk, "The Extinction of Races," Richard Lee reminded his listeners of the fate of the Tasmanians. The turn had now come of the Maori people of New Zealand, whose population had been halved in a few decades.

The reason for this could not yet be clearly given. Disease, insobriety, and "the antagonism between the white and the coloured population" were important external factors. But they did not explain why the female population diminished more quickly than the male, nor did it explain the large number of infertile marriages.

Whatever the reasons, everywhere around us we could see the way one world leaves room for another more highly developed world. Within a few years the surface of the earth will be quite changed. We civilized people know better how to the use the land that for so long has been "the black man's" undisturbed home. A new era is dawning that will multiply the undertakings of man.

The tide of European civilization is rising over the earth. Through its moral and intellectual superiority, the Anglo-Saxon race is sweeping away the earlier inhabitants. Light is consuming the darkness, said Richard Lee.

His opponent, T. Bendyshe, named the Philippines as one of the many examples of higher and lower races actually being able to live together without the lower being eradicated. So there was no question of any natural law.

The natives die out only where their land is taken from them and thus their means of earning a living. Although some Indian tribes of North America had been almost exterminated, there are sufficient numbers left to repopulate the continent—as long as they were given back their lands. For man reproduces himself regardless of race, according to Malthus's laws, said Bendyshe finally.

A.R. Wallace, the codiscoverer of the theory of evolution, maintained that the lower a race was the more land it needed to live off. When Europeans with their greater energy took over the land, the lower races could only be saved if they were swiftly civilized. But civilization could be acquired only slowly. So the disappearance of the lower races was only a question of time.

125

Later that same evening, in his lecture on "The Origin of Human Races," Wallace explained in greater detail how he looked on extermination. Quite simply, it was another name for natural selection.

Contact with Europeans leads the lower, mentally underdeveloped peoples of other continents to inevitable destruction, says Wallace. The European's superior physical, moral and intellectual qualities meant that he reproduces himself at the expense of the savage, "just as the weeds of Europe overrun North America and Australia, extinguishing native productions by the inherent vigour of their organisation, and by their greater capacity for existence and multiplication."

When Darwin read that, he heavily underlined the word "weeds" and added in the margin his own example: the rat. In *Descent of Man* he later wrote: "The New Zealander . . . compares his future fate with the native rat almost exterminated by the European rat." [63]

European animals and plants adapted without difficulty to the climate and soil of America and Australia, but only a few American and Australian plants, among them the potato, gained distribution in Europe.

These parallels from the worlds of plants and animals provided apparent confirmation of the belief in the biological superiority of Europeans and the inevitable decline of the other races.

But the parallels could also bring about doubts. Why did the weed spread more quickly and effectively in the colonies than any other European plants? Was it really through its moral and intellectual superiority that the European rat exterminated other rats?

126

We are having Christmas dinner with the Tideliuses across the street. I hardly reach the height of the table, which has been laid in the big salon with its black mirrored cupboard and formal high-backed oak chairs. The chandelier sparkles, the cutlery and porcelain, too. The tablecloth is of thick stiff white material, so it bulges a little at the creases and Mrs. Tidelius reaches forward to smooth out the bulge with her hand. A pitiful little squeak is heard, as when the mower exposes a mouse nest in the cornfield. In those days the fields stretched right up to the edges of our lawn. Uffe and I often hung around by the big barn of the manor house, where the rats were as natural as the barn cat. That is the direction our thoughts go as the rat squeaks and Mrs. Tidelius starts up with a shriek. Mr. Tidelius hurries to her rescue. He is twice as old as she is, an elegant, active old man, vigorous in his gait as every morning at six o'clock he takes a walk to the train to go to his ladies' tailoring business in Samuelsgatan. An excellent tailor, but no specialist in rats. He lifts the tablecloth to look underneath it—and whoops, the rat runs on along the crease, toward the center of the table, tipping over glasses on its way. A tremendous hullabaloo ensues as everyone tries to rescue glasses and plates, while they all lift the cloth, pull at the underlay, trying to trap the rat, now squealing with rage and terror and rushing hither and thither underneath the cloth, apparently growing each time it changes direction.

It is difficult to imagine my father doing what he now does. Later, in his old age, he became so mild and gentle. But when I was small, he was different. I still remember when that old rat, its fur quite gray, and as large as a small cat, coming leisurely gliding across our lawn. It was precisely the rat's untroubled way of moving as if it had a perfect right to that enraged my father. He threw open the terrace door, rushed down the slope, grabbing a piece of boarding in passing, caught up with the rat, which too late saw the danger, and killed it against the base of the fencing just as it was about to save itself. That is what he is like in his rage when he goes out into the kitchen for the big ax—we all still had wood-burning stoves in kitchens—raises it above his head and, to the joint squeals of bravo from the women, brings it down with all his strength straight through the bulge in the tablecloth. The cutting edge goes right through the damask and underlay and thuds into the dark oak table. It is sure also to have killed the rat, which is no longer rushing back and forth under the cloth, but is suddenly quite still. The shrieks stop. We all stand immobile, looking at the handle of the ax slanting up toward the ceiling and still trembling from the force of the blow. We can't continue Christmas dinner with the corpse of a rat on the table. The four parents clear the table. Finally they loosen the axe. Then they each go to a corner of the table and first lift the cloth, then the underlay. There is no sign of the rat. It has disappeared. But no one says anything. No one asks where it has gone. They all just stand there looking at the deep white bite the axe has made in the top of the table. "I'll cut a piece of oak," says my father, who is a woodwork master, "and stain it the same color. It'll hardly be noticed." His host and hostess thank him effusively. But dinner is eaten in an oppressive atmosphere and we do not stay late.

127

Even those who remained in the Ethnographical Society realized that the lower races were doomed to destruction.

On March 27, 1866, Frederick Farrar gave a lecture on "Aptitude of the Races." He divided the races into three groups: savage, semi-civilized and civilized. Only two races, the Aryan and the Semitic, were civilized. The Chinese belonged to the semicivilized, as they had once been brilliant but suffered from "arrested development." The savage races had always lived in the same ignorance and wretchedness. Farrar argued that:

> They are without a past and without a future, doomed, as races infinitely nobler have been before them, to a rapid, an entire, and, perhaps for the highest destinies of mankind, an inevitable extinction.
>
> . . . nor out of all their teeming myriads have they produced one single man whose name is of the slightest importance to the history of our race. Were they all to be merged tomorrow in some great deluge, they would leave behind no other traces of their existence than their actual physical remains.
>
> And I call them *irreclaimable* savages . . . [because] so far as being influenced by civilization, they disappear from before the face of it as surely and as perceptibly as the snow retreats before the advancing line of sunbeams.[64]

The Indians are an example. Or take a specimen from the hundred millions of Africa, not one of the most degenerate such as the Hottentots, but a real, pure-blooded Negro. What hope was there that he could be civilized? The great majority of Negroes will go under in a decline from which only a few can be saved.

Many races have already disappeared. These races—"the lowest types of humanity, and presenting its most hideous features of moral and intellectual degradation"—were doomed to go under. "Because darkness, sloth, and brutal ignorance cannot co-exist with the advance of knowledge, industry, and light."

128

What actually did happen when knowledge, industry, and light exterminated the inferior races?

Darwin knew. He had seen General Rosas's men butchering Indians, smothered in blood and vomit. He knew how eyes were gouged out when an Indian had sunk his teeth into a thumb and refused to let go, how women were killed and prisoners made to talk. He had a name for it. He called it the "struggle for life."

Darwin knew what the struggle for life was like. And yet he believed it developed and ennobled the species of man. Wallace shared his belief. The eradication of the lower races was justified, for it would gradually reduce the differences between races until the world would again be inhabited by one single, almost homogenous race in which no one was inferior to the noblest example of the humanity of the day. That is what Wallace believed.

But the strange thing was, he went on, that the little progress made toward this goal did not at all appear to be due to natural selection. Clearly "the best" were not those who were victors in this struggle for existence. The intellectually and morally mediocre, not to say deficient, in short, the weeds, succeeded best in life and reproduced themselves most rapidly.

129

Wallace had put his finger on a tender spot. William Greg took up the problem in an article in *Frazer's* magazine (September 1868), which Darwin read and commented on.[65]

What worried Greg was primarily that the middle classes, "who form the energetic, reliable, improving element of the population" have far fewer children than the upper classes and the lower classes, as both, though for opposite reasons, lack any grounds for restraint.

"The righteous and salutary law of natural selection" has been eliminated, and so our societies threaten to become overcivilized, like the ancient Greeks and Romans once became.

But fortunately the laws of nature are still alive in relations between the races, Greg goes on. Here the most favored are still the most capable and stronger. They are the ones who win the competition and "exterminate, govern, supercede, fight, eat, or work the inferior tribes out of existence."

Greg sees the struggle between the races as the only way of keeping civilized societies vital and capable of progress. Only by exterminating others can we avoid the racial decay that will otherwise be the consequences of civilization eliminating natural selection.

130

I have been cooking food on the computer. I cook it on the screen in the door of the microwave oven where it heats the food.

On my way home with dinner on a disc, I am jumped on in the underground by a man in ethnic clothing and a colorful little knitted cap. He takes the disc away from me. I try to stop him and wake up from having kicked a chair beside my bed with great strength. It still hurts when I walk.

131

Darwin's cousin, Francis Galton, continued the discussion in his book *Hereditary Genius* (1869). The history of geological changes, according to Galton, demonstrates how animal species have constantly been forced to adapt to new conditions of life. Civilization is the kind of new condition human species have to learn to live with. Many have failed. A large number of human races have been totally eradicated under the pressure of the demands of civilization. Galton further observes that "probably in no former period of the world has the destruction of the races of any animal whatever, been affected over such wide areas and with such startling rapidity as in the case of the savage man."

This should be a lesson to us. For even we who have created civilization are succumbing to it. Statesmen and philosophers and equally craftsmen and workers are today faced with demands they cannot master, Galton writes.

The conclusion is clear: if we do not want to go the same way as extinct animals and humans, we must seek to improve hereditary factors and through that increase our ability to survive the conditions of life civilization has created.

Galton devoted the rest of the century to studying and suggesting various methods of achieving such an improvement of hereditary factors. He had many followers, not just in Germany. The State Institute for Racial Biology in Uppsala was still in existence in the 1950s.

132

That passage in Galton is taken up by Benjamin Kidd in his hugely successful *Social Evolution* (1894), in which he observes that the Anglo-Saxon has exterminated the less developed peoples even more effectively than other races have managed to. Driven by the inbuilt forces of his own civilization, the Anglo-Saxon goes to the foreign country to develop its natural resources—and the consequences seem to be inescapable.

This struggle between races, entailing that the inferior are driven to subjugation, even eradication, is nothing distant and past. It is what is still happening in front of our very eyes, under the protection of the Anglo-Saxon civilization we are so proud of and like to link with the most elevated ideals.

For the race that wishes to keep its place in the competition, the eradication of other races is one of the stern imperative conditions. We can humanize those conditions, but not change them fundamentally—they are far too deep-rooted in physiological grounds, the effects of which we cannot shirk, writes Kidd.

133

Common to Wallace, Greg, Galton, and Kidd was their unease over society's terrain not tallying with the map. The wrong people were reproducing themselves. The selection did not favor those who ought to be favored. Then it was a solace to look on the struggle of the races. There, at last, the theory seemed to tally with reality. For it was precisely that reality which had once given rise to the theory.

Common to them was also their unease over changes in society, already very different from what they had experienced as children. Had we created a society which one day would break us as it had already broken the savages? Did it threaten us from within with creeping racial decay? Had we moved too far away from nature?

Common to them all was also the desire to excuse and approve genocide. Extermination was inevitable, apparently vitalizing the exterminators, and it had profound secret causes. Nor was it certain that it was particularly unpleasant for the victims.

To be exterminated could not be called "misery," Galton maintains. It was more a question of listlessness and apathy. The sexes simply lost interest in each other after contact with civilization, and thus their descendants diminished. It was unfortunate, but could hardly be called "misery". . .

But what caused the apathy? What were these profound physiological causes people talked about? At the beginning of the 1800s, in the days of Howison and Merivale, the answers to these questions seemed evident and clear.[66] In the 1890s they had vanished into a racist fog.

134

Put up to be shot from behind. Waiting for the shot, the pain, the end.

We are several. While we wait, we write. We stand writing before the shots are fired.

When our bodies are as cold as corpses, at last a postal order for two pounds arrives. "With thanks for your co-operation" it says on the counterfoil.

135

I believe I have demonstrated that one of the fundamental ideas of the nineteenth century was that there are races, peoples, nations, and tribes that are in the process of dying out. Or as the prime minister of England, Lord Salisbury, expressed it in his famous speech in the Albert Hall on May 4, 1898: "One can roughly divide the nations of the world into the living and the dying." [67]

It was an image that came frighteningly close to reality.

The weak nations become increasingly weaker and the strong stronger, Salisbury went on. It was in the nature of things that "the living nations will fraudulently encroach on the territory of the dying."

He spoke the truth. During the nineteenth century, Europeans had encroached on vast territories in northern Asia and North America, in South America, Africa, and Australia. And the "dying nations" were dying just because their lands had been taken from them.

The word *genocide* had not yet been invented. But the matter existed.

I do not maintain that Joseph Conrad heard Lord Salisbury's speech. He had no need to. It was enough with what he had read of Dilke's in *Cosmopolis*, in Wells's *The Wars of the Worlds*, in Graham's *Higginson's Dream*. Conrad could no more avoid hearing of the ceaseless genocide that marked his century than his contemporaries could.

It is we who have suppressed it. We do not want to remember. We want genocide to have begun and ended with Nazism. That is what is most comforting.

I am fairly sure the nine-year-old Adolf Hitler was not in the

Albert Hall when Lord Salisbury was speaking. He had no need to. He knew it already. The air he and all other Western people in his childhood breathed was soaked in the conviction that imperialism is a biologically necessary process, which, according to the laws of nature, leads to the inevitable destruction of the lower races. It was a conviction which had already cost millions of human lives before Hitler provided his highly personal application.

Lebensraum, Todesraum

"das Recht der stärkeren Rasse, die niedere zu vernichten"
[The right of the stronger race to annihilate the lower]

136

In the mid-nineteenth century, the Germans had still not exterminated any people, so were able to look more critically on the phenomenon than did other Europeans. The most thorough investigation into people threatened with extermination was made by the German anthropologist Theodore Waitz, in *Anthropologie der Naturevölker* (Anthropology of Primitive Peoples) (1859–62), which summarizes and analyzes information from reports by traveling scholars. His pupil, Georg Gerland, took up the problem of extermination in *Über das Aussterben der Naturvölker* (On the Extinction of Primitive Peoples) (1868).

Gerland goes through and evaluates every conceivable reason named in the debate: primitive peoples' lack of care of their own bodies and of children, taboos about certain foods, features of personality such as indolence, rigidity, and melancholy, sexual depravity and inclination to addiction to intoxicants, tribal warfare, cannibalism and human sacrifices, frequent capital punishment, an inhospitable environment, and finally influences from higher cultures and the whites' treatment of colonized peoples.

He concludes that the diseases of the whites have often been decisive exterminating factors. Even healthy whites can be infectious as they carry a "miasma," a "dust of disease," which was the name in those days for what we would call bacteria and viruses.

The miasma works more powerfully the farther away and more free of this dust a people has previously lived. The Europeans have slowly acquired a resistance to miasmas which peoples living in nature lack. So they die.

But an even more decisive factor is the hostile behavior of the whites, constituting one of the blackest chapters in the whole history of mankind. What could be called "cultural violence" is even more efficacious than physical violence, Gerland says.

The way of life of primitive peoples is so wholly adapted to climate and nature that sudden changes, however innocent and even useful they may seem, are devastating. Radical changes such as the privatization of land that had previously been public property disturb the basis of a whole way of life. Europeans destroy out of rapacity or lack of understanding the basis of everything the natives thought, felt, and believed. When life loses its meaning for them, they die out.

Physical force is the clearest and most tangible factor in extermination. The bloodthirstiness of the whites is especially frightening as it is exercised by intellectually highly developed people. It cannot be said that violence is taken to only by individuals who could be made individually responsible—no, "the cruelties have been carried out fairly uniformly by whole populations in the colonies or anyhow have been approved by them; yes, even today violence is not always condemned."

It is no law of nature that primitive people must die out. Hitherto only a few peoples have been completely exterminated. Nowhere have we found any physical or mental inability to develop among them, Gerland ends. If the natural rights of the natives are respected, they will live on.

Darwin read this book and refers to it in *The Descent of Man* (1871).[68] But he was more influenced by Lyell and Wallace and Greg and Galton, who had already drawn "Darwinian" conclusions for man and society from *Origin of Species* (1859). Darwin was forestalled by those who parroted him, and he seems to have been seduced by their higher bids.

137

At the turn of the century, the German authority in this field was Friedrich Ratzel. He devotes the tenth chapter of his *Anthropogeographie* (1891) to "the decline of peoples of inferior cultures at contact with culture."

It has been, he writes, a deplorable rule that low-standing peoples die out at contact with highly cultivated people. This applies to the vast majority of Australians, Polynesians, northern Asians, North Americans, and many peoples in South Africa and South America. "The theory that this dying out is predestined by the inner weakness of the individual race is faulty," Ratzel writes. It is the Europeans who cause the destruction; as "the superior race" is in a minority, it must weaken the natives in order to gain domination. The natives are killed, impoverished, and driven away, their social organization destroyed.

The basic feature of white policies is the assault of the strong on the weak, the intention to take their land from them. This phenomenon has taken its most grandiose form in North America. Land-hungry whites crowd in between the weak and partly decayed settlements of the Indians. In Ratzel's day, the still increasing immigration into native lands was contrary to treaties and one of the main reasons for the extinction of the Indians.

That far, Ratzel sounds just like Gerland. Since Waitz's day this had been the standpoint of German anthropology. After all, the Germans had no colonies.

138

However, at the beginning of the 1890s, colonial ambitions had also begun to arise in Germany. The same year that Ratzel published his *Anthropogeographie*, he became a founding member of the Pan-German League, a radical right-wing organization that had the creation of a German colonial empire highest on its agenda.

This gives rise to some contradictions in Ratzel's view on the extinction of the lower races.

The question is whether this "deplorable process" is not after all driven on by a certain "demonic necessity," he goes on. Violence and the theft of land are indeed the main reasons for the decline of native peoples, but the logic that this is precisely why they die out would be far too simple.

Anyone looking more deeply will see that the European assaults really only intensify an already existing evil. In peoples with little culture there are inner forces of destruction that are released for the slightest reason. Their decline can therefore not be seen only as a result of attacks by more advanced peoples.

No, those with little culture have fundamentally passive characters. They seek to endure rather than overcome the circumstances that are reducing their numbers. Contact with Europeans simply hastens an extinction already underway. Many peoples at lower cultural levels have died out for internal reasons, with no assaults from the outside.

Thus Ratzel has gone full circle. He now maintains what he began by denying. For a future empire builder, the new standpoint was undeniably more comfortable.

139

The Jews could not really be regarded as "a people of inferior culture" in the sense Ratzel meant. A standard accusation against them was the opposite, that their position in German cultural life was far too dominating. But in his book *Politische Geographie* (1897), Ratzel nevertheless is able to pair them with people who, according to him, are condemned to annihilation. Jews and gypsies are brought together with "the stunted hunting people in the African interior" and "innumerable similar existences" into the class of "scattered people with no land." [69]

Land with no peoples, on the other hand, no longer exists. Not even the deserts can today be regarded as ownerless empty spaces. So a growing people needing more land has to conquer land, "which through killing and displacement of the inhabitants is turned into uninhabited land."

Pericles depopulated the island of Aegina to prepare room for Attic settlers. Rome carried out the same transplantations. Since then these have become increasingly necessary as uninhabited land became rarer and, finally, nonexistent. "Colonization has long since become displacement."

The history of American colonization provides a great many examples of people being removed and displaced. "The higher the culture of the immigrants stands above that of the original inhabitants, the easier the process. . . ." The United States is the best example of swift spatial expansion: from 1.1 million square miles in 1783 to 2.9 million in 1803 and 5.7 million in 1867.

Europe is the most thickly populated continent and the one whose population is growing fastest. So colonies are for Europe a necessity.

But it is a mistake to think that colonies have to be on the other side of the oceans. Border colonization is also colonization. Occupations near at hand are more easily defended and assimilated than distant ones. Russia's spread into Siberia and Central Asia is the most important example of this type of colonization, Ratzel maintains.

Hitler was given Ratzel's book in 1924, when he was in Landsberg prison writing *Mein Kampf.*

140

There are toads for dinner. Live toads. I wake just as I am to bite the head off a toad. It is still throbbing in my hand.

141

What about international law, then? The British had always regarded their expansion as a self-evident right. The French expansion in Northern Africa and the Russian in Central Asia, on the other hand, they regarded as reprehensible aggressive acts. And the German expansion was the height of immorality—on that point, the French, Russians, and British were all in agreement.

Robert Knox drew the conclusion that might is right: "Whilst I now write, the Celtic race is preparing to seize Northern Africa by the same right as we seized Hindostan—that is might, physical force—the only real right is physical force."[70]

The British are now appalled by the French invasion and regard it as ruthless aggression. We forget, says Knox, that "laws are made to bind the weak, to be broken by the strong." Could we really expect mighty France to be content to be "cabin'd, cribb'd, confin'd" and stay within the borders that chance and fortunes of war had handed her? No, of course not.

And this even if France is regarded simply as a nation! If we look on it from a more elevated viewpoint and remind ourselves that France represents a race, then we realize that the French claims are fully justified. "The Celtic race of men demand for their inheritance a portion of the globe equal to their energies, their numbers, their civilization, and their courage," Knox wrote in 1850. The same argument was now used in Germany as a motive for German expansion eastward.

142

As lecturer in German at Glasgow (1890–1900), Alexander Tille became familiar with British imperial ideology. He "Germanized" it by linking Darwin's and Spencer's theories to Nietzsche's superman morality into a new "evolutionary ethic."

In the field of international law, this evolutionary ethic entails that the stronger are right. By displacing the lower races, man is only doing what the better organized plants do with the less well organized, and what more highly developed animals do to the less developed. "All historical rights are invalid against the rights of the stronger," writes Tille in *Volksdienst* (Service to the people) (1893).

In nature, the higher are everywhere victorious over the lower. The weaker races die out even if no blood flows. It is "the right of the stronger race to annihilate the lower." Tille further argues that "when that race does not maintain its ability to resist then it has no right to exist, for anyone who cannot maintain himself must be content to go under."[71]

These iron "laws" were so generally worded by Tille that they could easily be applied not only to primitive peoples on other continents but also to the economically less successful peoples of Europe.

The Pan-German League paper *Alldeutsche Blätter* in the following year, 1894, stated that the conditions of life for the German race could be assured only through "elbow room" stretching from the Baltic to the Bosphorus. In that process one should not allow oneself to be hindered by the fact that inferior peoples such as Czechs, Slovenes, and Slovaks would lose their existence, anyhow worthless to civilization. Only "peoples of higher culture" have the right to a nationality of their own.[72]

143

When the big boys go into attack, I entrench myself on the upper floor of my childhood home. I confront them on the stairs and defend myself by breaking off large bits of the banisters and the rail to use as weapons. But they are light and brittle as meringue and at once fall to pieces. I am overwhelmed in a flash.

Then the wallpaper comes away from the walls of my parents' bedroom and slips to the ground. Not that I have ever been particularly fond of that showy large-flowered pattern, but nonetheless it is frightening that it is falling off. A pattern is a kind of skeleton even if it is on the outside. An entire architecture of life has collapsed, leaving behind the bare walls.

144

In Southwest Africa in 1904, the Germans demonstrated that they too had mastered an art that Americans, British, and other Europeans had exercised all through the nineteenth century—the art of hastening the extermination of a people of "inferior culture."

Following the North American example, the Herero people were banished to reserves and their grazing lands handed over to

German immigrants and colonization companies. When the Hereros resisted, General Adolf Lebrecht von Trotha gave orders in October 1904 for the Herero people to be exterminated. Every Herero found within the German borders, with or without weapons, was to be shot. But most of them died without violence. The Germans simply drove them out into the desert and sealed off the border.

"The month-long sealing of desert areas, carried out with iron severity, completed the work of annihilation," the General Staff writes in the official account of the war. "The death rattles of the dying and their insane screams of fury . . . resounded in the sublime silence of infinity." The General Staff's account further reports that "the sentence had been carried out" and "the Hereros had ceased to be an independent people."[73]

This was a result the General Staff was proud of. The army earned, they stated, the gratitude of the whole fatherland.

When the rainy season came, German patrols found skeletons lying around dry hollows, twenty-four to fifty feet deep, dug by the Hereros in vain attempts to find water. Almost the entire people— about eighty thousand human beings—died in the deserts. Only a few thousand were left, sentenced to hard labor in German concentration camps.

Thus the words "concentration camp," invented in 1896 by the Spaniards in Cuba, anglicized by the Americans, and used again by the British during the Boer War, made their entrance into German language and politics.[74]

145

The cause of the rebellion was "the Hereros's warlike and freedom-loving nature," the General Staff stated.

The Hereros were not particularly warlike. Their leader, Samuel Maherero, over two decades had signed one treaty after another with the Germans and ceded large areas of land to avoid war. But just as the Americans did not feel themselves bound by their treaties with the Indians, equally, the Germans did not think that as a higher race they had any need to abide by treaties they made with the natives.

As in North America, the German plans for immigration at the turn of the century presupposed that the natives were to be relieved of all land of any value. The rebellion was therefore welcomed as an opportunity to "solve the Herero problem."

The arguments the English, French, and Americans had long used to defend genocide were now also put into German: "Existencies, be they peoples or individuals who do not produce anything of value, cannot make any claim to the right to exist," wrote Paul Rohrbach in his best-seller *German Thought in the World* (1912). It was as head of German immigration in Southwest Africa that he had learned his colonial philosophy:

> No false philanthropy or racial theory can convince sensible people that the preservation of a tribe of South Africa's kaffirs . . . is more important to the future of mankind than the spread of the great European nations and the white race in general.
>
> Not until the native learns to produce anything of value in the service of the higher race, i.e. in the service of its and his own progress, does he gain any moral right to exist.

146

From my place on the hotel roof terrace, I look down over the market place in Agadez. A black man is walking along wearing shiny reflector sunglasses and a gray corduroy suit. Has he any right to exist?

And that man in the black trench coat? Or him over there in a red jogging suit with white reveres? Everything suits a beauty, it is said, but that should be: everything suits a pride. These people move like kings, most of all the men of white shirts and flapping cloaks with turbans like eagle's nests on their heads. They often walk hand in hand. They carry nothing except possibly a toothbrush in their mouths or a sword at their sides.

Their way of life is threatened. The nomads are attacked from one direction by the assailing deserts, from the other by cultivators' fields, which today go right up to the borders of the desert.

When drought strikes, when the grazing vanishes and the wells dry, the nomads make their way to Agadez. Some return when the drought is over, but most remain—far too impoverished to take up the struggle against the desert again. They live in a circle around Agadez, crammed into small round tents of raffia mats, and have already tripled the population of the town.

They meet in the camel market. I sometimes go there when the dust has made it impossible to continue the day's work. The strong evening wind sweeps people and animals into a fog of dust. In this haze, heavily veiled men stand looking at each other's camels.

The camels protest against every change, with loud complaining screams. Their mouths are ash gray and evil smelling, their tongues as pointed as wedges. They hiss like dragons, strike like snakes, inflict hideous bites, and rise reluctantly on tall wobbling legs to stand there like some kind of outsized greyhounds with swollen stomachs and wasp waists at their loins, superciliously looking down on the world around them, their eyes filled with unspeakable contempt.

The same arrogance marks their masters. They often cannot even imagine abandoning their lifestyle. But nor can they live by selling their camels to each other. Nor can they live by transporting homemade desert salt from Bilma or Tueggidam in caravans, when one single truck carries a larger load than a hundred camels.

Tuaregs are not hunted as are the natives in the Amazon or the jungles of Borneo, but the basis of their life is disappearing like a melting ice floe. Many succeed in jumping over to other floes. The old camel yards have become repair workshops and diesel stations. As drivers, the Tuaregs find a use for their knowledge of the desert. Others despise such change or cannot cope with it.

147

A German schoolmaster is sitting on the roof this evening. For seven years he has spent his vacations in the Sahara and his idea of sport is to get as far south as possible before he has to return. Tomorrow he is to take the bus to Niamey, then fly back to Germany, where the neo-Nazis are attacking some refugee camps almost every night, his crackling transistor tells us. In Sweden, too, refugee quarters have been set on fire. In Paris, Le Pen is speaking on May Day.

"I've heard him," says a French engineer working for Michelin in Nigeria. "I thought that when Fascism came back, it would be disguised in bright friendly colors, so that it would be difficult to recognize. I didn't think it would come in a brown shirt and black leather. I didn't think it would be shaven heads, swastikas, boots, and officer's shoulder belts. I didn't think it would call itself 'national and socialist.' "

But just as recognizably, it is coming, swaggering with its heritage from Nazism. The same roar after every sentence when the leader speaks. The same hatred of aliens. The same preparedness for violence. The same wounded manhood.

"And the same soil," says the German. "After the war, *everyone* was afraid of unemployment. Everyone knew where that had led to and could do so again. That insight lasted for twenty-five years. Then it was forgotten."

The advantages are tempting. Unemployment rates of 5, 10, 15, or 20 percent give the employer a wonderful upper hand. The workforce stands on tiptoe, longing to be exploited.

And this is just the beginning. The great mass of unemployed are on the other side of Europe's Rio Grande, in Asia and Africa. Just wait until they come flooding in, said the German. Wait until the border falls just like the Wall fell and everything will be one great labor market. Who will then win elections?

148

The Pan-German League's "elbow room" was given wings when Friedrich Ratzel renamed it *Lebensraum* at the turn of the century.

The geographer Ratzel was originally a zoologist. In the concept of *Lebensraum*, he linked the biological theory of life with the geographical theory of space, into a new theory, charged with political dynamite.

Between the never-ending movement of life and the unalterable space of the earth lies a contradiction that always and everywhere gives rise to struggle, Ratzel writes in *Der Lebensraum* (1901, in book form 1904). Since life first reached the limits of space, life has been fighting with life for space.

What is called the struggle for existence is really a struggle for space. True "lack of space" we see most clearly in animals living together in colonies. The first to arrive take the best places, those who come later have to be content with the worst. Among them, infant mortality is greatest, and corpses lie scattered over the ground.

Similar courses of events arise in human life, says Ratzel. His readers knew what he was aiming at. Germany was one of the last to arrive among the European nations. In a world the colonial powers had already divided up between themselves, Germany had to be content with the worst places. This was why the children of the unemployed were dying in Berlin and Hamburg—that was the conclusion the reader was expected to draw.

As a young man, Ratzel had traveled in North America and seen the way whites and Indians fought over lands. This struggle became for him a paradigm, which he constantly returned to.

A few hundred thousand Indians, degraded and removed to unfavorable areas, had seen their continent Europeanized as to people, animals, and plants. The Spaniards built towns and ruled the crop-growing Indians. The Germanic and French settlers in North America took over the land from the natives in order to cultivate it themselves. "The result was an annihilating struggle, the prize for which was the land, the space."

This struggle is not only over *Lebensraum*, as when a bird builds its nest. It concerns the much larger *Lebensraum* needed to earn a livelihood. To conquer and hold sufficient *Lebensraum*, others have to be displaced, that is, lose space—which often entails the species weakening and dying out, leaving the space completely.

The shortage of living space on this earth makes it necessary for an old species to disappear to open the space for a new species to evolve. Extinction is a presupposition for creation and progress. "The history of primitive peoples dying out on the appearance of a people of higher culture provides many instances of this."

How much of the loss of space by the old species is due to inner reasons, such as declining life force, and how much due to the victorious progress of the new species is still an open question. What is certain is that the decline of a species is always expressed by it being crowded together into an increasingly smaller space.

One of the greatest riddles in the history of evolution is that some of the oldest and largest animal groups died out on the threshold of the Tertiary period. The reptiles dominating land and water during the Triassic, Jurassic, and Cretaceous periods died out in the Tertiary period and were replaced by mammals and birds.

We do not know why. From our starting point, Ratzel says, it is enough to establish what happened: an animal species replaced another in the space. Extinction is often preceded by a decline in numbers, which also suggests a reduction of the space.

Ratzel did not have to draw the conclusion himself. It was already clear: a people that does not wish to share the fate of the dinosaurs must constantly increase its living space. Territorial expansion is the safest, indeed fundamentally the only real sign of the vitality of the nation and the race.

149

Ratzel's theories were a good summary of what had happened during the nineteenth century. The spread of Europeans over four continents, the growth of the British, French, and Russian empires, such examples seemed to demonstrate that territorial expansion was necessary and favored the conquerors. A stagnant territory was considered as abnormal and as ill-omened as a stagnant economy is considered today.

But even in 1900, when the concept of *Lebensraum* was born, that approach was outmoded. Size of territory had been decisive for agricultural states, but for industrial states, other factors were much more important. Geographically insignificant, Germany developed her economy at the end of the 1800s as rapidly as the huge United States and considerably more quickly than the British Empire. Technology and education were already more important economic driving forces than spatial size.[75]

So the *Lebensraum* theory was backward-looking. Perhaps just because of that it became an enormous success. It appealed to the major power that had arrived last to imitate its predecessor. "The loser from 1870," as France was called in Germany, had since then built up the second largest colonial empire. Why not Germany? The Germans had lagged behind. Germany must catch up.

The *Lebensraum* theory urged Germany to use the strength the country had gained through new means of production (industry) to acquire more of the old means of production (land), roughly like the new industrial barons showing off their power by displacing the old nobility from their manors and estates.

An expanding people needs space, it was said. A people who cannot "feed itself" is doomed to die out. Why? No answer.

Hitler started the war to acquire more agricultural land a few decades before all the states of Europe began to pay their farmers to reduce cultivation.

150

When Adolf Hitler entered politics, one of the opportunities for Germany to expand had been closed. The British Navy ruled the seas and stopped every attempt to conquer new lands in the colonies.

There remained the continent. In *Mein Kampf* (1925–27) Hitler describes how Germany and England are to divide up the world between them. Germany is to expand eastward just as England had already expanded westward in America and south in India and Africa. The culmination of Hitler's policy of eastward expansion was the invasion of the Soviet Union in June 1941.[76]

German propaganda portrayed the war as an anti-Communist crusade. In that way, Hitler hoped to win sympathy among all those in western Europe and the United States who hated communism. But the crusade would never have come about if there had not also been economic reasons for it.

In the short term, by conquering the agricultural areas of the western Soviet Union, Hitler wanted to improve the food situation in wartime Germany. In this way an unknown number of millions of people (*zig Millionen Menschen*) in the Soviet Union were to die of starvation, which would also be a long-term advantage.

In the long term, Hitler intended to incorporate these agricultural areas into the German *Lebensraum*. The land, "which through killing and displacement of the inhabitants is turned into uninhabited land" (cf. Ratzel), would come into German possession. The decimated Slavic population, like the Hereros in Southwest Africa, would be the servants and workers of their German masters.

151

On the night of September 18, 1941, Hitler painted for his collaborators a rosy future in which the Ukraine and the Volga basin had become the breadbasket of Europe. There, German industry would exchange grain for cheap utility goods. "We'll send to the Ukraine kerchiefs, glass beads, and other things colonial peoples like." [77]

Of course, he was joking. But to understand Hitler's campaign to the east it is important to realize that he considered he was fighting a colonial war. For wars of that kind, special rules applied—those already laid down in *Politik* (1898) by the German extreme right's most beloved political scientist, Heinrich von Treitschke: "International law becomes phrases if its standards are also applied to barbaric people. To punish a Negro tribe, villages must be burned, and without setting examples of that kind, nothing can be achieved. If the German Reich in such cases applied international law, it would not be humanity or justice but shameful weakness."

Treitschke was only putting into words the practice European states had long applied and which Hitler now used against his future "colonial peoples" in the east.

In the war against the western powers, the Germans observed the laws of war. Only 3.5 percent of English and American prisoners of war died in captivity, though 57 percent of Soviet prisoners of war died.

Altogether, 3.3 million Russian prisoners of war lost their lives, two million of them in the first year of the war, through a combination of starvation, cold, disease, execution, and gassing. The first to be gassed in Auschwitz were Russians.

There is a crucial difference between these killings and the murders of Jews. Of non-Jewish Russians, only certain categories—first and foremost intellectuals and Communists—were totally exterminated. Among other Russians, according to the plans, some ten million or so were to be weeded out, but the remainder were to live on as a slave labor force under German command. On the other hand, the Jewish people as a whole were to be exterminated.[78]

In that, the Holocaust was unique—in Europe. But the history of Western expansion in other parts of the world shows many examples of total extermination of whole peoples.

152

My stomach is being filled with a great blood blister. My whole belly is full of black blood.

Just as a toenail blackens and falls off when the blood has coagulated under it, my body blackens and drops off.

All that is left is the throbbing blood beneath its membrane, thin and shimmering like a soap bubble.

An immense drop of black blood, for a moment still held together by its surface tension—that is me, before I burst.

153

"Many of the most horrendous of Nazi actions (especially the massacre of the Jews) . . . had comparatively little to do with the imperialist parts of the Nazi program," writes Woodruff D. Smith in *The Ideological Origins of Nazi Imperialism* (1986).

Smith is a great specialist in this field, but in my opinion he is wrong. Imperialist expansion gave the Nazis the practical opportunity and economic reasons to exterminate the Jews. The extermination project's theoretical framework, the *Lebensraum* theory, is part of imperialist tradition. To the same tradition belongs the historical model of extermination of Jews: genocide in the colonies.

When the mass murder of Jews began, there were only a quarter of a million Jews left in Germany. The rest had either fled or been banished. The great Jewish populations were in Poland and Russia. Hitler had the practical possibility of eradicating them only by attacking and capturing these areas.

The main intention behind the conquest was not to murder Jews, just as the Americans did not advance westward in order to murder Indians. The intention was to expand Germany's own *Lebensraum*. The Russian Jews lived in just those areas Hitler was after, making up to 10 percent of the total population there and up to 40 percent of the urban population.

To faithful Nazis, the killing of Jews was a way of implementing the most central point of the party program. For those less faithful, it was a practical way of reducing the consumption of food and making room for the future German settlement. German bureaucracy spoke of "de-Jewishing" (*Entjudung*) as a way of clearing out "superfluous eaters" (*überzähligen Essern*) and in that way creating a "balance between population and food supply."

Hitler himself was driven throughout his political career by a fanatical anti-Semitism with roots in a tradition of over a thousand years, which had often led to killing and even to mass murder of Jews. But the step from mass murder to genocide was not taken until the anti-Semitic tradition met the tradition of genocide arising during Europe's expansion in America, Australia, Africa, and Asia.

According to the *Lebensraum* theory, the Jews were a landless people, like the stunted hunting people of the African interior. They belonged to an even lower race than Russians and Poles, a race which could not lay claim to the right to live. It was only natural that such lower races (whether Tasmanians, Indians, or Jews) should be exterminated if they were in the way. The other Western master races had done just that.

The Nazis gave the Jews a star on their coats and crowded them into "reserves"—just as the Indians, the Hereros, the Bushmen, the Amandabele, and all the other children of the stars had been crowded together. They died on their own when the food supply to the reserves was cut off. It was a sad rule that low-standing people died out on contact with highly cultivated people. If they did not die fast enough, then it was merciful to shorten their suffering. They were going to die anyhow.

154

Auschwitz was the modern industrial application of a policy of extermination on which European world domination had long since rested.

To Zinder

The Nazi slaughter of the Jews, like every other event, however unique it may be, has to be seen in its historical context.

Arno J. Mayer, in his controversial book *Why Did the Heavens Not Darken? The "Final Solution" in History* (1988), goes right back to the horrors of the Thirty Years' War, the storming of Magdeburg on May 10, 1631, when thirty thousand men, women, and children were murdered, and even further back to the mass murder by the Crusaders of eleven hundred innocent inhabitants of Mainz in 1096, to find equivalents to the mass murders of Jews during World War II.[79]

On the other hand, there is no mention of the European slave trade, which forcibly moved fifteen million Negroes between continents and killed perhaps just as many. Nor are the nineteenth-century European colonial wars or punitive expeditions mentioned. If Mayer had as much as glanced in that direction, he would have found so many examples of brutal extermination based on clearly racial convictions, that the Thirty Years' War and the Crusades would seem to lie unnecessarily far back.

On my journey through the Sahara alone, I have been in two Mainzes. One is called Zaatcha, where the entire population was wiped out by the French in 1849. The other is Laghouat, where on December 3, 1852, after the storming, the remaining third of the population, mainly women and children, was massacred. In one single well, 256 corpses were found.

That was how one mixed with the inferior races. It was not considered good form to talk about it, nor was it anything that needed concealing. It was established practice. Only occasionally was there any debate—for instance, over the events taking place while Joseph Conrad was writing *Heart of Darkness* and the Central African Expedition was on its way toward Zinder.

156

The bus to Zinder leaves at 7:30. At dawn I find a man with a wheelbarrow to help me wheel away my word processor and suitcase. It is a windy and cold morning, some fires flickering over by the stalls across the street, a few lamps glowing faintly, overcome by the morning light.

After half an hour, the driver arrives and starts washing the windows of the big white Renault truck that has been converted into a bus. On the sides it says in giant red letters: SOCIETE NATIONALE DE TRANSPORT NIGERENNE.

Vendors of loose cigarettes and sticky lollipops start assembling. A shivering man is carrying round red nuts, already shelled and indecently naked on his tray. A bright yellow baby's cap frames his anthracite black face.

Toward half-past eight, the blind women come, all of them at once, all singing, all begging, all led by children, some of the women with newborn babies on their backs.

At nine, the passengers are called out according to the passenger list and each given a small piece of paper, which after another roll call is exchanged for the ticket already booked and paid for the day before yesterday.

A man stands on a barrel and flings the luggage up to the driver, who stows it on to the roof of the bus. After that the station supervisor gets into the bus and, standing inside where he is very difficult to hear, starts the third and determining roll call. It is not easy to predict how a name like mine will sound. I miss the name and thus lose my booked seat in the front of the bus. Only the seats at the back are left.

I can still change my mind. I can still jump off. Here at the far back I will never cope with the jolts. And once out in the desert there is no return. One has to go on, for eight hours, whatever happens. It is now, at this moment, and only now, I still have a chance to get off.

Always the same alloy of panic and joy at the moment of departure. It is like losing your foothold in a great love affair. What will happen now? I have no idea. All I know is that I have just thrown myself out into it.

157

At the head of the 1898 Central African Expedition were Captain Voulet and Lieutenant Chanoine.[80]

Paul Voulet, the thirty-two-year-old son of a doctor, had, according to his officer colleagues, "a true love of blood and cruelty coupled with a sometimes foolish sensitivity." He was, it was said afterward, a weak character dominated by two evil people, his black mistress and Chanoine.

Charles Chanoine, the son of a general, was described as impulsive, ruthless, and cruel—"cruel out of cold-bloodedness as well as for pleasure." Two years previously, in 1896, the two friends had conquered Ouagadougou in what is now Burkina Faso, and had shown themselves to be skilled at burning down villages and murdering natives. Faced with this new expedition, Voulet boasted to the governor of Sudan of how he would crush resistance by letting the villages burn.

So despite, or perhaps thanks to, his reputation, Voulet was appointed head of an expedition that was to explore the area between the Niger and Lake Chad and place it, as was said, "under French protection."

Otherwise his orders were vague in the extreme. "I don't pretend to be able to give you any instructions on which route to choose or how you are to behave toward the native chieftains and peoples," wrote the minister for the colonies modestly.

Voulet was given a free hand to use the methods for which he had made himself notorious.

158

It is 270 miles from Agadez to Zinder—270 miles of washboard, sanded over by high wandering dunes that lift the bus and throw it down with fierce, stunning jolts.

The driver maintains a good speed in order to get there before sunset. It is like sitting on a leaping compressed-air drill. The fat in my blood ought to be churned to butter by the vibration.

At the same time you have to be constantly prepared to rise in the saddle and receive the great jolts with your thigh and arm muscles instead of your spine. But I miss every fourth or every tenth one, not noticing in time that the driver has taken his foot off the accelerator, and I am suddenly hurled with full force down toward the center of the earth. All my vertebrae come tumbling down and the disks in my spine have to take the whole jolt.

For the first hours the wind is very strong. The dust turns day into white night, and the sand sweeps over steppe and savanna. The white steppe grass drowns, the bushes ride in despair on the waves of sand. The occasional tree is glimpsed in the blurred murkiness of the sand, and misty human figures struggle on, whipped by the sand in the air.

The sand seems to be the attacker when the desert comes, but it is the dryness that kills. Dead plants can no longer bind and stop the sand. We drive for hours through sparse forest where only every hundredth tree is alive. White tree trunks lie like distorted skeletons on the ground.

After five desert hours we are suddenly in among fields. The cultivation boundary has moved forward until it coincides with the boundary of the desert. The vulnerable living space the nomads once found between desert and field no longer exists.

159

Here on the edge of the desert, in 1898, marched the Central African Expedition. It consisted of nine French officers, seventy regular Senegal soldiers, and thirty interpreters and "agents." In addition, they had recruited four hundred "auxilliaries," Africans who went with the French and took part in the fighting for a chance to plunder. In Tombouctou, ninety Senegalese joined them, placed at the expedition's disposal by Lieutenant-Colonel Klobb.

Voulet took with him great quantities of arms and ammunition, but had not taken any means of paying the bearers. His men simply seized eight hundred black men and forced them to be bearers. The latter were dressed for the hot climate prevailing where they were captured and suffered severely from the night cold in the desert. A dysentery epidemic broke out, and 148 bearers died during the first two months of the expedition. Chanoine set an example by having anyone who tried to escape shot.

They requisitioned food from the villages, naturally without payment. What with baggage and mistresses, the expedition had grown to sixteen hundred people and eight hundred animals. It moved on like a swarm of locusts through areas normally living on the edge of starvation. Neither of the two commanders had any experience of desert areas. The expedition cruised between the water holes, dominated by the necessity of supplying men and animals with forty tons of water a day.

160

Meanwhile Joseph Conrad was sitting at his Chippendale desk at Pent Farm in Kent, penciling out his story about Kurtz, the story of outrages committed in the name of Civilization and Progress. He could not have been influenced by contemporary events in French Sudan, as he knew nothing about them.

Not until January 29, when Conrad had almost finished his story, was one of the French officers, Lieutenant Peteau, sent back owing to "lack of discipline and enthusiasm." Not until February 5 did Peteau write a fifteen-page letter to his wife-to-be in Paris to tell her of some of the atrocities he had been involved in.

The forcibly recruited bearers were maltreated and refused medical attention during the dysentery epidemic, Peteau writes. Those who were unable to continue were beheaded. Twelve bearers were shot for trying to escape, the rest bound together with neck chains, in groups of five.

To recruit new bearers, the French sent out patrols, which surrounded the villages at dawn and shot anyone trying to escape. As evidence that they had carried out their orders, the soldiers took the heads back with them. Voulet had the heads impaled on stakes and placed out to frighten the population into submission.

In Sansan-Hausa, a village already under French "protection," Voulet had given orders that thirty women and children were to be killed—with bayonets, to save ammunition. According to the chieftain, Kourtey, there were even more victims. "I had done nothing to them," he said. "I gave them everything they asked for. They ordered me to hand over six horses and thirty head of cattle within three days. I did so. And yet they killed everyone they could get hold of. A hundred and one men, women, and children were massacred."

161

Peteau's fiancée sent his letter to her deputy in parliament, and in the middle of April, the government intervened. The governor of Sudan gave orders to Lieutenant-Colonel Klobb in Tombuoctou to find Voulet and remove from him his command of the expedition.

Just as in Conrad's novel Marlow set off into the interior to find Kurtz, Klobb took up the hunt for Voulet. His tracks were easy to follow; they consisted of ruins and corpses, which increased in number appallingly the closer Klobb came.

Klobb found guides who had displeased Voulet and had been strung up alive, low enough for hyenas to eat their feet, while the rest of the bodies were left to the vultures. Outside the burned-out village of Tibiri, 120 miles west of Zinder, Klobb found the bodies of thirteen women hanging in the trees. Outside Koran-Kaljo, nearer to Zinder, hung two corpses of children.

On July 10, 1899, Klobb arrived at the little village of Damangara to be told that Voulet was only a few hours' march away.[81]

162

In the middle of the night, my father telephones. Surprised and confused, I rush across the hotel yard in the dark to take the call in Reception. When I lift the receiver I can hear nothing but a hollow crackling.

Nor could I expect anything else, I realize when I wake up. After all, Father is dead.

The heat enfolds me in its moist embrace. The heat in the Sahara stings like a whiplash, but only where the searchlight of the sun fell; in the shade it was cool, at night cold. Here in Zinder the summer temperature seldom goes below 105°F.

Your veins swell and snake along under your skin, pumping, throbbing, ready to burst. Hands and feet swell, the soles of your feet sting, fingers resemble small clubs, your skin is not large enough. Your face swells up, becomes porous and opens. Sweat spurts out through the pores, suddenly, just as when a heavy raindrop strikes your skin.

I can feel a burning heat on the inside of my lower arm and notice it is brushing my stomach. I have burned myself on my own body.

All flesh thickens, overflows, starts running. A movement and your body is soaked all over. Keep still and nonetheless you are soaked.

I drink so much, the salt balance in my body is disturbed. Then I eat salt, become thirsty, and have to drink even more. My belly swells, my body slops about, nothing helps.

Next morning I am sitting as usual in the library of the French Institute reading Klobb's journal.[82] But my mind stiffens like coagulated blood in my head, and the afternoons start earlier and earlier, sinking deeper and deeper into a hot torpor.

In the evening as I sit waiting for the news on the hotel owner's radio, I hear a sea moving in the rise and fall of the interference. Above me, filled with a wonderful cool, roll the huge roaring breakers of space.

163

The meeting between Klobb and Voulet was even more dramatic than the meeting between Marlow and Kurtz in Conrad's novel, by then already finished and published in *Blackwood's* magazine. Marlow did not after all have to make Kurtz come back with him. Kurtz was seriously ill and went with him after some persuasion. Voulet did not.

Klobb sent a sergeant and two soldiers with a letter that briefly and curtly told Voulet he had been removed from his command and was to return home immediately. Voulet replied that he had six hundred rifles against Klobb's fifty and would open fire if Klobb approached.

On July 13, Voulet had a hundred and fifty women and children executed as punishment for the death of two of his soldiers during an attack on a nearby village. On the same day, he once again wrote to Klobb and warned him not to come any nearer.

Klobb was convinced that neither Senegalese soldiers nor French officers would bring themselves to shoot at a superior officer. He counted on the ninety soldiers he had lent the expedition preferring to obey him rather than Voulet. What he did not know was that Voulet and Chanoine had kept his letter secret from the other whites and had sent them all out on various assignments in the vicinity, keeping with them only the black troops personally loyal to them.

On July 14, Bastille Day, Klobb's and Voulet's troops stood facing each other. Klobb gave his men strict orders not to open fire under any circumstances. Then he started slowly walking toward Voulet, who had his soldiers fire two salvos into the air. When Klobb was within earshot, he stopped and started speaking directly to the soldiers.

Voulet was furious and, threatening them with a pistol, forced his men to fire at Klobb. Klobb was wounded and fell—still calling on his men not to answer fire. The next salvo killed him.

164

Naturally, Voulet had not read Conrad's recently published story about Kurtz, the white man who, with terror and magic, had made himself king over a black realm in the heart of the continent.

But when the white officers returned that evening, Voulet told them what had happened and suggested a solution of exactly that kind: they would continue to Lake Chad and there set up their own kingdom, "a strong and impenetrable empire, surrounded by a waterless desert."

"I am no longer a Frenchman. I am a black chief," said Voulet.

The following day, the black sergeants decided to mutiny. Voulet was warned by an interpreter, who was immediately shot for not warning him earlier. Voulet mounted his horse and, with Chanoine, addressed the soldiers, firing at them at the same time. The soldiers answered fire and killed Chanoine. When Voulet tried to approach the camp the following morning, he was also shot.

The French officers held a council of war and decided to continue the expedition. They marched toward Zinder and captured the town.

165

The hotel owner sits all day in the yard talking to his parrot, his voice caressing and loving, quite different from the brusque commanding tone he otherwise uses in his contact with the outside world.

Sometimes he brings his two dogs here and exercises them in the yard. An adopted son takes up a middle position, a handsome black boy, son of his dead housekeeper.

I am the only guest.

I am engrossed in the history of Zinder. It turns out that a much larger French expedition, which had just crossed the Sahara in the summer of 1899, was on its way to Zinder. So it was quite superfluous for other Frenchmen to capture the town.

But the remains of the Central African Expedition got there first.

These were the troops to gain everlasting glory by occupying Zinder, the expedition's officers hoping their crimes would be forgotten.

They were right.

When the murder of Klobb became known in Paris, an official inquiry was set up on August 23. After having accumulated three huge cardboard boxes of statements and documents, they found only one conceivable explanation: the climate. Voulet must have gone mad in the African heat.

The crimes of the others were excused and forgotten, and France kept her captured possessions.

The French left wing took over in government in 1899 and had little interest in digging any further into the affair. The right wing had even less. The ugly truth stayed in the inquiry's cardboard boxes.[83]

166

Eventually the facts trickled out. Of course, educated Frenchmen knew roughly, or even quite precisely, by what means their colonies were captured and administered.

Just as educated Frenchmen in the 1950s and 1960s knew what their troops were up to in Vietnam and Algeria.

Just as educated Russians in the 1980s knew what their troops did in Afghanistan, and educated South Africans and Americans during the same period knew what their "auxilliaries" were doing in Mozambique and Central America respectively.

Just as educated Europeans today know how children die when the whip of debt whistles over poor countries.

It is not knowledge that is lacking. The educated general public has always largely known what outrages have been committed and are being committed in the name of Progress, Civilization, Socialism, Democracy, and the Market.

167

At all times it has also been profitable to deny or suppress such knowledge. Even today there are readers of Conrad's story who maintain it lacks universal application.

It has been said that the circumstances in the Congo of the Belgian monarch were unique. The novel cannot be seen as an accusation against the whole of the civilized world, as the oppressive Belgian regime in the Congo was a one-of-a-kind phenomenon already condemned by most reasonable people.

But during just those months when Conrad was writing the book, similar or even worse events were occurring by another river, the Niger, on the way to another chamber of the same dark heart.

No, the Belgians were not unique, nor were the Swedish officers in their service. Conrad would have been able to set his story using any of the peoples of European culture. In practice, the whole of Europe acted according to the maxim "Exterminate all the brutes."

Officially, it was, of course, denied. But man to man, everyone knew. That is why Marlow can tell his story as he does in Conrad's novel. He has no need to count up the crimes Kurtz committed. He has no need to describe them. He has no need to produce evidence. For no one doubted it.

Marlow-Conrad was able to assume quite calmly that both the listening gentlemen on the yacht, the *Nellie*, and the readers of *Blackwood's* silently knew quite enough to understand the story and in their own imaginations develop details the novel only implied. This knowledge is a fundamental prerequisite of the book.

This knowledge could be expressed in general and scholarly language. Imperialism is a biologically necessary process that, according to the laws of nature, leads to the inevitable destruction of the lower races. Things of that kind could be said. But the way it actually happened, what it really did to the exterminators and the exterminated, that was at most only implied.

And when what had been done in the heart of darkness was repeated in the heart of Europe, no one recognized it. No one wished to admit what everyone knew.

168

Everywhere in the world where knowledge is being suppressed, knowledge that, if it were made known, would shatter our image of the world and force us to question ourselves—everywhere there, *Heart of Darkness* is being enacted.

169

You already know that. So do I. It is not knowledge we lack. What is missing is the courage to understand what we know and draw conclusions.

NOTES

See generally Ian Watt, *Conrad in the Nineteenth Century* (London, 1980); and Patrick Brantlinger, *Rule of Darkness: British Literature and Imperialism, 1830–1914* (Ithaca, 1988). This English-language edition of *"Exterminate All the Brutes"* is a translation of the second Swedish edition.

To In Salah

1. The most recent geological period, which began at the end of the Ice Age.

2. Kim Naylor, *Guide to West Africa* (London, 1986), p. 193.

3. John Aubrey, *Brief Lives* (1949), p. 157

4. Joseph Conrad, "An Outpost of Progress" (1897).

5. B.W. Sheehan, *The Seeds of Extinction, Jeffersonian Philanthropy, and the American Indian* (Chapel Hill, NC, 1973); S.M. Stanley, *Extinction* (New York, 1987).

6. Richard C. Lewontin, "Fallen Angels," *New York Review of Books*, June 14, 1990.

7. Margaret T. Hodgen, *Early Anthropology in the Sixteenth and Seventeenth Centuries* (Philadelphia, 1964), p. 410.

8. Herbert Spencer, *Social Statistics* (1850), p. 416.

9. Eduard von Hartmann, *Philosophy of the Unconscious*, vol. 2, p. 12. Quoted in J.E. Saveson, *Modern Fiction Studies* 16, no. 2 (1970).

10. Ernst Nolte in *Historikerstreit: Die Dokumentation der Kontroverse um die Einzigartigkeit der nationalsozialistischen Judenvernichtung* (Munich, 1987), p. 33. See also Frank Chalk and Kurt Jonassohn, *The History and Sociology of Genocide* (New Haven, CT, 1990); and Ervin Staub, *The Roots of Evil: The Origins of Genocide and Other Group Violence* (Cambridge, 1989). None of these authors saw the connection between genocide by Hitler and European imperialism. However, Richard L. Rubenstein has done so in *Genocide and Civilization* (1987). I am grateful to Professor Sverker Sörlin, who drew my attention to Rubinstein's writing and to Helen Fein's bibliography, *Genocide: A Sociological Perspective in Current Sociology*, vol. 1 (1990).

11. K. Lange, "Der Terminus 'Lebensraum' in Adolf Hitler's *Mein Kampf*," *Vierteljahreshefte für Zeitgeschichte* 13 (1965), pp. 426–37.

12. Edgar Sanderson, *The British Empire in the Nineteenth Century: Its Progress and Expansion at Home and Abroad* (London, 1898); James Morris, *Pax Britannica: The Climax of an Empire* (London, 1968), chap. 1; Aaron L. Friedberg, *The Weary Titan: Britain and the Experience of Relative Decline, 1895–1905* (Princeton, NJ, 1988).

13. Keyaerts mentioned in Zdzistaw Najder, *Joseph Conrad* (1983).

14. *The Century Magazine*, September 1897.

15. Neal Ascherson, *The King Incorporated: Leopold II in the Age of Trusts* (London, 1963).

16. David Lagergren, *Mission and State in the Congo* (Uppsala, 1970).

17. *Regions Beyond*, May 1896, pp. 253ff.

18. Charles Dilke, "Civilization in Africa," *Cosmopolis*, July 1896, cited in H. Zin, *Joseph Conrad and Africa* (Nairobi, 1982).

19. Leonard Courtney, *Journal of the Royal Statistical Society* 61, no. 4 (1898), p. 640.

20. C. Lô, "Les foggaras du Tidikelt," *Traveaux de l'Institut de Recherches Sahariennes* 10, no. 2 (1953), pp. 139ff; C. Lô, "Les foggaras du Tidikelt," *Traveaux de l'Institut de Recherches Sahariennes* 11, no. 2 (1954), pp. 49ff.

Gods of Arms

21. Ian R. Smith, *The Emin Pascha Relief Expedition, 1886–1890* (Oxford, 1972). See also Richard Hall, *Stanley* (London, 1974); and Frank McLynn, *Stanley: Sorcerer's Apprentice* (London, 1991).

22. Philip Magnus, *Kitchener: Portrait of an Imperialist* (London, 1958). See also Trevor Royle, *The Kitchener Enigma* (London, 1985); Philip Warner, *Kitchener* (London, 1985); and P.M. Holt, *The Mahdist State, 1881–1898: A Study of Its Origins, Development, and Overthrow* (Oxford, 1970).

23. The execution of the wounded was defended in the *Saturday Review*, September 3, 1898, and September 10, 1898.

24. Geoffrey Parker, *The Military Revolution: Military Intervention and the Rise of the West, 1500–1800* (Cambridge, 1988).

25. Daniel R. Headrick, *The Tools of Empire: Technology and European Imperialism in the Nineteenth Century* (Oxford, 1981). See also W. Broadfoot, "The Lee Metford Rifle," *Blackwood's Magazine*, June 1898.

26. Martin Reuss, "The Disgrace and Fall of Carl Peters," *Central European History* 14, no. 2 (1981), pp. 110ff. See also *The Times*, April 26–27, 1897. For other German examples, see Lionel Decle, *Three Years in Savage Africa* (London, 1900).

27. William Tordoff, *Ashanti Under the Prempehs, 1888–1935* (London, 1965); Richard Austin Freeman, *Travels and Life in Ashanti and Jaman* (Westminster, 1898).

28. Michael Rosenthal, *The Character Factory* (London, 1986); Tim Jeal, *The Boy-Man: The Life of Lord Baden-Powell* (New York, 1990); Robert S.S. Baden-Powell, *The Downfall of Prempeh* (London, 1896).

29. Philip A. Igbafe, *Benin Under British Administration* (Longman, 1979). See also Felix von Luchan, *Die Altertümer von Benin: Veröffentlichungen aus dem Museum für Völkerkunde* (Berlin and Leipzig, 1919); R.H. Bacon, *Benin: The City of Blood* (London, 1898); and M.M. Mahood, *The Colonial Encounter* (London, 1977).

30. Robert S.S. Baden-Powell, *The Matabele Campaign* (London, 1897, 1901).

31. T.O. Ranger, *Revolt in Southern Rhodesia, 1896–97: A Study in African Resistance* (London, 1967), p. 121.

32. Darrel Bates, *The Fashoda Incident* (Oxford, 1984).

33. Norman Page, *A Kipling Companion* (London, 1984). See also Charles Carrington, *Rudyard Kipling* (London, 1955).

To Tam

34. Nicholas Delbanco, *Group Portrait: Joseph Conrad, Stephen Crane, Ford Madox Ford, Henry James, and H.G. Wells* (New York, 1982). See also Iain Finlayson, *Writers in Romney Marsh* (London, 1986); and Miranda Seymour, *A Ring of Conspirators: Henry James and His Literary Circle, 1895–1915* (London, 1988), chap. 5.

The Friends

35. *Chambers's Journal*, September 30, 1893; Bernard Bergonzi, *The Early H.G. Wells: A Study of the Scientific Romance* (Manchester, 1961). Wells and Conrad literary survey in *Journal of Modern Literature* (1986), pp. 37ff.

36. R.B. Cunningham Graham, *Mogreb-el-Acksa* (1898), pp. 25, 43ff.

37. R.B. Cunningham Graham, "Higginson's Dream," *Saturday Review* 1, no. 10 (1898). See also Cedric Watts, *Cunningham Graham: A Critical Biography* (Cambridge, 1979).

Cuvier's Discovery

38. *Mémoires de l'Institut national des sciences et des arts, Sciences mathématiques et physiques*, vol. 2 (Paris, 1799). See also Georges Cuvier, *Discours sur les révolutions de la surface du globe* (1812, 1985); and Dorinda Outram, *Georges Cuvier: Vocation, Science and Authority in Post-Revolutionary France* (Manchester, 1984).

39. Stanley, *Extinction*, p. 2 and passim. See also George G. Simpson, *Fossils and the History of Life* (New York, 1983), chap. 1 and 5.

40. Cuvier, *Discours sur les révolutions*, preface and afterword.

41. William Coleman, *Georges Cuvier, Zoologist* (Cambridge, MA, 1964), pp. 143–65.

42. Hodgen, *Early Anthropology*, pp. 408ff, 418ff.

43. Charles White, *An Account of the Regular Graduations in Man* (1799), p. 135.

44. Erik Nordenskiöld, *Biologins Historia* (The History of Biology), vol. 2 (Stockholm, 1920–24), pp. 45ff.

45. Charles Darwin, *The Voyage of the* Beagle (January 9–April 13, 1834).

46. W. Bölsche, *Ernst Haeckel* (Leipzig, 1900), chap. 9.

47. Coelman, *Georges Cuvier*, pp. 174ff.

48. Charles Darwin, *On the Origin of Species* (1859), chap. 9.

49. Letter to Lyell quoted in *Journal of the History of Biology* 10, no. 19 (1977). See also George W. Stocking, *Race, Culture, and Evolution: Essays in the History of Anthropology* (New York, 1968), pp. 113ff.

To Agadez

50. Alfred W. Crosby, *Ecological Imperialism: The Biological Expansion of Europe, 900–1900* (Cambridge, 1986), chap. 4.

51. Alfred W. Crosby, *The Columbian Exchange: Biological and Cultural Consequences of 1492* (Westport, CT, 1972). See also Woodrow Borah, *New Spain's Century of Depression* (Berkeley, CA, 1951); Russell Thornton, *American Indian Holocaust and Survival: A Population History Since 1492* (Norman, OK, 1987); Mörner Magnus, *History of Latin America* (Stockholm, 1969); and Lewis Hanke, *Aristotle and the American Indian: A Study in Race Prejudice in the Modern World* (London, 1959).

52. Adam Smith, *The Wealth of Nations* (1776), chap. 8.

53. Philip D. Curtin, *The Image of Africa: British Ideas and Action, 1780–1850* (Madison, WI, 1964), pp. 363ff, 373.

54. Darwin, *Voyage of the* Beagle, chap. 5.

55. James R. Scobie, *Argentina: A City and a Nation* (Oxford, 1964), chap. 1.

56. James Bonwick, *The Last of the Tasmanians* (1870; London, 1970). See also Robert Travers, *The Tasmanians: The Story of a Doomed Race* (Melbourne, 1968); and George W. Stocking, *Victorian Anthropology* (London, 1987), pp. 274ff.

The Birth of Racism

57. *Edinburgh New Philosophical Journal* 28 (1839), pp. 166–70.

58. D. Coates et al., *Evidence on Aborigines* (London, 1837).

59. Adrian Desmond and James Moore, *Darwin* (London, 1991), p. 26.

60. Curtin, *Image of Africa*, pp. 377ff, 364. "In time, the new racism was to become the most important cluster of ideas in British imperial theory. . . ."

61. Reade is also quoted in Zin, *Joseph Conrad and Africa*, p. 186.

62. *Journal of the Anthropological Society of London* 165 (1864), reprinted in A.R. Wallace, *Natural Selection and Tropical Nature* (1878).

63. John C. Greene, "Darwin as a Social Evolutionist," *Journal of the History of Biology* 10 (1977).

64. *Transactions of the Ethnological Society of London* (1867), p. 120.

65. Greene, "Darwin as a Social Evolutionist."

66. Howison and Merivale, see sections 115 and 116.

67. J.A.S. Grenville, *Lord Salisbury and Foreign Policy: The Close of the Nineteenth Century* (London, 1964), pp. 165ff.

Lebensraum, Todesraum

68. Darwin, *Descent of Man*, chap. 7. See also Woodruff D. Smith, *Politics and the Sciences of Culture in Germany, 1840–1920* (Oxford, 1991). This was not accessible to me until my own work was completed.

69. Friedrich Ratzel, *Politische Geographie* (1897), pp. 35, 119, 121.

70. Robert Knox, *The Races of Mankind: A Fragment* (1850), pp. 149, 198.

71. *Volksdienst* (1893), pp. 21ff.

72. *Alldeutsche Blätter*, quoted in Lange, "Der Terminus 'Lebesraum.' "

73. *Die Kämpfe der deutschen Truppen in Südwestafrika. Auf Grund amtlichen Materials bearbeitet von der kriegsgeschichtlichen Abteilung I des großen Generalstabes. Erster Band. Der Feldzug gegen die Hereros* (Berlin, 1906). Quote from preface and report by Oberleutnant Graf Schweinitz K. Schwabe, *Der Krieg in Deutsch Südwestafrika, 1904–1906* (Berlin, 1907). See also Woodruff D. Smith, *The German Colonial Empire* (Chapel Hill, NC, 1978); Helmut Bley, *Kolonialherrschaft und Sozialstruktur in Deutsch-Südwestafrika, 1894–1914* (Hamburg, 1968); and "Die Methoden der Menschenbehandlung haben auf das Mutterland zurückgewirkt," p. 314.

74. Andrej J. Kaminski, *Konzentrationslager 1896 bis heute* (Munich, 1990), chap. 2.

75. Paul Kennedy, *The Rise and Fall of the Great Powers* (New York, 1987), chap. 5–6.

76. Eberhardt Jäckel, *Hitler's Weltanschauung* (Tübingen, 1969). See also Reinhard Rurüp, *Der Krieg gegen die Sowjetunion, 1941–1945* (Berlin, 1991); and R.D. Müller, *Hitler's Ostkrieg und die deutsche Siedlungspolitik* (Frankfurt am Main, 1991).

77. Werner Jochmann, ed., *Monologe im Führerhauptquartier 1941–1944* (Hamburg, 1980), pp. 58ff.

78. Gerd R. Überschär et al., *Der deutsche Überfall auf die Sowjetunion* (Frankfurt am Main, 1991); Götz Aly and Susanne Heim, *Vordenker der Vernichtung* (Hamburg, 1991), pp. 115ff, 123; and Eberhard Jäckel and Jürgen

Rohwer, eds., *Der Mord an den Juden im zweiten Weltkrieg* (Frankfurt am Main, 1987).

79. Arno J. Mayer, *Why Did the Heavens Not Darken: The "Final Solution" in History* (New York, 1988), prologue.

To Zinder

80. J.F. Rolland, *Le grand capitaine* (Paris, 1976). See also Douglas Porch, *The Conquest of the Sahara* (Oxford, 1984); A.S. Kanya-Forstner, *The Conquest of Western Sudan: A Study in French Military Imperialism* (Cambridge, 1969); M. Mathieu, "La Mission Afrique Centrale" (thesis, Université de Toulouse-Miraile, 1975), pp. 40, 102, 151; *Documents pour servir à l'histoire de l'Afrique Occidentale Française de 1895 à 1899* (Paris); General Jolland, *Le drame de Dankori* (Paris, 1930): P. Vigné d'Octon, *La Gloire de sabre* (1900; Paris, 1984); and debates in chamber des deputes, June 21, November 23, November 30, and December 7, 1900.

81. Jean-François Klobb, *Dernier carnet de route* (Paris, 1904).

82. Ibid.

83. Cardboard boxes now in the Depôt des Archives d'Outre Mer, Aix-en-Provence.

TERRA NULLIUS

A Journey Through No One's Land

Sven Lindqvist

Translated by Sarah Death

CONTENTS

To Moorundie   193

The Secret of the Desert   201

To Kahlin Compound   234

The Dead Do Not Die   255

To Pinjarra   283

The Smell of White Man   302

The Ground   316

Chronology   359

Bibliography   369

Notes   377

Map of Europe enclosed in that of Australia.

To Moorundie

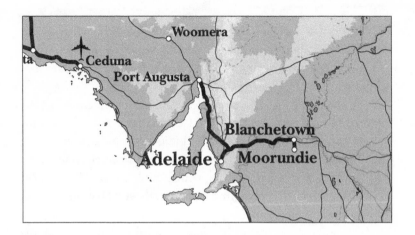

I

Terra nullius. From the Latin *terra*, earth, ground, land, and *nullius*, no one's.

Thus: no one's land, land not belonging to anybody. Or at any rate, not to anybody that counts.

Originally: land not belonging to the Roman Empire.

In the Middle Ages: land not belonging to any Christian ruler.

Later: land to which no European state as yet lays claim. Land that justly falls to the first European state to invade the territory.

Empty land. Uninhabited land. Land that will soon be uninhabited because it is populated by inferior races, condemned by the laws of nature to die out. Land where the original inhabitants are, or can soon be rendered, so few in number as to be negligible.

The legal fictions summed up as *terra nullius* were used to justify the European occupation of large parts of the global land surface. In Australia this meant legitimizing the British invasion and its accompanying acts of dispossession and the destruction of indigenous society.[1]

gov. refusal to recognize land of indigenous people

2

Moorundie? Morrundie? No, the RAC in Adelaide didn't know anything about it.

"Oh, but it was the site of the first fighting between whites and blacks in South Australia," I said. "A whole people was wiped out, the Ngaiawong people.[2] There must at least be a memorial or something."

No, the name wasn't on any of their maps or itineraries. They sent me to the South Australian Museum, which didn't know anything about Moorundie either. The indigenous population live in the museum's exhibition in a continuous now, in an eternally timeless, permanent present that has neither a future nor a history. On the subject of what the white invasion did to those who were invaded, the museum is silent.

"Oh, but it was where the explorer Edward John Eyre began his scientific investigation of the Aboriginal peoples of Australia. It was in Moorundie he collected the material for his treatise 'Manners and Customs of the Aborigines of Australia,'[3] which is the gateway to everything this museum has on show about them . . ."

No, the museum's information desk apologized and referred me to the tourist office, which sent me on to another tourist office, which didn't know anything either. Moorundie seemed to have been swallowed up by the ground.

3

All around me in Adelaide, Sorry Day was in full swing. "Sorry" said the placards. "Sorry" said fifty thousand white demonstrators. They were protesting against their government's refusal to apologize for the injustice that had been done, and was still being done, to Australia's Aborigines. Fifty thousand whites were showing their solidarity with the Aborigines by demanding that their government apologize.

Some of the 950,000 Adelaidians who didn't go on the demonstration took up the gauntlet and answered in the days that followed via the web and the letters columns in the papers. "Sorry" wasn't just a polite phrase, they pointed out. If the government apologized to the indigenous peoples, the present generation would thereby be accepting responsibility for the crimes of previous generations, for which the time limit for prosecution had long since expired. If the government as much as whispered "Sorry," the sluice gates would open and in would pour compensation claims from people who had nothing in common with the victims of those past crimes but the color of their skin.

"Apologize for what?" asked others. In the conflict there had most definitely been outrages committed on both sides. It was only natural that the technically and militarily more advanced civilization had beaten the technically inferior one. What happened in Australia had also happened in North and South America, in Siberia and Central Asia. Large areas of the globe are today populated by European immigrants who have ousted the original population. Who often in their turn have ousted even earlier inhabitants. Should they all be paid compensation? And in that case, who's to pay? For what?

4

I finally located Moorundie/Morrundie on a computer in the map section of the Department of the Environment. It turned out to be on the Murray River just south of Blanchetown.

One chilly, brilliant June morning, I drive out of Adelaide. The vineyards are turning green, the wheat is glistening in rust-brown fields, the bluebushes of the heathlands are strewn with stars. The occasional graveled road, bright white like those on the Swedish island of Gotland, tells of underlying limestone. The occasional long, treeless hill lends a Scottish air.

In this landscape we find neither spruce nor pine, neither birch nor lime, neither oak nor elm. Here we have acacia and eucalyptus, full stop. But in Australia, these two species seem able to assume whatever form they like. Since there are only two trees here, those two have arrayed themselves in all the rich variety of forms that on other continents are divided between many different species and families.

The crowns of the trees float like clouds in the sky. The foliage appears to hover in the air, resting lazily on nothingness. Suddenly, something that looks like the crown of a dill plant is sticking up above the other treetops. Just as suddenly, the landscape presents me with a bouquet of trees held together by the damp fist of a root-ball half buried in the ground.

Below Blanchetown, the river is sluggish and silty. It creates a lush, damp environment in the riverbed. A little gravel track runs by the waterside. The name "Moorundie" is associated above all with an island in the river, created by the silt.

5

John Eyre came here on June 15, 1839, and thought he'd found paradise. Here was every possible requirement for the good life: running water, tall trees, fertile soil, and thousands of birds and fish, in fact the ideal site for a settlement. He hurried back to Adelaide and bought 1,411 acres of land at Moorundie from the government of the newly founded colony. Now he was a landowner in paradise.[4]

An unspoken condition of the sale was that the land did not belong to anyone else; that it was what was called "terra nullius," no one's land.

There was just one catch: Moorundie wasn't uninhabited. The Ngaiawong people had been living there for at least five thousand years and had every intention of staying. Every time a herd of cattle was driven across the continent from the old penal colonies of Sydney and Melbourne in the east to the new settler colony of Adelaide, there was conflict when they reached Moorundie. A contemporary commentator summed up the situation: "Whenever the parties of whites happened to be of sufficient force, a great slaughter was sure to be committed upon the blacks."

Eyre noted in his diary: "But the only idea of the men was retaliation—to shoot every native they saw." Such shotgun progress may have eased their passage on that one occasion, but it created problems for the cattle herds to follow and for the whites who wanted to settle in the valley.

As predicted, the conflict intensified from year to year, culminating in 1841 in a massacre in which white troops mowed down a large group of Aborigines, regardless of their age or sex. The officially recorded death toll was thirty. According to the Aborigines the real figure was much higher. [5]

After the massacre, Eyre was appointed District Chief in Moorundie, with the task of getting to know the natives and resolving the conflict. On leaving his post three years later, he could boast there had not been a single instance in that period of Europeans suffering serious injury or being attacked by the indigenous people. Eyre also succeeded in preventing the whites' worst abuses of power. He introduced a paternalist regime with a monthly distribution of flour and sugar. But he could do nothing to stop Aborigine society disintegrating. The black people succumbed to white diseases, and the cramped conditions in the camps where they received their rations encouraged the rapid spread of infection. White men without women chased after black women and passed on sexually transmitted diseases. In 1841 these were still unknown in Moorundie; three years later, many were dying from them.

6

A few decades later, an entire people had vanished. No one spoke their language any more. No one preserved their holy places. There is not so much as a memorial left.

Was it genocide? If so, when did it become genocide? When they shot every Aborigine they saw? When they bought or raped the women and infected them with syphilis? Or even further back, when they took land at gunpoint and bought peace with rations of flour?

"Genocide was a concept that didn't yet exist," say those who don't want to apologize. It took another hundred years for the word "genocide" to come into use, and even longer for it to assume any legal force. It is anachronistic to judge the people of the 1840s by the laws and morals of our time. They couldn't know that what they were doing would at some future date be considered wrong. Genocide presumes intent. But those settlers in Moorundie didn't foresee the consequences of their actions. They didn't realize the natives would die out. They can't be guilty of something they were unable to predict.

But the truth is, the fate of the Aborigines could be all too clearly predicted. In 1837 a British parliamentary committee looked at the situation of the indigenous peoples of the whole empire, from Newfoundland, where the last native was shot dead in 1823, to South Africa and Australia, where whole peoples were en route to extinction. The committee found that the Europeans had unlawfully conquered the natives' territory, decimated their numbers, and undermined their way of life. "Injustice and cruelty" were the main causes of the extinction of the indigenous peoples.[6]

After three years in Moorundie, Eyre reached the same conclusion.

> It is an undeniable fact, that wherever European colonies have been established in Australia, the native races in that neighbourhood are rapidly decreasing, and already in some of the elder settlements, have totally disappeared. It is equally indisputable that the presence of the white man has been the sole agent in producing so lamentable an effect; that the . . . result must be that if nothing be done to check it, the whole of the Aboriginal tribes of Australia will be swept away from the face of the earth.
>
> To sanction this aggression we have not, in the abstract, the slightest shadow of either right or justice—we have not even the extenuation of endeavouring to compensate those we have injured, or the merit of attempting to mitigate the sufferings our presence inflicts.[7]

And that's why the calls are still echoing today round the buildings in Adelaide: Say sorry! Give redress! Make amends for the sins of the past!

7

As a very young man, I went to Iceland aboard a ship that stopped off in the Trondheimfjord to load herring barrels.

It was the summer of 1951, a lovely evening at hay-making time. The smell of freshly cut hay was heady and intense. The captain stayed aboard but the first mate and the Icelandic crew rowed ashore. They let me come along. The Icelanders had been there many times before and were welcome guests, invited in for coffee at farmstead after farmstead. There was much chatting and laughing and the mood was high-spirited—until someone caught sight of me sitting over by the door with a sugar lump between my teeth, drinking my coffee from my saucer as the custom was in those days.

"Who's that?"

"He's a passenger," the Icelanders replied. "Swedish."

"Swedish!" The whole room fell silent. All conversation stopped, every smile faded. They all looked at me. The silence seemed interminable. At last the great-grandmother said:

"Swedish, eh? Well what about the 1942 transits, then?"

What could I say? The transport of German troops through Sweden to Norway and back had in fact gone on for several years. But that was how she put it—"Well what about the 1942 transits, then?" And everybody was waiting for an answer. I tried to make light of it:

"I was ten in 1942. They didn't ask me."

"But big enough to share the booty," said the great-grandmother.

The silence became unbearable. I said thank you for the coffee and crept out with my tail between my legs. I thought it so utterly unfair. Why accuse little me for what the whole Swedish nation had done or not done? As if it was my fault. As if it was my responsibility.

I climbed down the steep edge of the fjord. It was a light evening, the scents were overpowering. The rowing boat we'd come in had dropped several meters with the outgoing tide. While I waited for the others, I silently composed a grand speech in my defense. "It's wrong to burden children with blame for their parents' actions. Every new generation is born free of guilt."

But of course that wasn't strictly true. The national debt is passed on from generation to generation. Just like the nation's assets, which amount to a great deal more than its debt. Simply by being born Swedish, I was born rich. It wasn't my own efforts that had made me better off than a Congolese or an Indonesian. It was as the heir to an undamaged society and a fully functioning economy; in short, it was as a Swede that I was well off.

And having accepted the advantages of being a Swede, how could I then disown the disadvantages? The ore consignments, the traffic of soldiers going on leave, and other gross breaches of neutrality were what enabled Sweden to keep on good terms with the Germans and avoid the war. It was my own country's cowardly appeasement policy I had to thank for never having been bombed or shot at or even having to go to bed hungry. Yes, the great-grandmother was right. I'd had my share of the booty, so I had to take my share of the responsibility, too.

The Secret of the Desert

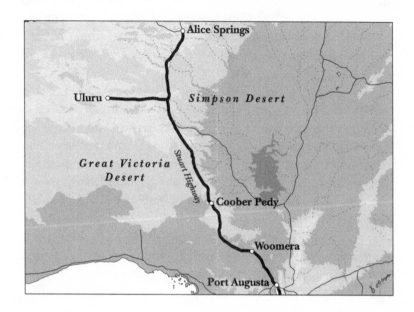

8

Swann Reach Hotel, not far from Moorundie, is shockingly over-priced for what it has to offer. The hollow, sagging beds seem designed for dromedaries. After a bitterly cold night, spent fully dressed under a double layer of covers, I fumble my way through the self-service breakfast. The morning mist over the river and the ferry berth are pewter gray, just like the heath.

Then the sun rises; at a stroke the whole scene is transformed. Suddenly you can *see* it all: Charon in his little car ferry across the river, the indecently naked trunks of the eucalyptus trees, the slender pepper tree beneath which the car is parked.

I continue north via Gladstone, through a Mediterranean landscape that gives way to waterlogged saltmarsh down by the coast. Port Augusta sits by a lagoon in the inner recesses of the bay.

I spend the night at the Pastoral Hotel. The reception desk is in the gaming hall, which is an electronic hell of flashing, bleeping slot machines. An Aboriginal woman is standing there changing her money into counters. She plays "The Desert Is in Flower" and "Lucky Clover," she plays "Blue Lagoon" and "Dingo Night." Outside in the street her daughter, who looks about six, sits waiting for her.

She's the first Aborigine I've seen on my trip. We avoid eye contact.

The steppe, flat and empty, starts just outside the town. To the west is the Great Victoria Desert, to the east the Simpson Desert.

It was the surveyor John McDouall Stuart who, in 1862, at the third attempt, successfully located the strip of steppe and savannah between the two deserts that makes it possible to cross Australia from coast to coast, south to north. He was applauded, fêted, given a noble title—and died, forgotten, as an alcoholic in London four years later.[8] But the road he discovered is still called the Stuart Highway.

A red road through dry, white grass. Nowhere is the horizon more important than in the desert. A sword-cut divides earth and sky. The landscape is vast, the skyscape even vaster.

9

Some miles east of the main highway lies Woomera, a small, symmetrical settlement of bungalows, planned as a single unit and built in 1947. The British needed somewhere to live while they were testing their intercontinental guided missiles. The huge test site extended from the launchpads in Woomera to the Australian west coast at Port Hedland—a stretch of 1,500 miles of no-man's-land with just a few farms, or "stations," as the Australians call them.[9]

White stations, of course. The blacks didn't count.

On six properties, the farmhouses were moved, relocated outside the risk area. Women and children were evacuated. Telephone warnings were given before each launch. Full compensation was promised for any injury.

When tests involving Black Knight missiles began in 1955, £30,000 was spent on building shelters at six farmhouses and

eleven outstations. A further £8,000 went on the extension of telephone lines.

The Aborigines had neither stations nor telephones. They were
scattered over an area the size of western Europe, no one knew quite
where. Most of this territory was "reserved" for the Aborigines. In
the 1930s it had been allocated to them "in perpetuity." Yet in the
1940s, the reservation was reappropriated and turned into a missile
test site. The natives had been given the use of the then worthless
land as some sort of compensation for everything else that had been
taken from them. Now the land was suddenly needed and at once
became a "prohibited area."

The welfare of the natives was entrusted to a police officer,
W.B. MacDougall. Stationed in Woomera, he was supposed to ensure the safety of everyone within an area of over 600,000 square
miles.

In practice, the whites' noise and refuse proved more dangerous
than their missiles. Along the roadsides and around the observation
points in the test site accumulated small mountains of the wealthy
world's rubbish, to which the Aborigines were drawn once the traffic had frightened off the game they hunted. The nomads of the desert took up residence as scavenging seagulls on the white landfills.

10

The abandoned missile launch town survives today as an internment camp for asylum seekers.

Asia has some of the world's most densely populated areas; Australia is the most sparsely populated continent. In fact, when viewed
though Chinese or Indonesian eyes, Australia seems virtually
unpopulated. The *terra nullius* doctrine used by the British when
they occupied Australia would give Asians the right to take over the
country.

But white Australians were determined to make the country
white. One of the first laws introduced by the Australian Federation
was the Immigration Restriction Act of 1901.

The part of it that proved particularly effective for the prevention of non-European immigration was the dictation test. The clause made no mention of race or religion but merely designated unsuitable anyone who could not take down an official fifty words of dictation in a European language. Faced with someone they wanted to let in, they allowed the applicant to choose the language. But they could exclude an Asian applicant with excellent skills in English, German or French quite simply by giving the dictation in some other European language, such as Hungarian.[10]

The dictation test was in use until 1958. Then the Migration Act came into force, making provision for any foreigner without a visa to be interned while his or her case was under consideration. Here again there was no mention of race or religion; in practice, however, the law was not applied to the fifty thousand or so whites staying illegally in Australia—some of them for decades—but only to boat people, refugees from Asia.

They came in the period 1989–94 from Cambodia, in 1994–97 from China, and after 1997 from Iraq and Afghanistan. The total number between 1989 and 1997 was fewer than 3,000, of whom 2,300 were refused entry after their internment.

The internees were considered not to have entered Australia despite their physical presence there; they were classed as "nonentrants," and detained in six camps in remote parts of the country, Woomera among them.

The first prisoners came here in November 1999. After over a year in detention and with their cases still unresolved, two hundred or, as some say, five hundred refugees broke out of the camp and disappeared. The authorities responded with barbed wire, water cannon, armed guards, and a ban on visitors. The internment camps became concentration camps.[11]

Men, women, and children stay shut up there for many years, kept in ignorance of their legal rights, deprived of contact with the world around them, in uncertainty, degradation, and desperation. The intention is to make internment so unpleasant that it will deter further refugees from seeking asylum in Australia.

"Australian detention practices involve a breach of international, civil, political and human rights," says Human Rights

Commissioner Christopher Sidoti. "No other western country permits incommunicado detention of asylum seekers."[12]

In January 2002, it was briefly reported in the world press that Afghan detainees at Woomera had sewn up their mouths to protest against their isolation. Outside the barbed wire there were protests, staged by and large by the same people who are demanding that the government apologize to the Aborigines.

II

According to my Religious Education teacher at secondary school, "contrition" is at the core of all religions. It's easy to make mistakes. Anybody can make mistakes, even commit crimes. The important thing is knowing how to feel contrition afterward. That was why he began every lesson with the same question: "What constitutes contrition?" To this day, I can still rattle off the answer in my sleep:

I realize I have done wrong.

I regret what I have done.

I promise never to do it again.

Today I tend to think these three criteria for contrition are far too introverted. "Realize," "regret," and "promise" can all be done internally, in complete secrecy, without betraying any outward sign of realization or promise. Such an internal contrition process is precious little comfort to the victim of the wrong I committed. And the promise is easily forgotten if nobody knows it was made. So the criteria should demand a more public process of contrition. Perhaps like this:

I freely admit that I have done wrong.

I ask forgiveness of those I have wronged.

I promise to do my best to make amends to them.

Here, the third criterion promises not only that I will not repeat the crime, but also that I will make efforts to put things right to the best of my ability. For the victims, redress is the most tangible result of my contrition and a measure of its sincerity.

Can we feel contrition for other people's crimes? Can we feel contrition for crimes we have not committed personally, but have subsequently profited from? How can we formulate the criteria for contrition to make them applicable to collective responsibility for historical crimes? Perhaps like this:

We freely admit that our predecessors have done wrong and that we are profiting from it.

We ask forgiveness of those who were wronged and of their descendants.

We promise to do our best to make amends to those who were wronged for the effects that still remain.

The larger the collective, the more diluted the personal responsibility. The less intimate the contrition, the greater the risk that it will just be hollow ceremony. A representative steps forward on our behalf, admits the wrong committed, apologizes, pays what it takes, and appoints a committee to "monitor our practices." Australia isn't even doing that.

12

Opal is a precious stone that was formed 30 million years ago where deep weathering had caused cracks and voids in porous claystone. In these cavities, the silica in the groundwater was able to accumulate, form a concentrated jelly and crystallize into grape-like, faintly gleaming opals. Australia is the world's greatest producer, and 70 percent of its production comes from Coober Pedy and adjoining fields along the Stuart Highway 220 miles north of Port Augusta.[13]

Rising above the mining fields are the red mesa mountains, "table mountains" raised above the "floor" of the surrounding plain and protected by a hard, ferriferous, silica-impregnated "tabletop." The landscape is perforated by the underground tunnels of the opal seekers. Holes everywhere—a quarter of a million holes. Everywhere there are spoil-heaps and warnings not to walk on the undermined surfaces.

The first opal was found in 1915 by a fourteen-year-old boy. In 1919, the demobilized soldiers returned from the First World War, experienced in digging trenches. By 1940 the deposits were considered mined out, and there were just a few pensioners left in Coober Pedy. But in 1956 mining operations were mechanized and the town burst back to life—a school in 1961, a small hospital in the same year, a larger, fully equipped one in 1982.

Coober Pedy today is a dusty, run-down gambling den of a town, ruined by alcohol. It is inhabited by three thousand fortune hunters from forty countries, who endure the summer heat and the winter cold by digging themselves into a modern version of catacombs.

They lived originally in abandoned mining tunnels or "dugouts," dwellings half buried in the hillside, earth cellars, which maintained a more stable inside temperature than walls of thin boarding could provide and were cheaper than proper timber houses. In Coober Pedy today, you can stay in an underground hotel, go to confession in an underground church, shop in an underground bookstore, and surf the web from underground Internet cafés.

But the smell on the town's breath comes from its bars and liquor stores. "It's no secret that many in our town have a weakness for alcohol that is slowly destroying both them and the town," writes the *Coober Pedy Times*. A team of five, appointed to consider appropriate measures, has put forward the following suggestions:

- Daycare provision for alcoholics, offering basic food, showers, laundry, health care, and activities.
- Alcohol-free premises where people can meet and socialize, free from temptation.
- Licensing restrictions for bars and liquor stores to make alcohol less readily available.
- A mobile patrol to identify and look after alcoholics who have been on a heavy drinking bout, until they sober up.

"Infringement of civil liberties," say those who make their money out of liquor or are dependent on it. So everything stays the way it is. In Coober Pedy, the very groundwater seems to consist of alcohol. The whole town smells of stale booze.

13

Fresh rain falls during the night, setting the desert ablaze with flowers, yellow, red, and blue. The plain turns green between meres and pools of red water and assumes an almost park-like appearance.

Plants and animals alike live in perpetual expectation of these rare and happy interludes and have developed various strategies for preserving their potential through the dry seasons and making instant use of them when the rains come.

The saltbush is particularly cunning. It has two sorts of seed, the soft and the hard. Termites and other insects prefer to eat the tasty and more accessible soft seeds. This leaves the hard seeds. The soft seeds are more inclined to take risks and will take the chance to grow at the first sign of any moisture. The hard seeds, on the other hand, are preserved in seedpods and seed-coats containing so much salt that the seed cannot grow until the pod has soaked sufficiently long in a sufficient amount of water for the salt to leach out.

So the hard seed remains sleeping in its salt until large amounts of rain have fallen. Then it grows and the plant quickly develops a deep root system that will allow it to survive even after the surface water that dissolved the salt has dried up.

Large mammals like the red kangaroo are equally well adapted to sudden changes in water supply. After rain, the female will give birth to her young in rapid succession. She will have one joey beside her on the ground, another in her pouch, and a third in the form of a fertilized egg inside her body. Each time a new baby is born, the previous one has to vacate the pouch, but it will continue to be suckled by its mother for four months.

The female will now have milk in one teat appropriate for the newborn in her pouch, and in another a different sort of milk suitable for the more mature joey. By producing two different kinds of milk, the kangaroo can make optimum use of the good times for rapid breeding. When drought conditions return, by contrast, fertilization is delayed and the juvenile's development toward sexual maturity slows. Some years later, new rains will trigger a fresh hormone storm and a new set of pregnancies, one after another.[14]

14

For the young, life is from the very outset a matter of extreme help-lessness and dependence.

A kangaroo baby is born deaf, blind, and no bigger than a little finger. The mother leans back so the baby can crawl up her belly into the pouch and latch on to a teat. The teat engorges to fill the baby's mouth, the edges of which simultaneously tighten so the baby is hanging from the teat. The baby is unable to suckle, so the female injects the milk into its mouth using a special muscle located directly above her mammary glands. She and the baby are so firmly attached that both will bleed if any attempt is made to separate them.

The people of the desert think human beings were originally just as imperfect as baby kangaroos. The Luritja people believe the first people were joined to each other. Their eyes and ears were not open and their arms were still attached along the sides of their torsos. Their legs were pulled up against their bodies. In this helpless state they were cared for by small birds called kurbaru, who fed them with little cakes made of grass seeds.

As a boy, I read about the Luritja people in Nathan Söderblom's *Gudstrons Uppkomst (The Origin of Faith in God,* 1914). I read it as a storybook and those stories about the original helplessness of mankind are the only ones I still remember.[15]

The Arrernte people, too, believed all humans were originally conjoined. They were rescued by a primeval creature called the Fly-catcher, who used his stone knife to carve out individual human beings. He cut eyes, mouths, and noses into their faces, opened their eyes, and separated their fingers. He showed them how to make fire and decided whom they could marry.

15

The little roadhouses along the Stuart Highway are a combination of country store, gas station, and café. Young people, chilled by the morning air, warm their hands on mugs of coffee. Wrinkled old cowboys, or stockmen as they are known here, sit with their hats on, as is the custom, having a few beers.

During the day I leave the state of South Australia and proceed into the Northern Territory. Here it has yet to rain. The road is flanked by great red boulders, cracking apart and on their way to crumbling to dust.

I stop to take a closer look at a floury white plant that has folded its leaves together to look like bowls. Some strange flying seeds are making their way on spidery legs ten centimeters long. A lettuce-like plant with muscular leaves the same color as well-hung meat. Thorny little fruits catch on my socks after only a few steps and carry swiftly on down into my shoes. You remove them at the cost of cutting your fingertips.

The main impression is of overpowering desolation. I wonder how Aborigine children would react to the Swedish forests. I know how Faeroese children reacted when they found themselves in Norway. In the 1950s on the Faeroe Islands there were some thirty trees all told. Traveling for hours through millions of trees proved too much for the children, who burst into tears. In much the same way, the emptiness of the interior of Australia can be overwhelming for those used to a livelier field of vision.

To me, this emptiness is liberating. The view in an urban street changes from one moment to the next. Its time is measured in fractions of a second. A stream of impressions bombards our consciousness. In the desert, there is little to see apart from geological formations that have been shaped over millions of years and take centuries to change.

The heart of the desert beats at a different pace from ours. Geology can't be rushed. When it occupies your whole field of vision, you feel first impatience, then oppression, and finally that sense of calm that only a blank space can create. The stillness that only the absolute provides.

16

Uluru is an inverse Grand Canyon. The same red sandstone, the same grandeur. But the Grand Canyon, unlike Uluru, is instantly

The effects of desert life on humans.
Illustration from *Bulletin* 1903.

comprehensible. You can see its cause—the river—and understand at once how it came about. Uluru is a visual mystery, lacking any perceptible cause. A huge red shape lies gleaming at sunrise and sunset. Its bulk is out of proportion with everything around it. It just rises up out of the ground, unexpectedly and for no apparent reason.

In places some geological knife seems to have cut slices out of the rock walls. There are keyholes, cavities, perhaps stamps or emblems—or possibly brands denoting ownership, like on a bull. You expect it to rouse from its fossil sleep at any moment and come rushing at you. But it just lies there, not even shaking off the climbers who, like ants on an ant trail, toil upward toward the bull's back.

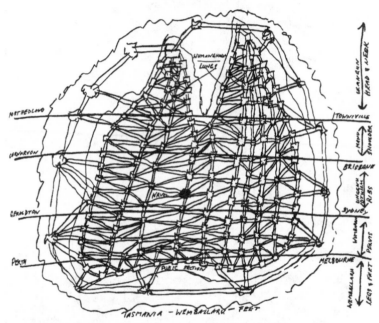

Bandaiyan, Australia as a human body with Uluru as the navel. The body is enclosed in a network of walking routes and mythical songlines. Drawing by David Mowaljarlai in Mowaljarlai and Malnic, *Yorro Yorro: Everything Standing Up Alive.*

Geologically speaking, Uluru is a so-called inselberg, an island in the surrounding flatness of the desert ocean.[16] The island consists of sandstone rich in feldspar, formed from a coarse gravel of gneiss and granite that came from the south about 600 million years ago. The Australian landscape is flat because it has been buried in the remains of its own geological decay. Why did this "leftover mountain" survive when nearby mountains like it have weathered away and

disappeared beneath the surface of the ground? One likely explanation is that Uluru was located at the top of a fold, where groundwater
and chemical weathering could not reach it from below.

The outer skin of the rock is hardened by the forces of weathering and gets its rusty color from the ferriferous sandstone. In some
places in the caves you can see fresh rock, pale grayish-white or pink.
Uluru is slowly being scooped out from the sides as the mountain is
undermined and slabs come loose and fall. It is also suffering severe
wear and tear from a continuous stream of ruthless climbers.

Uluru was "restored" to its original owners, the Anangu people,
in 1985. But only on condition they immediately leased back the
whole area to a park authority that makes it accessible to tourists.
Uluru has become a national symbol in the ever more aggressive
marketing of Australia as a tourist destination.

Large notices announce that Uluru is holy ground for the country's original inhabitants and urge visitors to refrain from going on
to the mountain. But the same people who would never dream of
setting foot on the high altar of St. Peter's in their heavy walking
boots, or climbing the holy black stone in Mecca—those same people think it the most natural thing in the world to climb up Uluru
and plant their boot on the bull's neck as if they had hunted it and
brought it down. They imagine themselves conquerors, but at this
distance they look more like dots on an Aboriginal painting.

17

Fortune seekers who saw the mountain glowing or "burning" believed they were seeing a mountain of gold, giving rise to endless
myths and legends.

Ernest Favenc's *The Secret of the Australian Desert* (1896) was
published in Swedish as part of the Fritzes Scout Library series, and
I read it as a boy. It was my introduction to Australia.

It's a novel about three friends who set off into the desert in
search of "the burning mountain" and discover what lies behind
"this yarn the niggers have." The question is: will the natives turn
out to be peaceable, or will they offer resistance?

"However, it's safest to act as though they were our enemies."

"Decidedly." [17]

Beneath the bare ground, the sound of running rivers can be heard. "There might be some Jinkarras living down there," remarks Charlie. "I wonder how this yarn of an underground race, the Jinkarras, originated." [18]

Before long, they find a hole in the ground, through which they can see down to a cave beneath, where the Aborigines are sitting eating.

"The thing that puzzles me," says Brown, "is—what do these natives live on . . . ? Within a hundred miles there isn't a feed for a bandicoot." [19]

"It is meat they are eating, but what meat?"

Morton shudders at the question put to him. Truth flashes across his mind.

"An awful feeling of horror came over the whole party as they realized their situation and possible fate. Their natural audacity, however, soon returned. At present they were masters of the situation; with their breech-loaders they could shoot down a score of the natives helpless in the cavern below, if so inclined. But affairs did not seem to justify armed intervention just then."

But a short time later, when they have forced their way into the cave and been witness to a human sacrifice, they open fire:

" 'Fire like blazes,' ordered Morton, setting an example which was followed by the others until the white smoke nearly filled the cavern. Madly and fanatically the natives dashed up the narrow passage; but with four breech-loaders playing on them, the terrible unknown lightning and deafening thunder smiting their foremost down, two and three at a time, the attempt was hopeless."

The white men manage to get out just in time to avoid a convenient earthquake that fills the cave with scalding mud, burying the black men, dead and alive.

18

When the white men have calmed down somewhat, they start to question their intervention:

"After all we had no business—according to their ideas—to interfere with their little rites and ceremonies. They treated us in a friendly fashion."

They even express passing concern about the outcome. The blacks are all dead. Only the chief is still alive, "Scarred, bleeding and burnt, a most miserable object, the only survivor of his tribe." [20]

"I cannot help feeling sorry for the old ruffian. He was a real plucky fellow."

Cooper's *Last of the Mohicans* in a new guise. Yet another representative of nineteenth-century literature's romanticizing of "the last of." The extermination of native peoples was in full swing, while the great reading public wallowed in sympathy for the last one, the only man left.

The next time the group of white friends encounter the Aborigines, they know they are dealing with cannibals. So driving them away with firearms is not enough. "Quick!" cries Morton. "Not one must get away!" [21]

The men on horseback pull up beside a "wounded savage." Then, "Morton slipped from his horse. Charlie turned his head away for he guessed what was going to happen. No quarter for the cannibals! He heard the revolver ring out. 'Perhaps it is all for the best, sad as it seems,' says Morton. 'Those six devils could not have kept their lust for murder under.' "

How did he know they were devils? Well, because the white men couldn't see enough food around to satisfy even a bandicoot, and because they couldn't see the animals hunted by the natives, or the grubs and roots they dug out of the sand, they assumed the natives must survive by eating each other. So the natives were cannibals, that is, devils who must be eradicated. That was their logic. Once the devils were gone, once the land had become no-man's-land, the deserts would turn into gardens.

"What a real desert!" exclaims Brown, gazing round on the dreary scenes.

"Yes, it's about as hopeless looking a picture as one could find anywhere, at present. No, burn this scrub off, or clear it somehow, and with a good supply of artesian water there are a hundred and one payable products one could grow here."

"You are an optimist, Morton."

"I am, as regards the future of Australia."

19

Fiction at times came close to reality.

By the end of the nineteenth century, white settlers had taken over most of the land around Alice Springs. Their sixty thousand cattle and sheep ousted the Aborigines from the waterholes. Competition for water led to conflicts in which the Aborigines' spears were no match for the settlers' modern firearms. Killing a black was considered no worse than shooting a dog. The town's mounted policeman William Henry Willshire (1852–1925) threw the power of the police wholeheartedly behind the whites.[22]

In 1881 there were only five white women in the whole of central Australia. Twenty years later, there were still only nine white women in Alice Springs. Conflicts between whites and blacks became common as white men broke down ancient patterns of marriage and blurred the distinction between bride-buying, prostitution, and rape.

Hardly able to contain his delight, Willshire recalls in his book *The Land of Dawning* (1896) how his police patrol happens on a "beautiful maiden savage," who runs away screaming. She is caught, but attempts to escape during the night by jumping into the river. The constable who apprehends her exploits her sexually until, as Willshire puts it, she is "over head and ears in love with the tracker who caught her."[23]

Reporting a white man for rape in Willshire's police station was not advisable.

The blacks were punished on the spot for their crimes; trials

"Native policemen disperse the blacks." Illustration
from Lumholtz's *Among Cannibals.*

were considered unnecessary. No suspects were arrested, no reports were filed; the natives, guilty or innocent, were summarily
dispatched.

One of the most violent punitive actions occurred at Owen
Springs, southwest of Alice Springs. A white witness later reported
that over 150 blacks were killed. The total number of black people
killed during Willshire's time at Alice has been estimated at between five hundred and a thousand. The crime for which they were
being punished was predominantly cattle-stealing. Willshire murdered human beings to protect cattle.

He boasted openly about what he had done, describing his massacres in a singular, baroque rhetoric:

> At 3 o'clock we came upon a large mob of natives camped
> among the rocks. They scattered in all directions. It's no use
> mincing matters—the Martini-Henry carbines at the criti-
> cal moment were talking English in the silent majesty of
> those eternal rocks. The mountain was swathed in a regal
> robe of fiery grandeur, and its ominous roar was close upon
> us. The weird, awful beauty of the scene held us spellbound
> for a few seconds.[24]

In February 1891 Willshire and his constables had, on some
flimsy pretext, opened fire on sleeping Aborigines not far from the
Temple Downs cattle station, killing two of them. This was done entirely as a matter of course. Afterward the murderers were casually
having breakfast with the settler, while his stockmen dragged away
the bodies of the Aborigines and burnt them.

It proved to be the straw that broke the camel's back. The telegraph station manager, Frank Gillen, intervened in his capacity as
magistrate and official Protector of the Aborigines. He went to the
scene of the crime, heard statements from the witnesses, and then
had Willshire arrested for murder. It was the first arrest made in all
Willshire's time as a police officer at Alice Springs.

Willshire was taken to Port Augusta, where he spent several
days under arrest while the cattle owners of Alice Springs collected

£2,000 for his court costs. He was acquitted, of course, but transferred to another posting and eventually given early retirement. He ended his days as a night watchman at the slaughterhouse in Adelaide, "a post for which his career made him admirably qualified," to quote historian D.J. Mulvaney.

20

Willshire's reign of destruction was not unique. Similar crimes were being committed around the world: in Canada and the United States, in South America and South Africa, in North Africa and Siberia, in central Asia and central Australia—in fact wherever European settlers were in the process of taking land from its original owners. The extermination of the Aborigines produced the no-man's-land, which according to the doctrine of *terra nullius* gave the white settlers rights to the land.

Most whites were convinced that those who had been murdered in this way were members of an inferior race, doomed to destruction. They could cite the foremost biological authority of the day: Charles Darwin. In chapters 5 and 6 of *The Descent of Man* (1871), he presents the extermination of indigenous peoples as a natural part of the process of evolution. Animal species have always exterminated one another; races of savages have always exterminated one another; and now that there are civilized peoples, the savage races will be wiped out altogether: "When civilized nations come into contact with barbarians the struggle is short, except where a deadly climate gives its aid to the native race. At some future period, not very distant as measured by centuries, the civilized races of man will almost certainly exterminate and replace throughout the world the savage races." [25]

Darwin had himself seen it happen—in Argentina, in Tasmania, in mainland Australia—and reacted strongly against what he saw. But in the context of his theory of evolution, the extermination of indigenous peoples no longer appeared a crime, but seemed to be the inevitable outcome of natural processes and the precondition for continued progress. Post-Darwin, it became the done thing to shrug

[handwritten margin note: land was being used and occupied by a complex society but the Australian gov. didn't wanna recognize that]

one's shoulders at extermination. Those reacting with disgust were merely displaying their ignorance.

"Nothing can be more unscientific," wrote George Chatterton Hill in his *Heredity and Selection* (1907), "nothing shows a deeper ignorance of the elementary laws of social evolution, than the absurd agitations, peculiar to the British race, against the elimination of inferior races." The truth is that the British race, "by reason of its genius for expansion, must necessarily eliminate the inferior races which stand in its way. Every superior race in history has done the same, and was obliged to do it." [26]

"If the workforce of a colony cannot be disciplined into producing the profits rightly expected by the mother country," writes Henry C. Morris in his *History of Colonization* (1900), "the natives must then be exterminated or reduced to such numbers as to be readily controlled." [27]

"The survival of the natives will only cause trouble," wrote anthropologist George H.L.-F. Pitt-Rivers in his *The Clash of Cultures* (1927).

> In fact, the Native Problem might well be defined as "the problem created by the survival of those native races or their hybrid descendants that have not been exterminated by the 'blessings of civilization.'" That is to say there is no native problem in Tasmania, and for the European population in Australia, the problem is negligible, for the very good reason that the Tasmanians are no longer alive to create a problem, while the aboriginals of Australia are rapidly following them along the road to extinction. [28]

Men like William Willshire practiced what these theorists defended or even recommended. Since 1949 it has been known as "genocide."

21

In the same year that Ernest Favenc wrote *The Secret of the Australian Desert*, a large research team, the Horn Expedition, traveled the same route as the three friends in his story. The expedition report contains a collective portrait of "the central Australian Aborigine" and what the scholars of the time knew about him:

> His origin and history are lost in the gloomy mists of the past. He has no written records and few oral traditions. In appearance he is a naked, hirsute savage, with a type of features occasionally pronouncedly Jewish. . . . He has never been known to wash. He has no private ownership of land, except as regards that which is not overcarefully concealed about his person. . . . Religious belief he has none . . . he has no traditions and yet continues to practise with scrupulous exactness a number of hideous customs and ceremonies which have been handed from his fathers, and of the origin or reasons of which he knows nothing. . . . Thanks to the untiring efforts of the missionary and the stockman, he is being rapidly "civilized" off the face of the earth, and in another hundred years the remaining evidence of his existence will be the fragments of flint which he has fashioned so rudely.[29]

The respect shown by John Eyre fifty years earlier has completely vanished. The scholars looks down on their subject with the unquestioned superiority of the occupying power.

When the natives deny the occupiers access to their records and traditions, scholarship declares that such do not exist. When the appearance of the natives differs from the norm among the occupiers, scholarship finds it an opportune moment for the airing of anti-Semitic prejudices.

When the natives adapt their hygiene to the lack of water and abundance of sand, scholarship sees merely an unwashed savage.

When the settler community has stolen the land from its original owners, scholarship finds that the natives have no land rights. And adds a jeering insult that shows a total lack of understanding of the natives' religious need for connection with the ground. Body paintings, ground paintings, myths, songs, and dances—for the scholars they are nothing but "hideous ceremonies" that the natives themselves do not understand.

This solid wall of white incomprehension ends with a death sentence couched in a tone of forced jocularity: they'll soon be gone. Soon, thank God, the problem will be disposed of for good. Soon the laws of biology will have made a reality of the fiction of *terra nullius*.

22

How did the recipients of this collective death sentence react?

After all, even a personal death sentence is hard to bear. So what must it feel like, living with the certainty that not only I myself but also everyone who speaks my language, lives as I do, believes as I do, and hopes as I do, that our entire world will be wiped out, that our whole people will shortly die and there will be no one to come after us?

The leading men of the Arrernte people[30] didn't read the Horn report. But they got the message. They realized something had to be done. Somewhere they had to try to break through the wall of white incomprehension. They had to make at least some of the occupiers understand their beliefs, their society, and their way of life.

Who? As manager of the telegraph station, Frank Gillen was one of the most powerful white men in the area. He had taken on the tyrant Willshire and won. He had long shown an interest in the culture of the occupied race. They had known him for almost two decades. They chose Frank Gillen.

Gillen, in his turn, chose Baldwin Spencer. He was a thirty-five-year-old biology professor from Melbourne who arrived in Alice Springs with the Horn Expedition. It moved on after three days, but Spencer stayed for three weeks to listen to what Gillen had to tell him. Gillen had experience, local knowledge, and local contacts. Spencer was educated, articulate, and had international contacts. They complemented one another, and together the two partners became the Arrernte people's way out to the world.

Leading men of the Arrernte decided to allow Spencer and Gillen to witness a grand seven-week cycle of ceremonies, which should

Baldwin Spencer took this photograph during a seven-week cycle of ceremonies in the telegraph station's backyard. He failed to realize he was part of one of the most successful publicity campaigns in history.

really have taken place at Imanpa en route to Uluru but was now moved to the backyard of the Alice Springs telegraph station to be easily accessible for the two researchers. From mid-November 1896 to January 8, 1897, Spencer and Gillen observed and documented an average of five or six ceremonies a day.

It has subsequently emerged that the ceremonies were carried out with many shortcuts and abridgements necessitated by the move to Alice and by the fact that many of the Aborigines who participated were not themselves members of the Arrernte people. Many misunderstandings also arose from the fact that the researchers didn't know the language and relied for the answers to their questions on interpreters speaking pidgin English.[31]

After Spencer had left, the Arrernte men carried on initiating Gillen into their secrets. He was soon able to send Spencer a further 110 pages of notes, which the latter incorporated into his field notes. Four months later, Spencer completed a summary, which was published in *Nature*. Through their two agents, the Arrernte people reached an international audience for the first time.

Spencer was also working on a book called *The Native Tribes of Central Australia*, which he finished in March 1898. Gillen read it and gave his comments chapter by chapter. The book was also read and edited in advance of publication by two of the leading ethnologists of the day, Edward Tylor and James Frazer. It was published on January 13, 1899, and caused an immediate international sensation.

"Since the publication of their first volume, half of the total production in anthropological theory has been based on their work and nine-tenths affected or modified by it," wrote Malinowski in 1913.[32]

The men of the Arrernte had sung and danced for Gillen and Spencer and tried to explain the ideas embodied in their community and way of life. They only partially succeeded. Spencer retained a lifelong conviction that the Aborigines were a race doomed to extinction. He failed to notice that the natives he viewed as study objects were in fact using him as an instrument in one of the most successful publicity campaigns in history.

The Arrernte, an unknown desert people in the heart of the world's most remote continent, suddenly emerged as the best-known, most discussed natives in the world. They wouldn't let themselves be exterminated in silence. They were showing the world that their *terra* was not *nullius*.

23

The Alice Springs of today reminds me of Tamanrasset in the Sahara: the same dried-up riverbed running right through the town; the same road running south–north; the same feeling of huge distances in all directions; the same cosmopolitan character; the same sharp contrast between sun and shade, between white and black.

But Tam is that much dustier, poorer, and tougher than Alice, which is a pleasant town, at least in winter. The winter climate is sunny and warm, with slightly chilly nights. I buy books in the Aranta Bookshop, run by two old ladies who treat the store as their living room and the customers as company. I buy a salad from Woolworths for my lunch, read Freud and Durkheim in the library, obtain maps from the Department of the Environment across the street, and have dinner sitting outside at the Sports Café before going back to Alice Springs Resort on the other side of the bridge.

Alice is in permanent contact with outer space and the world metropolises. This remote spot in the desert is part of an international network that monitors all the satellite conversations, faxes, and e-mails between the cities of the world. The American base for electronic espionage at Pine Gap has more than a dozen monitoring globes that since 1970 have been picking up satellite signals from radio transmitters, telephones, and radar all over the world. If a sigh is heard over a mobile phone anywhere on earth, it will also be heard in Alice Springs.[33]

The livelihood of the town depends on it. The base at Pine Gap owns more than six hundred houses in Alice and purchases £4 million worth of goods and services a year. That makes quite an impact in a little town of only 25,000 people, and helps give it a white, middle-class feel.

The Aborigines make up just over 2 percent of the population of Australia. But in the Northern Territory, they make up 30 percent. The prophecy of the Aborigines dying out has not come true.

This is not because they are long-lived, in fact just the opposite. Life expectancy is just sixty for black men and sixty-six for black women. White people live on average seventeen years longer than black people.

No, it's the children who are causing the black proportion of the population to rise. The average age among Aborigines is twenty-one. An aging white population is living side by side with an increasingly youthful black one.

At the office of the Discrimination Commissioner, the job is considered done: the official view is that there is no longer any discrimination against black people in Alice Springs.

"But then how can the unemployment be accounted for?" I wonder. "And is there a place where white and black people meet on equal terms?"

The atmosphere between white people is open and friendly. People nod and say hello in typical small-town fashion. But a black person will never say hello unless the white person has offered a greeting first. Are they shy? Oppressed? Uninterested? Hostile?

Aborigines are to be found working in private and government offices, as shop assistants, janitors, and parking attendants, and as troublesome drunken layabouts in the parks. I see them as clients at court, as hospital patients, as artists in art galleries, and occasionally as restaurant guests, usually in the company of white people. I see them in the library, reading, listening, and watching videos. I practically never encounter an Aborigine in any situation offering an opportunity or reason for "meeting," "talking," "going for a coffee," or even acknowledging one another's existence. Strict rules demand advance written permission to visit an Aborigine settlement, photograph an Aborigine, or reproduce what an Aborigine says.

Why? Well, why should a long-despised people, now it is no longer faced with certain annihilation, go about longing to socialize with its former annihilators and despisers? Why should a long-exploited people be prepared to offer itself as an exotic, unpaid bait in the tourist traps?

24

That night, I dream that all the high ground in Stockholm is suddenly linked together by a system of light, slender footbridges.

I make my way on foot above the waters of Riddarfjärden from Mariahissen to Kungsklippan. I walk above the traffic of Götgatan, from Helgalunden to Sofia Church. Another bridge links Sofia with Mosebacke, and Mosebacke with Mariaberget.

A spider's web of bridges, built of thin, pliable wood, covers the entire city. It is like that system of underground passages which in Charles Fourier's imaginary city links the workplaces and the lovers. What's more, the bridges afford wonderful views that make it a delight to walk up there, high above the time- and profit-driven traffic.

The surprising combinations, the connections as swift and straight as a bird flies—each new bridge is hailed as a victory for reason and its imagination. All Stockholm is crisscrossed like a brain by these winding, airy gangways, where body moves as easily as thought.

25

How did human beings become human beings? That was the great question Darwin posed to his readers. If mankind was not created by God but has gradually evolved from animal to human by natural selection, then which were the qualities in the animal that allowed it to become human?

Was it speed, strength, and cunning in constant, life-or-death gladiatorial combat? Was it our ability to exterminate each other that made us human? That notion did feature in Darwin's work, and in the course of the second half of the nineteenth century it became increasingly prevalent in European consciousness under the name of "Darwinism."

But Darwin also offered an entirely different answer to this question. Mankind has achieved its current superiority over other species of animal above all by means of its social skills, its capacity for cooperation and mutual help. This aspect of Darwin's theory found its leading exponent in Petr Kropotkin.[34]

Kropotkin was a member of the Russian aristocracy and became known for his expeditions to Siberia. There he went looking for examples of competition and combat between individuals of the same species, but instead found innumerable examples of cooperation. Cooperation is what enables weak animals to protect themselves against predators, look after their young, and organize migration to new areas. Of course strength and speed are important for survival in certain circumstances. But cooperation is a far more significant factor in the battle for life, Kropotkin argued in his book *Mutual Aid: A Factor of Evolution* (1902).

Spencer was able to make a significant contribution to this discussion. He described the Arrernte people as "naked, howling savages" unable to shape a clay pot, make a garment, or appoint a chief. But they didn't remotely resemble the accepted "Darwinian" picture of primitive man as violent, uncontrolled, and interested only in gratifying his own egotistical urges.

Their religious life, as described by Spencer and Gillen, centered on "Intichiuma," a ceremony to increase the food supply. The remarkable thing about it was that each clan would attempt to increase the supply of the plant or animal that the rules of taboo expressly forbade them to eat. Why invest so much ceremonial force to an end from which you could not yourself benefit? That was what James Frazer asked in a long letter to Spencer.[35]

And he gave the answer himself: although the individual clan cannot benefit from the results of its own Intichiuma ceremony, it will benefit from the results achieved by all the other clans. The combined effect of the efforts of all the clans will be an increased supply of food, from which all can profit.

Spencer and Gillen's Arrernte didn't live in the "war of everyone against everyone"; they had a complicated system based on avoiding conflicts over food by extending family solidarity to an ever-growing circle of more and more distant relatives. They had strict marriage laws intended to minimize men's conflicts over women.

In short, Kropotkin's ideas were affirmed. Natural selection led not to combat and competition but to a quest for practices that avoid conflict. This applied to both animals and humans. Society already existed before human beings; but there were no human beings before society.

26

The most famous interpreters of Spencer and Gillen's data were Émile Durkheim and Sigmund Freud. Both used the Aborigines as windows onto the origins of human culture. Both took Darwin as their starting point. Like Darwin they wanted to create their own grand, comprehensive model of interpretation extending far beyond its original sphere. Freud saw himself as the Darwin of the soul, Durkheim as the Darwin of society.

Freud was born in 1856, Durkheim in 1858, Spencer in 1860. Spencer became a professor in Melbourne in 1887, the year in which Durkheim became a university lecturer in Bordeaux and Freud a doctor in Vienna. Durkheim published first: two epoch-making works of sociology in the mid-1890s. A few years later, Freud published the work with which he made his name, *Die Traumdeutung* (*The Interpretation of Dreams*, 1899), and Spencer's *Native Tribes* appeared the same year. [36]

Both Durkheim and Freud grew up in poor Jewish families in which traditional religion and a close sense of community played a central role. Both of them abandoned the faith of their fathers but continued to feel its attraction throughout their lives. Both were fascinated by the primitive society described by Spencer and Gillen, in part because it resembled the narrow societies, driven by internal imperatives, in which they had grown up themselves. [37]

Durkheim's life's work culminated in *Les Formes élémentaires de la vie religieuse* (*The Elementary Forms of Religious Life*, 1912), a case study of the beliefs of the Arrernte people, seen as the most primordial and fundamental of all forms of religion and thus as the key to them all.

As the Australian Aborigine's ceremonies fill him with reverence and elate him to a state of rapture, he is not falling prey to

delusions. Admittedly Durkheim takes the view that the Aborigine is mistaken in believing an animal or a plant is working the
miracle within him. But no more than Durkheim's own father was
mistaken when he believed it was Yahweh. The animal and Yahweh are merely metaphors for a genuine sensory experience, the
experience of the society to which the believer belongs. A society
capable of much more than the individual, a society that supports
and helps the individual but also makes demands and administers
punishments.

His whole study, writes Durkheim, is based on the conviction
that the collective experiences of believers through the ages cannot
be mere imagination. There is a "religious experience"—but the
very fact that believers at different times and in different parts of
the world have had widely diverging perceptions of the basis of this
religious experience makes it less likely that any one of them could
be "right."

But the experience remains. There is a reality behind the articles
of faith. That reality is society.

With this solution, Durkheim had reconciled himself with his
father and the environment in which he grew up, and incorporated
them into the new world of sociological concepts in which he was
now living. He believed he had proved that what his father had spent
a lifetime seeking, namely God, was identical to what he had devoted his life to studying: society.

27

In the autumn of 1896, when Spencer was in the backyard of the
Alice Springs telegraph station observing the ceremonies that the
theorists would subsequently interpret, Sigmund Freud's father had
just died. The death of his father gave Freud the impetus to begin
the self-analysis that would later become "psychoanalysis."

One of his core discoveries was that even as a child he had sometimes wished for his father's death. After a further ten years of an-
alyzing sons' desire to kill their fathers and marry their mothers,
Freud was able to posit the "Oedipus complex" as lying at the heart

of all neuroses. And in *Totem und Tabu* (1912–13), patricide itself becomes, through a reinterpretation of Spencer and Gillen's data, the creative act that leads to the emergence of civilization.

Once again the central focus is the Arrernte people's Intichiuma ceremony. For Freud it is significant that the ceremony concludes with a feast where it is permitted, indeed decreed, that the participants eat of their own totem animal, which at all other times is strictly taboo.

"Let us now envisage the scene," Freud writes, giving his fantasy free rein.[38] The clan kills the totem animal and consumes it raw. During these proceedings, the clan members are dressed up as the animal they are eating and mimic its sounds and movements, as if to emphasize the identification of the humans with the animal. This act, individually forbidden to every participant, becomes obligatory when everyone does it together. No one is allowed to refuse. Once the totem animal has been consumed, it is mourned and tears are shed for it.

"Psychoanalysis has revealed to us that the totem animal is really a substitute for the father," writes Freud. This leads to a hypothesis which may seem fantastic," he admits, but which establishes "an unexpected unity among a series of hitherto separated phenomena."

The Darwinian conception of the primal horde is dominated by a violent, jealous father who, wanting to keep all the females for himself, drives all his sons away. This primal state has never been scientifically observable anywhere. The most primitive societies we have observed, for example that of the Aborigines, consist of associations of men, within which all members are relatively equal. How, Freud asks, have these associations developed out of the primal state?

"By basing our argument upon the celebration of the totem, we are in a position to give an answer: one day the expelled brothers joined forces, slew and ate the father, and thus put an end to the father horde. Together they dared and accomplished what would have remained impossible for them singly."

It seemed quite natural to these savage cannibals that the father should be consumed. By each eating part of the father's body, they were appropriating his strength for themselves. The totemistic feast at the Intichiuma ceremony, "perhaps mankind's first celebration," became in that context a commemoration of the crime, the patricide, which gave rise to social organization, to ethics and religion.

For once the father is dead and eaten, the sons' hatred gives way to tenderness and contrite fear. "The dead now became stronger than the living had been." The brothers grow "subsequently obedient" and forbid one another to kill or eat the father substitute, the totem animal. They also forbid one another to "use" (as Freud puts it) the women made available by the killing of the father. The guilt-ridden brothers deny themselves the fruits of their crime as a way of seeking reconciliation with the dead father.

As Freud sees it, we still seek that reconciliation today. We seek it in holy communion when we consume the body and blood of Jesus in remembrance of the original totem meal, when the sons gorged themselves on the body of the dead primal father. We seek it in society and culture. Everywhere we seek to make amends for the original crime: the killing of the father. Freud ends his book with the assertion "In closing this study . . . I want to state the conclusion that the beginnings of religion, ethics, society and art meet in the Oedipus complex."[39]

"Impressive," said the mouse, when they told him the moon was made of green cheese.

28

These were truly impressive theoretical towers that Freud and Durkheim constructed with Spencer and Gillen's building bricks from the backyard of the telegraph station—without ever having been there, without even having seen an Aborigine.

Both based their work on fundamental assumptions that have proved incorrect. They believed the Arrernte people to represent a specific "primitive" stage in human development that other peoples had already passed. But there is no proof that all peoples develop in the same way, nor that the Arrernte people should be considered more "primitive" than others.

On the contrary, the Arrernte are highly unusual, even by

Australian standards; in particular, the ceremony that includes eating the totem animal is not found among other Aboriginal peoples. Bang goes the first half of Freud's hypothesis. Studies of the social life of primates don't bear out Darwin's belief in hordes dominated by a single, jealous male. Bang goes the second half.[40]

Durkheim ascribes to what Freud termed "associations of men," and he termed "clans," a role that in reality is played by other social groupings: the family (which lives together), the "horde" of families (which sometimes live together) and the "tribe" or "people," who speak the same language and control a common territory. The clans, on the other hand, live scattered over wide areas, only meet on ceremonial occasions, and are not the social unit that Durkheim imagined. The "society" he saw as the solid foundation underlying religious experience dissolves on closer inspection into a whole series of different "societies."[41]

And which of them merits the name of God?

To Kahlin Compound

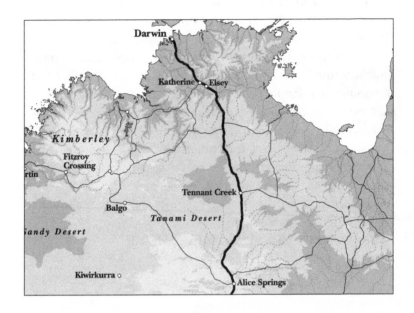

29

I'm driving north with the sun in my face (this being of course the southern hemisphere, where the midday sun is in the north). Just after Alice I pass the Tropic of Capricorn and am in the tropics. Red termite mounds rise from the ground and I'm surrounded on both sides of the road by whole copses of acacias, their flower spikes full of yellow pollen.

The road is so straight it's wearisome. I can see much farther than the eye is able to see. Way off in the distance, beyond my range of vision, everything's lost in a hazy flickering. Even so, it's hard to keep your eyes off that point, since that's precisely where any danger would come from. No one drives with their lights on as they would in Sweden, and often the reflection of the sun on an oncoming vehicle is the first and clearest indication that it's there.

One of my dreams from the night before is haunting me. It's

about my white parrot, who has been given a tidbit by the waiter. She takes it in her beak and deposits it on her back. Retrieves it, eats a little, and pops it under one wing. Takes it again, eats a bit more, and pops it under her other wing. Soon the tidbit is all gone. But the parrot has already forgotten this. Over and over she searches for it on her back and under her wings, but in vain. "No tidbit!" she shrieks desperately. "No tidbit!"

30

LIVE MORE! DRINK LESS! runs the slogan in giant letters above the road into town. With fourteen pubs, of which eight are also liquor stores, Tennant Creek is the Australian town with the greatest density of drinking establishments. But it is also the town in which the Aborigines have declared war on alcohol.[42]

Most Aborigines in Tennant Creek don't drink alcohol. But those who do drink too much. The drinkers are drawn to each other, so whole suburbs are laid waste by alcohol abuse. The children grow up without parents and are alcoholics before they start school.

How did things get like this? Tennant Creek was once called Junkurrarkur and was a holy site where the Warumungu people's songlines and footpaths intersected. The whites built a telegraph station there in 1872. White sheep farmers took over the land. What little remained was set aside as an Aboriginal reservation in 1892.

In 1932, a black boy called Frank Jupurrula found a nugget of gold six miles south of the telegraph station. Three years later, a locust swarm of white prospectors had drained the waterhole dry, destroyed the hunting and grazing grounds, and made the "reservation" a joke. The booze flowed and prostitution became a major industry.[43]

In 1934 the anthropologist William Stunner discovered that mining rights had been granted illegally inside the reservation in some fifty cases and that the telegraph station had five hundred cows grazing on Aboriginal land, exploiting their waterholes. The following year the reservation rights were simply annulled and the Warumungu people forced to move twenty-five miles north to Manga

Manda, notorious for its scorpions, red spiders, and perpetual water shortage. Twenty years after that, the Warumungu were moved on again, to Ali Curung, far from their traditional lands.

The reason for these repeated moves was the need to evict the Aborigines from land that had become valuable. The thinking was, too, that desert people, as nomads, should be used to moving around. In actual fact, the enforced transportation and accommodation in camps destroyed their original lifestyle. For many, only drink remained. "We walked to paradise—Wycliff Well Hotel. It was a long way. But we walked for that grog." [44]

Times got even worse at Tennant Creek when the abattoir closed and mining declined. The population shrank from 9,000 to 3,500. Pubs and liquor stores lost a large proportion of their customers. To stay in business, the pubs began offering credit. The first drinks were free of charge, but the pub owners charged all the more once the customer was drunk.

In the 1990s, the Aborigines started a campaign against the pubs. The whites don't shoot us any longer, they poison us with liquor. They've always wanted to be rid of us. Alcohol is just the latest ploy for achieving a *terra nullius*. The unregulated sale of alcohol in Tennant Creek, according to the Julalikari Council, is "a state sanctioned act of genocide against Aboriginal people." [45]

The Julalikari Council represents Aborigines from sixteen different language groups in ten different suburbs. The program of the organization has four main points:

- The fight against drug abuse
- Education and employment
- Land and housing
- Culture and traditions. [46]

The first point is seen as critical for the other three. The demand is for stricter control of when alcohol can be served. The pub owners should not serve customers who are spilling their drinks and having trouble finding their mouths. Alcohol should not be sold on credit. One day each week should be alcohol-free, preferably the day

pensions and social security benefits are paid out. The
also demanding a tax on alcohol to finance the treatment of
tims of alcoholism.

On the way home, beneath the pink neon lights of the ma
street, I pass the Fernandez Bar and Restaurant, which entices customers with "shooters" at $6 a shot: "Slippery Nipple," "Blow Job,"
"Cock Sucking Cowboy," and "Orgasm."

The pub war continues. Above the road out of town flutters the
slogan DRINK LESS! LIVE MORE!

31

Cool morning turns into hot afternoon. I've passed the "tick limit,"
where cattle used to have to be dipped before they could be taken
any farther; I've passed the palm limit and the limit for rainy-season
flooding. The copses have grown into forests: the patches of green
have spread and cover the ground entirely.

A century ago, Elsey was a remote cattle station that Jeannie
Gunn wrote into Australian hearts with her two bestselling books,
The Little Black Princess of the Never-Never (1903) and *We of the Never-
Never* (1908). Today it lies just a couple tarmacked miles from the
main highway.

The little black princess is Mrs. Gunn's maidservant. "She didn't
sit—like fairy-book princesses—waving golden sceptres over devoted subjects, for she was just a little bush nigger girl or 'lubra,'
about eight years old. She had, however, a very wonderful palace—
the great lonely Australian bush."

The tone of the tale, familiar, intimate, jocular, is established
from the outset. "It takes a good deal of practice to tell a King at a
glance—when he is naked and pulling up weeds." [47] The white people call the king Goggle Eye: "He was very proud of his 'white-fellow
name', as he called it. You see he didn't know what it meant." Little
jokes like this at the expense of black people are all part of the kindly,
condescending attitude. They are portrayed as childishly pathetic
and comical. The reader is invited to admire their tracking abilities, while laughing at their poor English and defective arithmetic.

...zations abound: on one page we read that no
...t beyond two; on the next the "black-fellow"
...many eggs are laid by different bird species.[48]
...children's book with no violence in it. But
...ou don't leave the house unarmed. When the
...oronation of King Edward with a gun salute,
...ic-stricken; they throw down the flour and
syrup and run away. "We shouted to them to stop and said we were
only having a 'playabout'; but they did not wait to hear. We ran after
them, but that only made matters worse."[49]

The incident is related as an example of the comic misunderstandings that can arise between white and black people, and of
black people's laughable lack of courage and self-control. But why
were they so scared? Did they perhaps have good reason for taking
fright? What had experience taught them about drunken white men
firing revolvers? Mrs. Gunn doesn't so much as touch on the subject.

32

For all its defects, *The Little Black Princess* was Australian literature's
first full-length portrait of a young black girl.[50] It took another half-
century for the first autobiography of a black woman to be published:
Tell the White Man: The Life Story of an Aboriginal Lubra (1949).

Readers immediately know where they are when Buludja describes her childhood on the ranch: it's Elsey Station in Mrs. Gunn's
time. "She was the first white lubra I had known and I well remember her arrival."[51] Buludja hides under the veranda so she can listen
to the whites and learn their language. She is old King Goggle Eye's
favorite. She has a playmate and best friend called Taclammah.
They go swimming at sunset every day. A hundred little details link
the two works. Behind the first literary character and the first autobiography we sense the same black woman: Buludja.

Her story is far less idyllic than Mrs. Gunn's. She tells of killing
her first two children: "I did not want any children. They would be
a nuisance. . . . As soon as it was born I closed its nostrils between
two fingers and held my hand over its mouth so that it could not

breathe. . . . It was much easier to get rid of the baby than have the trouble of looking after it. . . . A few years later I had a new baby which I smothered as soon as it was born."[52]

Her employer finds out what is happening and worries about the future labor supply for his station. He decides that from then on, every newborn baby's arrival will be celebrated with the slaughter of an ox and the baking of bread using a whole sack of flour. The little children will even come to the main house to be fed bread and milk. "So I killed no more." Buludja bore five children, of which three survived.

So the first time a black woman has a chance to give an account of her life, she admits having murdered two of her children out of sheer laziness and having stopped the killing only as a result of her white employer's resourceful intervention.

One small problem remains. It wasn't Buludja herself who recorded her story. It was done by her employer, H.E. Thonemann, whose name is also given as author of the book. It's true he claims to have kept faithfully to Buludja's story and described everything from her perspective. But he often forgets himself and sees things from a white male point of view. It's conceivable that he saw his own steps to prevent infanticide as more important than they really were. It's even possible he was duped.

The first time infanticide is mentioned, it's with reference to "light-coloured piccaninnies," that is, children of black mothers and white fathers. If anyone gives birth to such a child and doesn't kill it, the police can come and take it away, Buludja says. "We do not understand why they should take our piccaninnies away from us and never let us see them again. They tell us it is the white man's law. We do not like our children being taken away from us, so sometimes we hide and sometimes we kill them."[53]

These are the words of another kind of mother, not an indolent girl who can't be bothered to look after her babies but a mother who wants at any price to stop the police getting the child. What is she to say? If she says, "I've hidden it," it's an invitation to the police to carry on looking. If she says, "I've killed it," perhaps she'll be able to keep it.

[handwritten margin note: was not her own account was the account of a white man but she clarified her reality]

33

Why were the police on the lookout for fair-skinned children? Well, at the beginning of the twentieth century white society was concerned about the growth in the number of so-called half-castes. It was becoming increasingly common for white men to have children with black women and then play no part in their upbringing. There could be no question of forcing white men to take responsibility for their "illegitimate" children, so the children were to be removed from their black families and put in institutions. The justification given for the policy was as follows: "The half-caste is intellectually above the aborigine, and it is the duty of the State that they be given a chance to lead a better life than their mothers. I would not hesitate for one moment to separate any half-caste from its aboriginal mother, no matter how frantic her momentary grief might be at the time. They soon forget their offspring."[54]

So the police's hunt for fair-skinned children was undertaken in part for the children's own good, in part to make the best use of the valuable gene pool the white men left behind them in the Aborigine camps. Taking the children into custody would also contribute to the final solution of the race question. White society spoke in terms of "breeding out" the blacks, rather than killing them off by shooting them. Making black women bear fair-skinned children who were immediately confiscated and incorporated into white society would hasten and facilitate the process of black extinction.

In the Northern Territory, the Aboriginals' Ordinance of 1911 gave a protector, appointed by the whites, blanket authority to take into custody any Aborigine or "half-blood" whenever he considered it expedient. The ordinance came into force when Baldwin Spencer was Protector of the Aborigines. He wrote: "No half-caste children should be allowed to remain in any native camp, but they should all be withdrawn and placed on stations . . . even though it may seem cruel to separate the mother and child, it is better to do so, when the mother is living, as is usually the case, in a native camp."[55]

The ordinance remained in force until 1957, yet the number of children in custody didn't start to decline until the 1970s. It was only in 1995 that a national inquiry was set up and exposed the full extent of the crime.

34

When I was little, I was taught to call every adult man "uncle." It was usual in those days, and nobody took it as proof that every adult male really could be my father's brother or that my paternal grandmother had practiced group sex.

My grandmother was a member of the Betania mission society, where it was customary for people to call each other "brother" and "sister." This habitual form of address didn't give rise to any hypotheses about the congregation engaging in group sex either.

But when the wealthy American businessman Lewis Henry Morgan found out that certain North American Indians called each other "brother" and "sister," he was prompted into novel and titillating trains of thought.[56] Perhaps, Morgan speculated, this is a form of address surviving from an earlier era when everyone of the same generation could be biological brothers and sisters because their parents lived in group marriages and practiced group sex.

Maybe, Morgan conjectured further, this didn't only apply to a specific group of Indians. Perhaps all primitive peoples had at some early phase of their development lived in group marriages, the women belonging not to a single man but to all the men in the group.

Seeking evidence for his thesis, Morgan sent a questionnaire to places all around the world, and received an answer from a missionary in Australia. The latter reported that some Aborigine women used the same form of address for their husband's brother as they did for him. They called them all the equivalent of "my husband." This was conceivably a practice surviving from a bygone era when brothers owned all their women in common.

The idea that humankind had originally lived in a state of sexual communism was transmitted on from Morgan's *Ancient Society* (1877) via Karl Marx, who read the book and noted down extracts from it in his final years, 1881–82, to Friedrich Engels, who found

Marx's notes after his death and used them as the basis of his *Der Ursprung der Familie, des Privateigentums und des Staats* (*The Origin of the Family, Private Property and the State*, 1884).

Engels begins with an enthusiastic account of Morgan's ideas, including the idea that for some Aborigine peoples marriage is a union of two groups rather than two individuals. For Engels, this assertion applies not to some hypothetical prehistoric age but to current and continuing practices.

In fact, Engels sees group marriage as the key to the process of becoming human. [57]

The human animal would never have survived without its capacity for interfamily cooperation. The most serious obstacle to this suprafamilial organization was jealousy. The transition from animal to human occurred when the males abandoned their claim to sexual monopoly and started sharing females between them. Human beings only became human by means of an uninhibited sex life in a society where all the adult men and women belonged to each other.

This was something of which my grandmother was blissfully unaware.

Those who introduced the Aboriginals' Ordinance of 1911 had certainly never read Morgan, Engels, or their many successors. But the hypotheses and speculations of those theoreticians seeped into society in the form of rumors of loose living and group sex. The rumors hardened into prejudice: black women would have sex with a man as soon as look at him and didn't know who the fathers of their children were. Thus they couldn't love their children, so they killed or mistreated them. It was a blessing for the children to be saved from the sexual snake pit where they had been born, and where they would soon be forgotten again.

35

In 1913, all Europe was discussing the indigenous peoples of Australia. It was among those peoples that all the theory merchants—Morgan and Engels, Frazer and Spencer, Kropotkin, Durkheim, and

Freud—hoped to find the point at which human beings became human. It was there they sought the origins of civilization, the cradle of culture, the birth of society, the roots of religion. Then along came a young Polish anthropologist called Malinowski and turned everything on its head with his thesis *The Family Among the Australian Aborigines* (1913).

He differed in two crucial respects from all who went before. [58]

First, he questioned the search for a primal state. He rejected the validity of the very question that everyone else was trying to answer. He doubted that all humans had passed through the same stages in the course of their development. Conditioned by their climate and their environment, the Aborigines created social institutions exerting mutual influence over each other. Their society is worth studying for its own sake—not as a preliminary stage of Europe but as one of many potential solutions to the basic problems common to all humankind.

Second, he maintained that a critical approach to sources is as vital for the ethnographer as it is for the historian. He takes as an example the assertion "It is the group which marries the group and begets the group." [59] To whom does this refer? A particular Aboriginal people, all Aborigines, or perhaps all primitive peoples? Does it apply to the present, the past, or primeval times? How does the source know this? Personal observation? Second- or thirdhand account? In which language? What are the language skills of the parties? Who was the interpreter? What interests did the narrator have in the matter? The interpreter? The researcher? How did his theory influence his gathering of facts? And so on.

After this scrutiny of the evidence, nothing much remained of the original assertion. Sexual infidelity, yes, of course. That occurs in most societies. A man with several wives, yes, frequently. But no one has ever seen "the group which marries the group and begets the group," and the circumstances leading to that conclusion have other, far more likely explanations.

Once the source material has been immersed in this acid bath, what is actually left of our knowledge of the family life of the Aborigines? Do we know anything definite at all? What are emotional relations between parents and children like, for example? Do the parents care for the children?

Yes, replies Malinowski, on that point all the sources are unanimous. Conflicting observations are made on other questions, but when it comes to parental love, the sources all agree. The observations are concrete. Parents are kind to children who need help and show great patience with them. Both fathers and mothers look after their children conscientiously and very seldom punish them.

There are innumerable accounts testifying to parents' love for their children. A father exposes himself to mortal danger to rescue his son. A mother is a broken woman as she mourns her son. A man searches desperately for his lost son (despite claims that individual paternity doesn't exist among his people). In these accounts, it's never a group of fathers and mothers anxious or grieving or risking their lives—it's always the individual mother or father of a specific child.

Malinowski established that all that was really known about the family life of the Aborigines in 1913 was that they love their children and are deeply attached to them. Simultaneously, a policy was being introduced in Australia that was taking tens of thousands of children from their black parents, brothers, and sisters on the grounds that black parents don't really care about their children: "They soon forget their offspring."

36

Aboriginal children grew up in great freedom, loved and cherished. White Australians had often known very different childhoods. Most came from Great Britain. Many remembered a childhood of hard work, sleeping on the factory floor under the machines. Others remembered a childhood without parents, abandoned in bullying boarding schools. How did they react when they saw black children growing up unpunished, surrounded by loving parents, siblings, and other relatives?

Even Malinowski couldn't resist raising a warning finger to the Aborigines for not beating their children. He saw it as a shortcoming in their child-rearing methods, "for it is impossible to conceive of any serious education without coercive treatment." [60]

Other whites must have reacted even more sharply to what they perceived as laxity in Aboriginal children's upbringing. What a provocation the Aborigines' whole lifestyle, particularly their interaction with their children, must have been to the British! A childhood without shame, without guilt, without punishment! Surely a great sense of loss must have welled up inside them, a sense of missing all these things they were now condemning as neglect, defective hygiene, lack of manners and discipline. When they took fair-skinned children from their black mothers, was it because those children were getting something they themselves had never had, and they felt a bitter sense of lack when they saw others getting it?

The matter came to a head when a white father and a black mother lived together and two widely differing notions of child-rearing had to be reconciled. We get a glimpse of the conflicts that could then arise in Catherine Martin's classic novel *An Australian Girl* (1890).

Old Thompson, on his deathbed, tells the story of the biggest mistake of his life. [61] He had heard that a half-caste inherits the worst qualities of both races, so he would anxiously scan his son by a black woman called Caloona for any sign of negative traits. The boy was sharp, all right, and so funny his parents fell over laughing. But whenever his father tried to teach him manners, he would play dumb or start crying and his mother's hands would tremble. One day, when the boy was seven, he let a young dog loose among the newborn lambs.

> I took him by the hand to the hut, and before punishing him I asked him why he did such a thing. His mother stood there shiverin', looking at us, and the boy burst out cryin' and denied it hard an' fast. He said he was callin' the dog off. This riled me so much that on the instant I give him a bad thrashin'—worse, I know, nor I should have—so that the mother turned on me very fierce like. I got into a bad Scot, an' told her if she did not let me bring up the boy proper

she had better clear. In course, I never meaned a word of it, and never thought as Caloona would take it to heart. But the boy sulked and would eat no food, an' made believe he was very badly hurt. God knows, perhaps he was, though I didn't believe a word of it, an' felt very hard agin him for telling such barefaced lies. Next day his mother stayed in the hut with him and wouldn't even look at me when I was going out. When I came home that night they were both gone, an' from that day to this I never set eyes on them.

37

Children's fear of being separated from their parents, parents' dread of losing their children—these are universal human feelings occurring in all times and cultures. But in one particular place, Australia, and at one particular time, the second half of the nineteenth century, literary fiction becomes obsessed with the subject of "the lost child," writes Peter Pierce in his book *Country of the Lost Children: An Australian Anxiety* (1999).

The definition of lost children in this context is: "Boys and girls of European origin who strayed into the Australian bush." [62] The literature of the period is full of stories of children who disappear; their courage and fortitude; their hunger, thirst, and other sufferings; their parents' despair and frantic search; and the children's eventual rescue or doom.

Why? The aim of the stories, it was said, was to warn young children against going off on their own or straying too far from home. But the intense preoccupation with this theme has far deeper roots, according to Pierce.

He sees the lost child as symbolic of an Australia peopled by lost Englishmen who, finding themselves on the other side of the globe, felt too far from England and were afraid they'd never find their way back home. They felt lost in a *"terra nullius"* that belonged neither to them nor to anyone else. They imagined themselves forgotten and abandoned by their mother country, and expressed those emotions in stories about lost children.

That, at least, is Pierce's interpretation. It makes him limit his investigation to white children and white parents, since Aborigines would hardly have gone around longing to be back home in England. It makes him end his investigation of the motif at the start of the twentieth century, when Australia became independent.

In other words, he breaks off his investigation of the "lost child" theme at the very moment when children really did begin to disappear—not just a few odd cases but wholesale, in the thousands and tens of thousands, not by mistake or by accident but as a deliberate result of a federal and state policy voted through by the settler democracies.

How was the disappearance of Aboriginal children reflected in literature? Was their resilience and heroism somehow different from that of the white children? Were their black mothers indifferent to their loss or did they experience the same hopelessness and despair as white mothers? Pierce doesn't tell us.

If dread of losing children was a white Australian obsession in the second half of the nineteenth century, might that have been one motivation for starting to steal black people's children, forcing them to experience the same dread, the same nightmares, that the whites had suffered for a quite different reason? Might their underlying aim have been that of freeing themselves from their own dread by transferring it to the others, to black people?

Questions of this kind are totally absent from Pierce. He shuts up shop in 1900 and opens for business again in 1950, with a punctuality that enables him to ignore completely how the systematic abduction of fair-skinned Aboriginal children is reflected in fiction, if it all.

38

One of the remarkable novels to fall into Pierce's void is Catherine Martin's *The Incredible Journey* (1923). The writer was seventy-five when she broke a long silence with one last book. Why did she write it? Perhaps because the state of South Australia, where she lived, was about to implement the Better Protection, Care and Control of

Aboriginal Children Act, which would extend the state's powers to take children of black mothers into custody.

Martin takes us to an Aboriginal camp by the fictional Jane Creek, close to "the naked heart of Australia." The Aborigines speak the Arrernte language. A short distance away there is a grand house, whose white inhabitants know what it means to lose a child. Two of their own had gone astray in the forest, and it was only with the aid of the Aborigines' tracking skills that they were found and brought home. Thus far, the story adheres to the nineteenth-century model: if lost children are found, it is nearly always by black trackers.

But then comes something new. A white man, Simon, kidnaps a twelve-year-old black boy, Alibaka, and takes him far off into the desert, where he's completely in Simon's power. His mother, Iliapa, is initially paralyzed by the loss of her son. "She lay stone-still, unable to shed a tear." [63] But the next morning she meets her friend Polde, who has already crossed the desert once. Together they set out on foot to try to track down the boy. The "incredible journey" begins.

The two black women are depicted neither as comic and helpless, nor as infanticidal monsters, but as adult human beings who know what they are doing and are able to make use of their exceptional range of talents. They find snakes and lizards to eat and know where to dig their sticks to find water; they keep away from men, black and white, and enter into alliances with women, black and white. They survive a sandstorm by rolling up all their belongings close beside them and lying facedown. They locate water by watching the flight of birds. At length, they reach the (fictitious) town of Labalama, where the boy is being held prisoner by Simon, a short, fat man with a face the color of old brick.

" 'This is my mother who has come for me,' says Alibaka proudly.

" 'The cheek of niggers! Do you really mean to tell me that you think you are going to take this boy away from me?'

" 'That is why I come.' " [64]

The police side with the white man and decide the boy should stay with Simon until Iliapa can prove she's the child's mother—however she's supposed to do that. The days go by; nasty bruises appear on the boy's face, and Iliapa realizes he's being beaten. She's on the verge of giving up. But through a combination of furious love and skillful diplomacy, she finally gets the better of the white man.

Catherine Martin returns to the theme of "the lost child" but puts a black woman at its heart. The book was bound to cause an indignant outcry among many white readers. Martin knew this, as is obvious from both her preface and her narrative tone. But it would have been "a sort of treachery," she writes, to leave the black women's side of the story untold. "A fellow can't be allowed to steal a child from a black mother any more than from a white one." [65]

39

In the second half of the twentieth century, the lost child of literature gives way to "the abandoned child." Instead of hunting frantically for their lost children, parents (according to Pierce) try in every conceivable way to get rid of their offspring. But here Pierce, once again as a result of the limitations he has imposed on his study, misses the most important piece of evidence for proving his thesis.

Xavier Herbert's *Capricornia* (1938) marks the breakthrough of modern literature in Australia. It tells of two brothers who shortly after the turn of the century arrive in the town now known as Darwin. Oscar dresses in white, moves in the best circles, and rises up in the world. Mark finds himself in bad company, drinks to excess, and fathers a child with a black woman.

> On a downy sheet of paper-bark beside her lay a tiny bit of squealing, squirming honey-coloured flesh. Flesh of his own flesh. He set down the lantern, bent over his son. Flesh of his flesh—exquisite thing! He knelt. He touched the tiny heaving belly with a fore-finger. The flesh of it was the colour of the cigarette-stain on his finger. Smiling foolishly he said with gentle passion, "Oh my lil man."

> The thought of anything bad happening to his son makes him rigid with fear. "S'pose some feller hurtim belong me piccanin. I'll kill every blunny nigger in the camp. Savvy?" [66]

But once the initial joy of fatherhood wears off, he loses interest and leaves. Some years later, he finds his son playing with an emaciated mongrel dog. The child's mother is dead; people call him Noname.

"He was unutterably filthy. Matter clogged his little eyes and nose; his knees and back and downy head were festered; dirt was so thick on his scaly skin that it was impossible to judge his true color; and he stank." [67]

Mark is filled with remorse. He tells a woman to wash the child. He gives him food and clothing. Soon the boy's eyes no longer look like those of a hunted animal. He grows "fat and bold and beautiful."

But then Mark is away for a year, and on his return he has a new black woman who drives Noname away. What the boy doesn't learn from his mother's people, he learns from the dogs.

The years pass, and the next time Mark meets his abandoned son, Noname has virtually turned into a wild animal. Mark catches the boy and sells him as a slave to his friend Jock.

Mark's successful brother Oscar has bought a cattle station, and Jock decides one day to send Noname there because he has become too difficult. His howls of misery are keeping the dogs awake at nights. The author's alter ego, Peter Differ, tries to persuade Oscar to keep the boy:

"Don't send the kid to the Compound, Oscar. It will mean the ruin of him. He'll grow up to learn nothing but humility. . . . Think of the life before the kid. . . . Life-long humiliation. Neither a white man nor a black. A drifting nothing." [68]

Oscar is increasingly charmed by the boy; he says his parents are dead and adopts him. [69]

40

Peter Differ drinks himself to death, and from his deathbed sends his beautiful "half-caste daughter" Connie to the local Protector, begging him to take care of her. The Protector, whose duty is to protect the interests of the Aborigines, promptly gets her pregnant. He promises that if she never tells anyone who the father of her child is, he will come and fetch her and they will live happily ever after. Connie, alone with the child, becomes just one more black prostitute along the railway.[70]

One day, railway worker Tim O'Cannon comes along the rails on his inspection trolley.

> He trundled on, up grade and down, through dripping cuttings where golden catch-fly orchids grew in mossy nooks and tadpoles wriggled in sparkling pools, over culverts where smooth brown water sped over beds of grass, past towering walls of weeds that stretched out leaves and flowers to tickle his face and shower him with dew and touch him— as though he were a flower to be fertilized—with blobs of pollen.[71]

In the midst of this paradise, he suddenly sees a white child. And there at the foot of the railway embankment lies Connie. "She was lying on a bed of leaves, clad only in a sugar bag, thin as a skeleton, black with filth and flies."

"She began to cough. She coughed till her body heaved, till dust was flying from her wretched bed, till it seemed her poor thin frame must burst into leatherly fragments, till she fell back gasping, with tears streaming from her eyes, bloody spittle from her mouth."

He takes her to the compound. When he goes to see her the next day, the doctor still has not visited. Whaddya mean, sick and dying? This is no proper woman, just a half-caste whore, so why are you making such a fuss, Mr. Busybody?

Connie is put in isolation in the venereal disease ward. They say she will die within a few days. Tim creeps in at night and rescues her little daughter Tucky.

Shortly afterward, Tim has a fatal accident during one of his heavenly trolley rides. His whole family, including Tucky, ends up in the compound.

41

Today, Kahlin Compound in Darwin is just an empty building site by the beach, where Gilruth Avenue crosses the road to Myilly Point. This is where Baldwin Spencer set up a camp under his protectorate in 1913 for the collection and holding of Aborigines. In those days it was out of sight of the town itself but still close enough to provide an easily accessible labor supply for the town's middle class. Soon they began to sort them into "half-bloods," who were kept, and "full-bloods," who were moved on to other camps farther away.

A committee formed in 1923 found that public opinion in Darwin demanded the "half-castes" be taken from their native parents at the earliest opportunity, to be "reared in a more healthy and elevating environment." But people did not want them in the town itself, where they constituted "a danger to health" and exerted "an undesirable influence on white children." The challenge was to isolate the "half-castes" from their black families and from white children while keeping them accessible to white employers.[72]

Once the fair-skinned Aboriginal children had been separated from their parents, they would have their native identities scraped away. The children were to be trained, the boys learning handicraft skills and ranching, the girls housework. At fourteen they would be sent out to work, unpaid, in order to learn their place in the lowest stratum of white society. In practice, there was never enough money for anything except keeping the children locked up and sending them to work.

Xavier Herbert spent six months in Darwin in 1927–28, where he came into contact with racism in its most virulent form. He met a mailman who had a little black boy as his "gate opener" and kept him chained under the cart at nights to stop him running away. He met Dr. Cecil Cook, who wanted to solve the Aborigine problem by means of eugenics. All Aboriginality was to be bred out by pairing "half-caste" women with suitable white men—a method crudely known as the "fuck 'em white policy."[73]

During his first stay in Darwin, Herbert met most of the people who later featured in his first novel. The book was virtually finished when he returned to Darwin in 1935 as the acting superintendent of Kahlin Compound. The camp was in a sorry state and Herbert was obliged to begin by installing latrines and organizing school classes. He soon found himself in conflict with other authorities locally, because he defended the Aborigines and identified with their problems in a way that the whites in power found intimidating. Herbert's provisional appointment was not renewed.[74]

"The Compound" is the geographical and emotional center around which everything in *Capricornia* revolves. The novel was published in 1938. Kahlin Compound was closed down in 1939.

42

Twelve years after his adoption, Noname, now called Norman, qualifies as an engineer at the technical university in Melbourne, where nobody cares about the color of his skin. But when the time comes for him to return to Oscar on the station, he gets no farther than the ticket window before attitudes start to change. He gets a cabin right in the stern of the boat. He notices his fellow passengers leaving him more and more alone, the farther north the boat gets. He disembarks and is addressed as "nigger."

He's able to laugh it off. But once he gets to Darwin, he's spoken to in pidgin English in spite of his dazzling white suit and the university diploma in his pocket, and is asked to wait outside. It isn't funny anymore.

Rejected by the whites, Norman is drawn to the Compound and meets Tucky, now fourteen. Always hungry, she sneaks out at night to look for crabs on the beach. She gets found out and is sent to a mission station. When she runs away, the police hunt her across the whole of the state. Norman hides her in a disused water cistern on his cattle station. The missionaries find her, pregnant, and demand that Norman marry her. But the Protector does not approve the marriage: "Norman was disqualified because of his 'superiority to the girl.'" So she is to be returned to the Compound.

Norman is beside himself: "What's she got to grow up to? I'll tell you, all of you, you pale-faced cows—to be a colored slave to high and mighty whites—to the likes of you that can be masters just be-cause your faces are damn well white—to be humble—to keep her place—to . . . to. . . ."[75]

This outburst costs Norman three months in jail. Tucky is wait-ing for him when he returns to the cattle station. When the police turn up once more, Norman thinks they have come for the heavily pregnant Tucky and tells her to hide. But this time it's him they are looking for. He is taken away, accused of murder, and only released after an extended trial.

Back at the station, ruined by the cost of the trial, he sees two crows flying up out of the old cistern.

> Dry grass rattled against the iron. Dry wind moaned through rust-eaten holes. He stepped up to the tank and peeped through a hole. Nothing to see but the rusty wall beyond. He climbed the ladder, looked inside, saw a skull and a litter of bones. He gasped. A human skull—no—two—a small one and a tiny one. And human hair and rags of clothes and a pair of bone-filled boots. Two skulls, a small one and a tiny one. Tucky and her baby!

Thus the story ends. The once abandoned child Noname finds the abandoned child Tucky, daughter of the abandoned child Con-nie, and her own abandoned child, still nameless.

And what does he call his child? He calls it "her baby." Tucky's baby.

This is the final, and presumably unintentional, betrayal in Xavier Herbert's great novel about deserting fathers and abandoned children.

The Dead Do Not Die

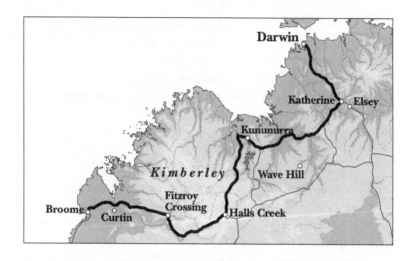

43

After a holiday week in beautiful, modern Darwin, which the cyclones keep permanently fresh and newly built, I long to get back to the dust and emptiness of the interior.

I drive south and stay overnight in Katherine, a small town with a population of ten thousand, an important crossroads with a bank, a post office, a police station, and a main street crammed with the usual inland amusements.

There's Popeye's Pizza and the Bucking Bill Burger Bar Tasty Takeaways. "Come in and see Aboriginal artists at work." Cheek by jowl with Newton's saddlemakers is Jen's Place, the fashion boutique. EVERYTHING MUST GO. The florist offers a wide selection of artificial flowers; the felt hats at the hatmaker's are guaranteed genuine and the Beauty Factory gives professional massages and beauty therapy. The southern end is shared by the newsagent and estate agent. No prices in the window.

If you cross the street and turn back north, the first thing you see is the Northern Land Council, then the butcher's, which also sells fish, and Hotel Crossways, which has most things. This evening they're featuring Love Entertainment & Co. On Friday it gets even more exciting. At 8 p.m. there's a show with "toe-sucking cowgirls." On the next block is the office of Tim Baldwin, MP for Victoria River; his colleague, the Member for Katherine, has his quarters across the street. Anyone still not satisfied can continue to the Christian Outreach Center, which this evening offers "confidential advice."

I go to bed early. The next morning, I drive into the heartland of the great cattle empires.

44

The Victoria Highway between Katherine and Kununurra runs through former Vestey property, which occupied something over sixty thousand square miles of Northern Territory. That's more than three times the size of Belgium.

The jewel in the crown was Wave Hill Station.[76] The land was taken from the Gurindji and other Aboriginal peoples at the end of the nineteenth century. The peoples, or what was left of them, stayed where they were. They could not leave their holy places and the land that it was their traditional task to tend. They had to stay, but to be able to do so they had to work for the new owner, Vesteys. Their wages reflected the situation. In practice, northern Australia's meat production was achieved by use of a native labor force whose pay consisted of the right to remain on the land that had been stolen from them.

The racial divisions were acute and insurmountable. But in the mid-1960s, word spread of the black unrest in the USA. The American civil rights movement sprouted offshoots in Australia. The North Australian Workers Union began organizing black workers, and the Council for Aboriginal Rights formulated a program with the following main points:

- Equal pay for equal work
- Social insurance payments to go not to the employer but directly to the worker

- Living accommodation for Aborigines to meet the same standards as that for whites
- Aborigines to be treated with as much respect as whites. Offensive racist expressions such as "nigger" not allowed.

The press published pictures of ramshackle workers' accommodation at Wave Hill. The company replied that the pictures were not representative—all their other accommodations were better than this particular example. The press published profit figures and claimed the company could afford to pay black people the same wage as white people. The company at first answered that it paid low wages out of consideration for the Aborigines, who did not know how to handle money. When this argument was scoffed at by the papers, the company maintained that the difference in wages was a competence issue. But it proved difficult to explain why every white worker, without exception, had displayed greater competence than every single black worker.

"For eighty-five years our people have accepted these conditions and worse, but on August 22, 1966, the Gurindji tribe decided to cease to live like dogs," said Vincent Lingiari, and led the black workers and their families in a "walkout" from Wave Hill to Wattie Creek. It became one of the most famous strikes in Australian history. Initially, the focus was on the question of equal pay. But the underlying issue of land rights soon surfaced. In April 1967, the Gurindji people wrote to the Governor-General and demanded back a small part of the land that had been taken from them. They declared themselves willing to pay the same annual fee that Vesteys had paid up to that point. If Vesteys demanded compensation for handing over the land, the fifty years and more that the Aborigines had worked unpaid or for derisory wages should be considered compensation enough.

The Legislative Assembly set up a committee that declared: "There are strong moral arguments to support this people's demand for the restoration to them of a small share of the much larger area which they have regarded as their own since time immemorial."

In August 1975, the Labor prime minister took part in a ceremony at Wattie Creek in which the right of ownership to 2,000 square miles of land was returned to the Gurindji people. It was celebrated as a famous victory. But 96.8 percent of the problem remained. The battle for land had only just begun.

45

Victoria Highway runs along the boundary between wetlands and dry areas. A distinctive feature on the dry side is the spinifex, a sort of grass spear the height of a man, emerging point outward from a clump at the base. Armed grasses that know how to defend themselves, resinous grasses that burn well, especially in the wet.

Another characteristic of the dry side is the trees' habit of shutting down some of their foliage during the winter season. Just as we lived in the warm, fragrant kitchen in the wartime winters of my childhood, keeping the living room closed off to save fuel, or as the farming communities of my childhood kept their best parlors shut and unheated until guests arrived, so these trees let half their foliage stand withered and deactivated over the winter, while their other half stays green.

The most distinctive vegetation on the wet side is the boab tree, which in Africa is known as the baobab. Looks like a bundle of branches stuck into a thick thermos flask. These trees are quite often hollow, their trunks roomy enough to be used as places of detention, as in Timber Creek, where I lunch in the shade of the former police station, which is now a museum.

Kununurra, with its population of five thousand, is a modern, fully planned, single-story development, important for fruit-growing and sugarcane production. Middle-class bungalows and shopping centers, administrative buildings, services, a country club, and a tourist office—all of the latest design. The face Western Australia likes to show to the world. I have bed and breakfast at Duncan House, a trim little *pension.*

46

In my dream, I'm still staying at Duncan House. The years are passing. I'm taking it easy. There's nothing to do but wait in the permanently

The boab tree. Illustration from J. Lort Stokes's
Discoveries in Australia (1846).

blowing wind. A tall young woman asks to borrow my bicycle. I'd forgotten that I had one. But her muscular back is impressive. Her ver-
tebral column is magnificently flexible. Her backbone makes a dark
runnel in her flesh. She swings herself up on to the bicycle and disappears. I stay sitting there, so impensioned that the newspaper bursts
into flames in my hands. A tongue of fire licks upward, the news instantly blackens and is borne away on the wind in great flakes.

47

From Kununurra it's twelve miles or so to the Great Northern Highway, which runs south across a wonderful white tableland—silver
white, gray white, creamy white, blue white, dry white, green white,
white white—always against a background of red soil punctuated by
the occasional black-green tree.

Two hundred and ten miles later I reach Halls Creek, an old gold-digging town where cattle transport routes converge before going on east toward the Tanami Desert. There are double-decker road trains parked everywhere, loaded with cattle and engulfed in dense swarms of flies.

This was how Vesteys decided to invest its way out of the problem when it could no longer keep its black workforce in serfdom. Anthropologists Catherine and Ronald Berndt proposed investment in modern worker accommodation, day nurseries, maternity care, and child allowances. The landowners opted instead to put their money into running the cattle station with helicopters, and transport by means of road trains. Their former stockmen now swell the ranks of the unemployed in all the small settlements edging the Great Sandy Desert.

After Halls Creek there are long, straight sections; great stretches with evidence of fire damage; and numerous dead kangaroos at the roadside, traffic-accident victims, with birds of prey hovering above them. Now and then a hill, surrounded by material from landslides. Occasional turnoffs to solitary stations, like in Patagonia.

On the main highway, absolutely nothing happens for 180 miles.

Fitzroy Crossing is a newly built, well-designed town a short distance from the ruins of the old one. In the big supermarket and shopping center, black people predominate. The Fitzroy Lodge Hotel is raised on pillars, with parking places below and a swimming pool in the middle. I sit writing on the loggia outside my room in the cool of the sunset. A few insects. A swell of rowdy, inebriated voices from the hotel's all-white bar. I glimpse the occasional woman, but mostly I see nothing but men in hats. They have become virtually unthinkable without hats. Do they make love in their hats? Do they even take them off to go to sleep?

Most of them are truly drunk, and don't come weaving up to their rooms until three in the morning when the bar closes. The female occupant of the room next to mine turns in with a crash. Just before seven the next morning, she starts her car and drives away, heavily made-up to hide the ravages of the previous night but still alive.

48

North of the Great Northern Highway lies Kimberley, wooded and hilly. A remarkable chapter in the history of Swedish scholarship was played out here, the "Swedish Expedition to Australia 1910–11," led by the zoologist Eric Mjöberg (1882–1938). The planned activities of the expedition were to include "an attempt to bring back as many skeletons as possible of the interesting Australian negro race, which is increasingly dying out."

The Swedish expedition seems oblivious to the scientific debate of the time about Aboriginal social systems. The only thing of interest to Mjöberg is their skeletons.

Collecting these was a delicate undertaking involving considerable inconvenience and difficulty, according to Mjöberg. "Nothing is so risky as stealing people's dead from them." On New Year's Day 1911, he succeeds nonetheless in "snatching an exquisitely well preserved skeleton which in accordance with local custom had been laid to rest on a bed of eucalyptus logs up in the crown of a eucalyptus. But only a few days later the negroes tracked me down, and news spread like wildfire all over the district that I had desecrated their dead."

Thus runs Mjöberg's preliminary report in the scientific journal *Ymer* of 1912. In his more popularly written travelogue *Bland vilda djur och folk i Australien* (Among Wild Animals and Peoples in Australia, 1915), he describes "the Australian aboriginal" with thinly concealed distaste: "His nose is broad, flat, repulsively ugly, his nostrils wide, the root of the nose somehow pushed inwards. His eyes are deep-set, bloodshot, his look sly and shifty."[77]

In the chapter entitled "Hunting for the Bones of the Dead," he relates the episode of the dead body in the crown of the tree:

> I climbed up into the tree and found I had a good view of the deathbed. The smell was in truth anything but pleasant.
>
> Safely back on the ground, I did a quick tally [of the bones] and found that they were all there, with the exception of one little bone from the base of the hand.

This was the first anthropological material and a splendid acquisition for my collection.

On the way home, Mjöberg passes a burial place called Skeleton
Hill and finds a number of dead bodies in a cave. "I managed to ex-
tract two lovely skulls. The bottom jaws were missing, however, and
I only located them after a long search."

"In the depths of the dark caves, generations of aboriginals lay
buried. No white man had ever before disturbed the peace of the
natural grave vaults."

"Pleased and tired, I set off on my homeward journey . . ."

He has hidden the bones in sacks. His companions are worried
that the "negroes" will realize what is in the sacks, but Mjöberg tricks
the Aborigines into believing they are just kangaroo bones. "I was
laughing inside as the three niggers walked ahead of me in cheerful
conversation, carrying the remains of their dead comrades."[78]

49

The Aborigines warn him not to desecrate any more graves. They
"express their indignation at my activities," Mjöberg writes. In his
capacity as a scientist he realizes that their view of the dead is linked
to religious ideas, but sees no need to respect these. "It was only to
be expected that these ideas and feelings would be deeply rooted
amongst a people by no means liberated from the dark reaches of
suspicion, superstition and primitive notions."

So when a young man dies of fever, Mjöberg sees his chance and
asks to attend the burial. His request is refused. Mjöberg however
follows the funeral procession at a distance. "They were clearly sus-
picious of my presence. But I for my part was firmly resolved not to
let such an exceptional opportunity slip through my fingers."[79]

In view of the "negro's" nature, as he saw it, Mjöberg was thereby
exposing himself to great personal risk: "A negro never kills in an
open or honest combat. No, that is too much at odds with his wily,
treacherous nature. It is the ambush that is his strength and his
weapon. And when he kills, he kills unerringly."

Zoologist and grave robber Eric Mjöberg (1882–1938).

From a distance, Mjöberg observes the dead man being laid to rest in a tree. "What a splendid opportunity for me after a while to retrieve Sambo from his airy bier and add his bones to my collection, I thought to myself."

What he is planning "was in the eyes of the blacks a grave crime." They can guess his intentions, and when he comes to fetch the skeleton, he finds the grave empty. "Evidently rumour and suspicion had conspired to upset my plans. In future skeleton hunts I would need to exercise even greater caution, for the Australian negro is very unreliable, and highly fanatical in all his superstition."

At Cherubin's cattle station in Kimberley, Mjöberg meets a young "negro," whom he "cultivates with all the means at my disposal" until he reveals where the dead of the area are buried. "He was a cheaply bought Judas Iscariot."[80]

"Despite all my precautions, it had leaked out that I was hunting the dead, and groups of negroes gathered round the station with grim and threatening expressions." They had also as a precaution taken the bodies of their dead and hidden them.

Mjöberg is on the verge of giving up when his companion points to a hollow eucalyptus tree. "I stuck in my hand and it came up against a skeleton, semi-decayed and still in one piece."

At this point his helper refuses all further involvement. "Single-handedly I had to work loose the individual parts, so they could be packed in the smaller sacks I had brought with me.

"With this, I was able to add another valuable skeleton to my collection."

Mjöberg knew that "there is a strict law forbidding all export from Australia of the Australian negroes, skeletons or parts of them." But he considered that as a scientist he was above the law and describes with pride his conscious breaking of it. Altogether he triumphantly took home six skeletons and some skulls, which were added to the collections of the Stockholm Ethnographical Museum—where they lay untouched for ninety years, while scholarship went in other directions.

After a debate in the national daily *Dagens Nyheter* in the autumn of 2003, Sweden declared its willingness to return the skeletons stolen by Mjöberg. State museums were required to carry out inventories of all the human remains in their possession and offer to return them to any surviving descendants.

50

The Great Northern Highway continues along the fringes of the Great Sandy Desert, but not much of it is to be seen—the landscape is so flat that the smallest bush obscures the view. The only things offering any variety are the flares of burning grass and bushes, and the birds of prey circling above the flames, waiting to hunt down small animals as they flee.

On the road into Derby there's a thousand-year-old prison tree, as big as the Runde Taarn tower in Copenhagen. It's a boab with a diameter of fourteen meters, which was used to detain Aborigine prisoners on their way to the police jail in Derby. The jail, too, is now a historic monument, open to visitors. That's what you find in town after town. In both Sweden and the United States I've seen former prisons converted into hotels, but Australians in these remote parts seem sold on prisons and police stations as signposts to the past. Not schools, nor churches, nor bridges and other constructions— but specifically jails. Maybe a fixation from Australia's time as a penal colony? Maybe it's the infrastructure of state violence that best represents history in this part of the country?

Twenty-five miles from Derby at Curtin lies the Australian Air Force base that from 1999 to 2002 was also a so-called detention center—that is, an internment camp—for 1,400 asylum seekers from Afghanistan, Iran, and Iraq. The camp was run by a private company, Australasian Corrective Services (ACS), which on paper was under the control of the Immigration Department. In practice, treatment of the inmates was left entirely to the company.[81]

The internees were kept first in tents, then in sheet-metal barracks. All accommodation was subject to searches and reallocation at any time of day or night. Contact with the world outside was strictly rationed. Hundreds of internees had to share one newspaper and one television set. Any articles critical of Curtin would have been cut out of the newspaper in advance.

Visitors had to apply in advance in writing for permission to visit a given prisoner, and include written evidence that the prisoner himself had initiated contact and asked for the visit. Of three hundred telephone lines, only six payphones could be used by the 1,400 internees. Incoming calls had to be approved in advance by both the Department and the camp authorities. If you weren't on the list, your call wasn't connected.

Even faxes were blocked, if they weren't from the Department or a legal representative—something most of the asylum seekers lacked. All faxes from families, lovers, friends, and other prohibited contacts were immediately shredded. In many cases, this destroyed crucial evidence in the asylum seekers' cases.

The first hunger strike came five months after the opening of the camp and lasted for nine days. The next hunger strike lasted twenty-six days before it was violently crushed. Suicide and attempted suicide became increasingly common.

"The Freedom Bus" was the name given to an activist initiative to provide legal help to the asylum seekers. The bus traveled around Australia in 2002, visiting all the internment camps. After protracted correspondence, the lawyers were half promised a visit to Curtin. The day of the planned visit arrived. The activists had to walk three miles in searing heat. Reaching the fence, they were informed that the only personnel able to take decisions were "out fishing." Permission to visit was categorically refused.

Two days later, two women from the Freedom Bus were allowed a two-hour meeting with five internees at an abandoned airstrip nine miles from the camp. The camp staff seized their gifts and documents, claiming that these would be kept safe and, subject to approval by the camp management, given to the internees if and when they were released.

The visit was supervised and videotaped by the camp staff. The internees spoke in whispers, with frantic intensity. Four of the five were on hunger strike, along with two hundred other internees. Desperately they tried to explain their plight in a language they could barely speak. Requests for interpreters were not granted. Nor were the internees permitted to hand over the forty-page document they had prepared about conditions in the camp.

Soon after this, the desperate asylum seekers set fire to the camp. It was closed in September 2002 and the last internees were transferred to other camps or to the prison at Broome.

51

Broome is the pearl of the west coast, in more than one sense. It was pearls that created the town and made it as rich and pleasant as it is today.

It all started with black boys diving for mussels in the bays along the coast. Sometimes they found pearls, which white men happily took in exchange for a little tobacco or an old penknife. Later, companies were formed, which "employed" native divers. "A sack of flour and a hank of tobacco bought a human life." The cattle-station owners got £5 for every boy they hired out and did good business. Agents rounded up boys from way out in the desert, boys who had never seen the sea. They were lassoed and dragged after the horses if they refused to come voluntarily.

The boys were taken to the island of Lacepedes, north of Broome. No one there cared how they had been hired. "One nigger was as black as another." They all signed with a cross the contract that in practice became their death warrant.

After the contract ceremony, the boys were taken to the ships and sent out in small boats at dawn, one white man to eight to ten naked boy divers. One after another they climbed over the rail, turned in the water, and swam to the seabed. Ten meters was the norm, but sometimes they were forced to dive as deep as eighteen meters. They were down there for thirty seconds to a minute. Then the shining heads broke the surface and the mussels were thrown into the boat. A few minutes' breathing space, then came a rap on the knuckles with the oar: down again! If they lost a boy, there were always plenty more to replace him. Most of them didn't even last two years as divers. Those who survived were often lame or invalids by the time they were put ashore to make their way home as best they could.[82]

In the Protector's view, six was a suitable age for a black boy to be hired out as a pearl fisher. If he managed to run away, he would be brought back to his employer by the police.

It took harsh discipline for a single white man to be able to force ten Aborigine boys to do deadly dangerous work they loathed. The divers were forbidden to talk to one another in the boats; they could only reply to the white man's questions. The whole day could pass without a word being uttered. If anyone refused, two experienced divers would grab him tightly by the wrists and swim to the bottom holding him between them. After that brutal initiation, no one made a fuss again.

The trick was to stay down long enough to gather enough mussels, but not too long. The instant a diver can no longer hold his breath, his upward motion is arrested and his body starts slowly sinking. Quick action from his comrades could sometimes save him, but many divers never came back up. Even the most experienced were risking their lives with every dive.

The local bishop reported boys whose hands had been smashed on the boat's rail because they were taking too long between dives, and children who were whipped and left to die on the beach when the bends had rendered them useless.[83]

There was no question of wages. The blacks "didn't understand money," the boat owners said. A shirt and a pair of trousers at the start of the season, food and tobacco while they were working—this was the usual remuneration. Rumors spread about what it was like on the boats, and boys had to be taken from deeper and deeper in the desert, and with ever rougher methods. Firearms, ox whips, and neck-irons became standard items of equipment for the agents recruiting "volunteers" to the pearl boats.

In the town museum, it is only fitting that the pearl has pride of place. But there they let the story begin around 1900, when the industry starts employing highly specialized, highly paid Japanese and Malayan divers with modern technical equipment. Not a word about the black boy divers.

52

I and my cousin was at the post office with my Mum and Auntie. They put us into the police ute [a small flatbed truck] and said they were taking us to Broome. They put the mums in there as well. But when we'd gone about ten miles they stopped and threw the mothers out of the car. We jumped on our mothers' backs, crying, trying not to be left behind. But the policemen pulled us off and threw us back in the car. They pushed the mothers away and drew off, while our mothers were chasing the car. When we got to Broome they put me and my cousin in the Broome lock-up. We were only ten years old. We were in the lock-up two days waiting for the boat to Perth.[84]

This happened in 1935, by which time the police had already been abducting children for over twenty years. Black boys were no longer being kidnapped into slavery on the pearl boats; instead, the fairer-skinned "half-bloods" were being kidnapped and taken to institutions where they were brought up as cheap labor, as farmhands or maids for the whites. The justification for this, here as in the Northern Territory, was the need to make the most of the supposedly superior "white" gene pool among the mixed-race children, to lift them out of the black slums and assimilate them into white society.

The children were taught to despise their own language and culture. All ties with parents, relatives, and friends were severed. They were even separated from their brothers and sisters. If two children from the same family happened to be placed in the same institution or white family, the fact that they were siblings was denied. Many have testified to discovering only later that they were sharing a "home" with their brother or sister.

53

I spend a few days in pleasant Broome. Visit the pioneering Aborigine publishing house Magabala Books. Make purchases in the well-stocked bookshop. Eat at Matsos Café & Store where the deep veranda offers shade and catches the wind. Stay at the Mangrove Hotel, from whose windows, evening after evening, I see the bush fires glowing on the other side of the mangrove swamp.

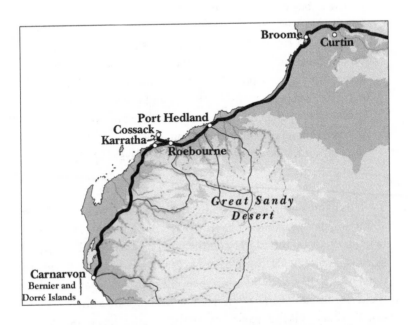

The Great Northern Highway running south looks on the map as if it's squeezed between the desert and the sea with a clear view over both. In actual fact, it starts off so utterly flat that you see nothing but thicket and brush, brush and thicket. For almost 250 miles, it's like the littered remnants of a forest after a gigantic clear felling project.

No other part of Australia has given me such a powerful sense of no-man's-land. There are no roads leading out into the desert, no roads leading down to the sea; nothing happens along the road except the grubby and dilapidated little Sandfire Roadhouse, totally free of any redeeming features. There's a turnoff down to an equally charmless campsite by the beach, from which you are grateful to return to the main highway.

And then it happens. After 250 miles, the landscape suddenly opens out, the undergrowth disappears and a magnificent, majestic monotony takes its place. Endless miles between hedges of yellow mimosa. Endless miles across plains of dry, sparkling white grass. And way off in the distance, right on the horizon, a caravan of mountains looking like humpy camels.

It's the flatness that can make you think of Australia as ugly and empty. The flatness keeps you captive in the bushes. But as soon as the road rises a little and lets you see over the top of the thicket, fantastical landscapes are revealed. White salt lakes rimmed with red foam and beaches of red sand. Round. Meandering. Long and narrow. Luminous. Dry lakes where the salt is all that is left of the fresh water. Lakes that grow, spread out, form whole landscapes of white veils, of pink patches, of long stripes.

Australia is *striped*. My whole field of vision is filled with *lines*. Left by water that once ran there? Or did the wind draw them in the sand?

Grooves. Scratches. Claw marks. Like those torn by the inland ice into the flat rock surfaces of Sweden. All in the same direction. In this divine monotony, it looks just as though an army of pastry wheels has advanced across thinly rolled, light red biscuit dough.

54

Nearer Port Hedland, the salt lakes of the desert give way to artificial salt lagoons producing one of the town's most important exports. The west coast of Australia exports salt, meat, and iron ore on a large scale through Port Hedland docks. The townscape is dominated by cranes and huge conveyors. The town itself is only two or three streets across and situated on a peninsula surrounded by tidal mudflats. I check into the Mercure Inn and lie there listening to the hum and buzz. Six thousand miles separate me from Woomera, where I heard the sparrows taking a dust bath. I've reached the other end of the world's biggest firing range.

"The library? It's opposite the detention center," the lady says, just as anyone else might say, "It's opposite the cathedral," or "opposite the town hall." The internment camp is the natural point from which people take their bearings here.

"What's a detention center?" I ask with all the innocence of a foreigner.

"The House of Correction," she replies in surprise. (And I read in her face the inaudibly added remark: "Don't you know *anything*, blockhead?") "Though it's the boat people they keep there these days."

It was my first prison of the day. Then I got to Roebourne. And where was the tourist information office if not in "the Old Gaol," now a museum? I went on to Cossack, where they serve sandwiches in the Old Tollhouse, now a café. And what was there to see in the place? The Old Gaol, of course. A stone building with three cells and barred windows. The rest of the town has gone; only the street names are left, clearly marked by street signs in the vast emptiness.

Everyone knows that eastern Australia was historically a place to which British convicts were deported. But even here on the west coast, which was never a penal colony, the prisons are the only permanent features to survive, the only things stable enough to weather all the storms. Even on this coast, there's a strong sense of Australia as a penal culture.

55

On September 28, 1983, sixteen-year-old John Pat was taken into custody after a clash between Aborigines and police at the Hotel Victoria in Roebourne. He died in a police cell the same night.

Roebourne is an old port town with ingrained racial antagonism, particularly between white police officers and black youths. In the words of one district judge who regularly presides over court proceedings in Roebourne, the police terrorize the town's Aborigines. "This is a town on the boil," he added.[85]

When no explanation was given for the sudden death of a healthy young man, tensions boiled over. On October 7, some hundred black

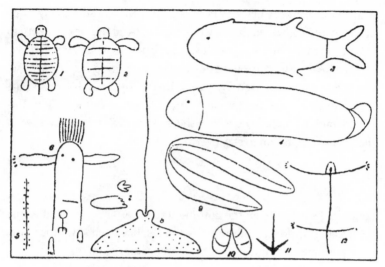

Rock carvings from Port Hedland. Illustration from
Herbert Basedow's *The Australian Aboriginal* (1925).

people, chanting, "Murderers, murderers," attacked the Hotel Victoria, vandalized the restaurant, and emptied the bar of strong liquor.

To calm the mood, a police investigation of the death was
launched. Five officers were accused of manslaughter but released
in 1984. The family thought it could see a pattern. All too often, apparently healthy young men died without warning after being taken
into police custody. No one was guilty, no one had done anything
wrong; the incident was simply inexplicable.

Five families that had fallen victim set up a committee and began collecting facts to fill in the background: repeated harassment,
continuous arrests for minor offences, open racism, threats, beatings followed by sudden deaths in police cells or jails that were never
investigated, intimidation of witnesses, contradictory police evidence and key evidence mysteriously "lost." In two cases, even the
heart and brain of the deceased were "lost" after autopsy.

"The overall imprisonment rate in Australia is 60 per 100,000,
but for Aborigines it is 726 per 100,000," committee chair Helen
Boyle pointed out at a meeting in Perth on the third anniversary of

John Pat's death. A black person is twelve times more likely to be
arrested and convicted than a white person. And the risk of dying in
custody is many times higher if you are black.

Five years after John Pat's death, a wide-ranging inquiry was set
up, and the resulting report, "Black Deaths in Custody," raised national awareness of the problem of racist police violence. The Victoria Hotel in Roebourne is still there. The pub's worth a visit, but
there's no temptation to stay overnight.

56

Today, the sky has been the dominant feature. The ground has just
been a short little strip at my feet—the rest has been sky. I recall my
disappointment when I bought my first camera and started taking
pictures; I found that all those glorious views consisted of nothing
but a thin line of ground under an immense curtain of sky. I lost
faith in photography, gave my camera away.

Giralia is a station that offers bed and breakfast on the long,
empty stretch between Karratha and Carnarvon. The accommodation consists of four portable metal huts with toilet and shower.
Three of them are divided into five cabins with two bunks in each.
There's just enough room to put your feet on the floor between the
bunks, and just enough room for your bag between the end of the
bunk and the short wall. Electric power is provided by a diesel motor
that stops its noisy chugging about nine at night, and then by batteries charged by solar energy during the day. A well for water and
its own private water tower. The whole station is being rebuilt after
the last cyclone. It had twenty-five thousand sheep before natural
disaster struck, and now has eighteen thousand.

There's nobody staying in the cabins around me, except for a
road scraper called Tom and his wife. He moves from station to station and scrapes their roads for them. It turns out we were born in
the same year, so Tom greets me effusively, lets me see his index finger with its top joint missing, shows off his flat stomach and abun-
dant hair, and shares with me his rich experience of life as a cattle
herder, truck driver, and road scraper. He's got a small property up

north, where he's thinking of going to live in a few years. But he can't imagine stopping work. Work keeps your stomach flat, your hair long, and old age at bay. Work is an insurance policy against death. From the proposition "If you're working you're not dead," it's just one short step to "If you're working you won't die."

Dinner consists of vegetable soup, chicken out of a package, and crème caramel. For breakfast next morning, we each get a big sausage with scrambled egg. In the meantime it's night, dark, clear, and starry. The moon lies splashing in its bathtub. The Milky Way is a vastness of scrambled stars, really a mush of stars covering virtually the whole sky. A small horse and a few solitary sheep are grazing near the buildings. I sink like a stone into sleep.

57

In my dream I see the sea, the utterly calm sea.

I see the coast, the utterly still coast.

When this utterly calm sea meets this utterly still coast, huge breakers are suddenly thrown up.

Two sorts of stillness touch one another and explode in roars and foam.

58

Off the town of Carnarvon lie two long, narrow, red sandstone islands called Bernier and Dorré. The Dutch explorer William de Vlamingh came here in 1696 and found that there was no water on the islands. The British explorer George Grey came here in February 1839 and was forced to drink rainwater, which his men sucked out of the sandstone and spat into a pail. There wasn't a tree or a blade of grass. The fauna was predominantly mosquitoes and rats. A cyclone tore across the islands with such force that grown men were knocked down like children. After the hurricane, all the supplies were contaminated by seawater, the ammunition was damaged, the clocks no longer worked, and the boats seemed impossible to repair.[86]

At the start of the twentieth century, these two islands were selected for the forcible internment and treatment of Aborigines suffering from sexually transmitted diseases, above all syphilis. This illness was unheard of before the whites arrived, and the infection was spread mainly by male white settlers chasing after black women, but it was considered more appropriate to intern the natives, especially women, in order to reduce the risk of infection for white men.[87]

The proposal was put forward in 1903 by the Aborigines' Protector in Western Australia. He claimed coercive measures needed to be taken against the Aborigine women to prevent them from "pandering to the lusts of Asiatics, who are so numerous and ubiquitous." So the blame was put on the women and the Chinese, but the proposed measures were intended to protect the very people who were the primary source of the illness: the white men.

In the villages of the outback, it was the police who made the diagnoses and decided which of the indigenous people needed treatment. The police lined up the men and above all the women and inspected their sexual organs. Those who were considered sick were treated as criminals and held captive in neck-irons during long marches through the desert. The number of arrests was determined by the number of neck-irons available on the chain. They were marched from place to place until all the neck-irons were taken. It was not unusual for women in neck-irons to be raped by the police or fellow prisoners. Those who weren't sick when they were seized fell ill on the march.

The police were in no great hurry to deliver the patients they had rounded up to the hospital. Some of those taken prisoner because of sickness remained in chains for three years, carrying out hard physical labor in tropical heat. As late as 1958, the police of Western Australia were defending use of neck-irons by claiming the natives preferred them.

A large proportion of the costs to the state of Aboriginal welfare went toward salaries for a doctor and a couple of nurses for several hundred black patients on the two islands. The first of them arrived in October 1908. The method of treating sexually transmitted diseases at that time involved painful injections and operations, usually ineffectual. Experiments were carried out on the patients; they were given a series of different injections, some of which probably killed more than they cured. The majority of those taken to the islands never returned.

Framboesia, from the French word for raspberry, is a tropical skin disease that occurs and spreads particularly among undernourished children living in conditions of primitive hygiene. Spongy, raspberry-like growths decompose, leaving sores. In 1914, a new doctor found that most of the patients on Bernier and Dorré were suffering not from syphilis but from framboesia. The diagnosis had been wrong, the treatment misdirected, the internment unnecessary, and the alleged threat to the white population far less than had been feared. Financial support was cut drastically, and by 1918 there was nothing left on "the Islands of the Dead" but the graves of all the patients who had died during treatment.

59

All the great men of ideas who between 1910 and 1913 were seeking the answer to the puzzle of the birth of mankind among the indigenous peoples of Australia had one thing in common: none of them had been to Australia. Morgan and Engels, Frazer and Freud, Kropotkin, Durkheim, and Malinowski all happily discussed the Aborigines' way of life without themselves ever having seen an Aborigine.

The young postgraduate student Malinowski did at least realize this was a problem, which he tried to solve by means of a rigorously critical approach to sources. His professor, William Rivers, had a background in the experimental sciences and wanted to go still further. The study of the original inhabitants of the world had always been an "amateur science," he maintained, and would remain so for as long as it was dependent on chance observations by explorers and missionaries. Scholars should make personal contact with the natives, and confine themselves to studying their family relationships, because the extended family provided the basis for their whole social life.

The main advantage of the "genealogical method," as Rivers called it, was that it was self-checking: incorrect information would easily be identified, because it would soon be contradicted by information from other family members. This methodology would make ethnology the only branch of social sciences able to achieve results with a scientific precision to match that of the natural sciences, Rivers declared in his lectures in 1910.

Rivers was an inspiration to a young man called Alfred Brown, who would later become famous under the name Radcliffe-Brown. He traveled to Western Australia, equipped an expedition, set off inland, and near the small town of Sandstone found an Aboriginal encampment where he began his genealogical research.

The peace was soon shattered by the police, who one night surrounded the camp and rode to and fro, trampling huts and campfires, shooting their weapons in the air, and shouting orders to the natives to line up for inspection. A murder that had taken place hundreds of miles away was used as an excuse for terrorizing Aborigines all over the state. While they were at it, they took the opportunity of inspecting the women's sexual organs and taking some of them away to Sandstone, where other unfortunates were waiting to begin the long march to forcible treatment on the islands.[88]

The police action destroyed any chance of success for Radcliffe-Brown's work in Sandstone. He decided to go to the islands instead, where he would be able to question the natives in peace, without any police disturbance. And no one would be able to sneak off to avoid being questioned. The scene was set for the first experiment to employ the genealogical method.

60

Radcliffe-Brown concentrated on terms for expressing relationship in the Kareira people, which at the time of the whites' arrival appear to have comprised some seven hundred individuals, of whom about a hundred were left by 1911.[89] They were linked together by a complicated system of family relationships, as can be seen from the following mini-dictionary:

Maeli   Paternal grandfather, paternal grandfather's brothers, maternal grandmother's brother, spouse's maternal grandfather, and (if the speaker is a man) son's son and son's daughter.

Kabali   Paternal grandmother, paternal grandmother's sisters, spouse's maternal grandmother, and (if the speaker is a woman) son's son and son's daughter.

Mama   Father, paternal uncle, maternal aunt's husband, and spouse's maternal uncle.

Nganga   Mother, maternal aunt, paternal uncle's wife, and spouse's paternal aunt.

Kaga   Maternal uncle, paternal aunt's wife, and father-in-law.

Nuba   If the speaker is a man: my wife, my maternal uncles' daughters, my paternal aunts' daughters, my brothers' wives, and my wife's sisters. If the speaker is a woman: my husband, my maternal uncles' sons, my paternal aunts' sons, my sisters' husbands, and my husband's brothers.

This little lexicon only includes the most important terms and their primary meanings. The term *mama*, father, is for example also used for all those my father calls brothers, as well as my maternal uncles' wives' brothers and the maternal uncles of my brothers-in-law. The list of who has the right to be called *mama* can be extended almost ad infinitum. But ask a man: Who is your *mama*? and he will reply with the name of his father, or if applicable his foster father, although there is a whole series of other people he also calls *mama*.

Thus, just like us, the Kareira people distinguish between close and distant relatives. But the distant relatives' position in the family network is of far greater significance for the Kareira. Their society consists in its entirety of more or less close or distant relatives. The Kareira address small children by name; everyone else is addressed in terms of the relationships—father, mother, grandfather, grandmother, etc. As a member of the Kareira you cannot have social relations with anyone other than relatives, since it is the relationship between you that determines how you should behave toward each other, and other forms of intercourse do not exist. It is highly unusual for there to be no family connection whatsoever between two Aborigines, but if that is the case it implies a latent threat.

Spencer and Gillen, who studied the totem rites of the Arrernte people, found that their totemic relations were the basis of the tribe's social life. In Radcliffe-Brown's work, the totem system is peripheral. He studies family terms among the Kareira people and finds, not surprisingly, that "the entire tribe's social life is determined by kinship."

61

In his questioning of the island internees, Radcliffe-Brown used a fifty-year-old Irishwoman, Daisy Bates, as an intermediary. Much later, she wrote in her autobiography that the Islands of the Dead were the saddest thing she had experienced in all her long life with the indigenous people of Australia. [90]

She could never forget the anguish and despair in their faces. They were taken from their homeland without knowing why or where they were going. After marches of hundreds of miles in neck-irons, they were shipped in fragile little craft across the sea, which they had never seen before, to those desolate islands where no one but strangers awaited them.

They were frightened of the hospital, with its endless tests and injections; they were frightened of each other, both alive and dead; they were frightened of the sea and of the hurricanes that heaved the sea in over the islands. They were undernourished, as weeks could go by without essential supplies when stormy weather prevented ships from putting in. Many succumbed to mental illness and tried to walk on the water to return home or sat for days on end pouring sand over their heads. Others cried night and day in an interminable monotony of grief. Even death offered no consolation since their souls, so far from home, would be among none but enemies.

Used to extremely close family ties but cut off from all contact with their people, they would often stand in silence at the farthest point of the promontory, in the vain hope of catching a glimpse of a loved one somewhere out there, on the far shore.

To be forcibly moved and forcibly treated for alleged sexually transmitted diseases on a remote island in the ocean, bereft of all contact with family, relations, and friends—that would have been bad enough if it had happened to you or me. For the Kareira, a people whose "social life is determined by kinship," isolation on the islands was even more dreadful. But Radcliffe-Brown never drew that conclusion.

The newly introduced policy of taking fairer-skinned children into custody and sending them to what in my childhood were called "reformatories" would have been cruel enough treatment for anyone. But abducting children from a people like the Kareira, for whom kinship plays such a crucial role, was dealing a fatal blow to the heart of their society. Radcliffe-Brown never drew that uncomfortable conclusion either.

When in 1913 he began reporting the results of his studies in the *Journal of the Royal Anthropological Institute*, he was somewhat reticent in his description of the concentration camps where he had collected his data. He wrote that they had been "obtained during a journey through the country of the tribes referred to." Full stop.

Radcliffe-Brown was alone among the scholars of 1913 in visiting Australia and meeting Aborigines. But there is nothing to indicate that he really saw them. Perhaps he was so obsessed with

his "genealogical method" that he failed to make the connection between the significance of family and the sufferings of the Aborigines around him. Perhaps he thought it undiplomatic from a career
point of view even to hint at the connection?

Sure enough, Radcliffe-Brown became Australia's first professor in his subject. Daisy Bates, with equal logic, ended up in a tent in
the desert where she spent the following twenty-five years as guard-
ian angel to her black friends.

To Pinjarra

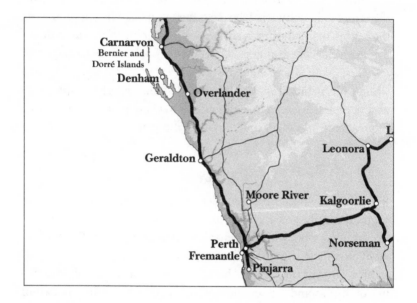

62

Another cool, sunny day. There's still water on the ground after yesterday's rain, throwing a sudden cascade of blue flowers along the verges. Fleshy leaves with claws along their veins; well-defended thorny stalks; the whole plant spangled with delicate, sky blue flowers. It all has the air of an overnight improvisation, produced by the rain and already about to go to seed.

The ants bring sand to the surface and deposit it in red rings around their holes on the gray ground. The resulting landscape is as full of red spots as an Aboriginal painting.

After Overlander I swing out toward Denham. The beach is covered in pulverized shells. Little white shells, a few of them whole, but the majority crushed. The roads are long, straight, and as dizzyingly beautiful as aerial photographs, the road rising and falling.

Hamelin Pool is known as the home of the world's largest colony of the world's oldest life form, single-celled creatures on the boundary between the plant and the animal kingdoms, halfway between algae and bacteria. Their excretion creates formations like tiered cakes, sometimes several meters high and known as stromatolites. It was the stromatolite builders who 3.5 billion years ago began producing the oxygen that is the precondition for all other life forms. Remains of this primeval life are protected in Hamelin Pool, a world heritage site.

At Monkey Mia, the dolphins come every morning to play for a while with us humans. They seem to like our delightful spontaneity, but their demeanor throughout is that of busy parents with more important things to do, and they soon move on.

63

Radcliffe-Brown and his disciples extended their mapping of Aboriginal family ties right across Australia. He summarized the results of his work with the genealogical method in *The Social Organization of the Australian Tribes* (1930–31).

The basis of traditional Aboriginal society is the family, consisting of a man and one or more wives, plus their children. Two or more families constitute a "horde," who together own and control a specific territory where they hunt and gather. Most hordes belong to a "clan," which carries out rites in holy places within the territory of the horde. In these rites, the participants reincarnate mythical ancestors and dramatize their feats.

Hordes that speak the same language form a "tribe," or more correctly a "people." A people is unified by language and custom but is not under the orders of any central leadership. Most peoples are divided into named halves, "moieties," which in turn are usually also divided into halves. A man from one half must always take his wife from the other half, sub-half, or sub-sub-half.

Every child is born into a complicated kinship system that is considered more important than both horde and people. Everybody knows how everybody is related to everybody else and the rights and obligations this entails.

The underlying principle is that of sibling relationships. A man and his brothers are classed together, as are a woman and her sisters.

Those we would call "uncle," the Aborigine calls "father." Aunts are called "mother"; cousins are called "brother" or "sister."

Another basic principle is that those who marry into the family are treated like blood relations. The wife of every man I call "father" I will call "mother," although she did not give birth to me and originally belonged to another family entirely. In the same way, the husband of a woman I call "mother" will become my "father." Thus I may have many mothers and fathers, who in their turn may have many mothers and fathers, all of whom I call "grandfather/grandmother" (on both the maternal and the paternal side).

The third principle is that there is no limit to the application of the two previous ones. They do not cease to apply beyond the horde or the people. Kinship crosses all boundaries, so every Aborigine is in some way related to every other. Which before the white invasion meant that every human being was in some way related to every other human being, and thereby had the right to be treated as "father," "mother," or some other close relative. [91]

Radcliffe-Brown presents these conclusions quite baldly, without a single word to indicate how he arrived at them. Occasionally he refers to his own, unpublished notes of 1911–12, but he never describes a concrete situation.

Nor is there any concrete reference to the rights and obligations that family kinship implies. Which were the problems the family system was designed to overcome? Was it perhaps at heart a pension system? Might it have been a way of organizing childcare or distributing welfare benefits? It is, after all, inherent in the system that the relationships of the close family, of one's own home, are metaphorically extended to the whole family, the whole nation, in fact to every fellow man or woman. Wasn't it in fact a family-based but unlimited welfare state, uniting family members across all boundaries, that the Aborigines were trying to create in the deserts of Australia?

64

Mary Montgomerie Bennett's father, Robert Christison, owned a vast sheep station, but the sheep had a mysterious tendency to disappear. [92] One day when he was out looking for missing sheep, he caught sight of four Aborigines carrying something heavy between them in a kangaroo skin. What was it? Believing he had caught a gang of sheep stealers red-handed, he galloped at full speed toward the Aborigines, who set down their burden and ran.

When the skin was opened, he found to his amazement not a dead sheep but a human being: a very old, severely handicapped woman. Her hair was white, her teeth worn right down. But she appeared well nourished and cared for. She was so terrified that she could not utter a word. The black farmhands recognized her, however, explaining that she had been crippled from birth and that members of her family took it in turns to carry her as they covered long distances on foot.

The incident gave Christison food for thought. For his daughter Mary, it was life-changing. Everything she had ever been told about brute savages and childishly irresponsible natives was turned on its head. She realized with astonishment that the blacks would not think of abandoning one another but took responsibility even for the most helpless and vulnerable members of their family. It was brought home to her with all the force of a bolt of lightning that black people really were human.

Mary expressed her new conviction in the title of her book *The Australian Aboriginal as a Human Being* (1930). In the Australian outback, it was still a provocative and controversial thesis.

While Mary Bennett was working on her book, a group of police officers and settlers went into the Forrest River reserve in Kimberley and killed all the Aborigines they could find. When Pastor Gribble discovered and reported the mass murder, threats were made on his life. An investigation revealed that at least eleven Aborigines had been shot, probably while in chains. The perpetrators could not be convicted because no whites were prepared to testify against them, although they boasted openly of what they had done. The police officers returned to their duties with full authority. Pastor Gribble, on the other hand, was transferred elsewhere. [93]

The following year, 1928, the great drought in central Australia led to disputes over water. The Aborigines tried to stop the whites letting their cattle drink and pollute the water they needed for their own survival. A white dingo hunter named Brooks was murdered, giving the police the excuse to massacre the Aborigines indiscriminately. They were shot by the same policemen appointed to be their protectors. In this case, too, police action was found to have been justified, although the Aborigines who had been killed were innocent of Brooks's murder. [94]

In the end, the only guilty party was deemed to be one Sister Lock, who had been working among the native women and children of the area for twenty-five years. An investigation found her to be "a woman missionary living amongst native blacks, thus lowering their respect for the whites," and her conduct was said to be the primary cause of the incident. [95]

Mary Bennett appealed to the growing number of enlightened, humane Australians shocked by the administration of such "justice." She was supported by both British and Australian women's organizations when, at the age of fifty, newly widowed, she returned to Australia to devote the rest of her life to the struggle for Aboriginal rights, especially those of the women. [96]

65

Personally I have never taken much interest in so-called blood ties. My paternal grandmother, Anna, and my uncle Gustav have been important people in my life, as have my parents, daughter, son, and grandson. But I've never understood why my siblings and my parents' brothers and sisters and their children and grandchildren should necessarily be any closer to me than my friends and their children and grandchildren.

I'm not tone-deaf. But I may be a little kin-deaf.

I ponder this as I drive south along the coastal road to Geraldton. Here, in 1945 in a sand dune behind the hospital, a girl named Millicent was born. [97]

From the word go, Little Milli was handicapped in kinship terms. Both her parents were "half-castes," i.e., they had white fathers, who normally do not acknowledge any responsibility toward black children or grandchildren. So Milli lacked a grandfather on both sides. Their part of the family tree was totally unknown to her.

The black hole expanded and swallowed up everything. In 1949, since Milli was relatively fair-skinned, she was taken from her mother and father, her six brothers and sisters, and the rest of her relations. At the age of four she was put into Sister Kate's Children's Home in Perth and not permitted to see her family again or hear any news of them.

That same year saw the publication in Paris of Claude Lévi-Strauss's epoch-making dissertation *Les structures élémentaires de la parenté* (*Elementary Structures of Kinship*, 1949). He builds on Radcliffe-Brown's genealogical tables and is fascinated by the intricate patterns that emerge when the concept of "paternity" also embraces uncles' wives' brothers and brothers-in-law's uncles. He sees the Aborigines' kinship culture not as a kind of social insurance but as an art form.

Perhaps different civilizations have chosen to develop different aspects of human life, he writes. Greek antiquity reached its zenith in drama and sculpture, our own civilization in technology and the control of nature. Australia's Aborigines chose instead to develop kinship relations and in them reached "le point culminant de leur civilisation." [98]

But in Geraldton they didn't read Lévi-Strauss. No one realized it was the culmination of a whole civilization they were violating when they tore apart the kinship network around Milli. They just took her.

"Child Welfare said we would have a better life and future brought up as whitefellas away from our parents in a good religious environment. All they contributed to our upbringing was an unrepairable scar of loneliness, mistrust, hatred and bitterness."

The sibling group was systematically split up and sent to different institutions. Milli's brother Colin was placed in another section of Sister Kate's Home, so the children would meet only rarely. Sunday was visiting day. But their families never came.

"We spent each Sunday crying and comforting one another as we waited for our family. Each time was the same—no one came. That night we would cry ourselves to sleep and wonder why."

The intention was clear: to make the children feel rejected and abandoned, thus crushing the very core of their Aboriginality. "They told me that my family didn't care or want me and I had to forget them. They said it was very degrading to belong to an Aboriginal family and that I should be ashamed of myself." 99

Ashamed of what was her birth and her innermost sense of belonging. Ashamed of everything she was.

To become what?

66

At sixteen, Millicent was sent to a station as a maid. It soon transpired that her employer also expected sexual services. "The man of the house used to come into my room at night and force me to have sex. I tried to fight him off but he was too strong."

She fled to Sister Kate and told the whole story. After several clips around the ear, she had her mouth washed out with soap and was ordered back to the station. She prayed and begged to be excused, but to no avail. "This time I was raped, bashed and slashed with a razor blade on both of my arms and legs because I would not stop struggling and screaming. The farmer and one of his workers raped me several times."

She was sent back to "the Home" and once more told them everything. She was beaten, had her mouth washed with soap again, and was kept isolated from the other girls. "They constantly told me that I was bad and a disgrace and that if anyone knew, it would bring shame on Sister Kate's Home."

When it became apparent that she was pregnant, she received further beatings. "My baby was taken away from me just as I was from my mother."

This happened in 1962. It happened in one of the Anglo-Saxon democracies, under a freely elected government carefully scrutinized by a free press. It was one among tens of thousands of similar fates suffered by children of the "stolen generations."

It is not clear from Millicent's testimony whether she finally got to see her parents and siblings again. Was she ever able to reconnect with the extended vascular system of kinship relations that is the circulating blood of her people's social life? The only thing we know is that in 1996 Milli received an unexpected inquiry from the South Australian authorities concerning a woman, born in 1962, who was searching for her mother. It turned out to be Milli's daughter Tony. The two have now been reunited after thirty-four years without family, without kin, without belonging anywhere.

67

What is it that makes us into human beings? That was the great question Darwin posed and Freud, Durkheim, and the rest of the class of 1913 tried to answer with reference to the Australian Aborigines.

Claude Lévi-Strauss took up the challenge issued by his eminent predecessors. His answer was that reciprocity (*réciprocité*) was the key to humanity and civilization. If I give you a gift, you owe me a gift in return. The mutual exchange of gifts is the creative act that makes an animal into a human. Reciprocity is the common principle behind war and peace, trade and marriage—in brief, the premise on which all social life is based. The principle manifested itself first and most distinctly in the kinship system of the Aborigines.

This was not an entirely new idea.[100] But no one argued the case of reciprocity with more tenacity and rhetorical imagination than Lévi-Strauss. Nor did anyone else have his pretensions.

Lévi-Strauss does not study relationships between people and groups of people but models resembling economists' ideal models of market functions.[101] Like many economists, Lévi-Strauss and his adherents believe the study of models offers knowledge of a deeper, truer reality than experience, which is all too often contaminated by specific circumstances. "To reach reality one has first to reject experience."[102]

To make anthropology properly scientific, Rivers wanted in 1910 to limit it to what can be studied using the self-checking "genealogical method." In 1949, Lévi-Strauss goes one step further and limits his branch of science to studying models of hypothetical genealogies. With the Aborigines' kinship terms as his building blocks, he creates a world of his own, free from all contradictions and reference to other worlds. In the preface to the second edition of *Les structures élémentaires* (*Elementary Structures*, 1967), he writes: "Is there any need to emphasize that this book is concerned exclusively with models and not with empirical realities?"[103]

68

Reciprocity as the defining characteristic of humanity sounds fine. But what did it mean in practice?

Lévi-Strauss's model is constructed, like all others, on certain assumptions. These assumptions are often forgotten, or remain unstated for other reasons, when the model is presented.

1. The reciprocity that creates societies is always a relationship between men. Only relationships between men are social. The male–female relationship is biological, and relationships between women are not worth mentioning.
2. The reciprocity that creates societies presupposes men's power over women, particularly a father's and a brother's power to control and give away a daughter or sister.

When male animals learned to exchange goods and other useful articles with each other, they became human beings and created societies. The most highly valued exchange article, that which renders life possible and enjoyable for man, is woman. Exchange of sisters is therefore the origin of society.

The basis for symbolic thought, and human culture in general, is the uniquely human phenomenon of a man being able to enter into a relationship with another man by exchanging women with him.

Two boys meet and get on well together. Each has a sister at his disposal. They agree to give each other their sisters as wives, once the girls reach sexual maturity. The two brothers-in-law thereby create between them an alliance that begins to work immediately, often many years before the agreed marriages take place. This alliance is, according to Lévi-Strauss, the concrete expression of reciprocity and the very core of society.

"It is no exaggeration to say that this is the archetype of all other manifestations of reciprocity, and is the basic, immutable rule assuring the existence of the group as a group."

"The prohibition of incest is less a rule forbidding marriage to mother, sister or daughter, than a rule obliging a man to give away his daughter, sister or mother to others. It is the rule of gift-giving *par excellence.*" [104]

A woman can be seen, according to Lévi-Strauss, from two incompatible points of view. On the one hand she is an object for my, the man's, needs and arouses sexual desire in me. On the other hand, I note that she arouses the same desire in other men, therefore offering me the possibility of entering into alliance with them. The prohibition of incest means that I am obliged to choose the alliance over immediate sexual gratification. And I get the beginnings of a society in the bargain.

The idea that the woman herself might have some inclination in one direction or another is totally ignored. The rules of marriage are intended to satisfy "a deeply rooted polygamous tendency found in all men." [105]

By not using his own sisters and daughters sexually but instead giving them away in marriage, the man enters into an alliance with other men, creates society, and holds it together.

How do we know this? Lévi-Strauss does not claim that any brother consciously finds himself in the situation of choosing between two different ways of using his sister. The assertion deals only with the—for the brother—unknown, unconscious significance of marrying off his sister. But Lévi-Strauss has no anthropological equivalent to psychoanalysis that could make the Aborigines' unconscious principles knowable to him.

His own unconscious principles are almost comically sexist. [106] Women are viewed only as resources owned by men. Their needs are treated as nonexistent or negligible. Women's needs are satisfied within the biological family; it's men's needs that demand the

formation of societies. If we want societies,
rule of fathers and brothers, ultimately even
the logical conclusion of Lévi-Strauss's model

294

clay was
physi

69

When forcible treatment on the islands off Carnarvon
the buildings were pulled down and taken to Moore River north of
Perth. They formed the basis for the Moore River Native Settlement,
a school for children who had been taken from their black mothers.
Under the leadership of the Aborigines' Chief Protector, Octavius
Neville, nicknamed "the Devil" by the Aborigines, Moore River became Western Australia's equivalent of the dreaded Kahlin Compound in Darwin.[107]

Neville was a competent man of many parts. He sang in choirs,
played golf, and loved gardening. His policy was to let the "full-
bloods" die out. There was no point trying to civilize them. The
"half-bloods," on the other hand, needed saving. He considered
his authority to extend to anyone with the least drop of Aboriginal blood in their veins: they were to be isolated and controlled. In
1944, he summed up his philosophy as follows: "The native must be
helped in spite of himself! . . . the end in view will justify the means
employed."[108]

White people wished to avoid being disturbed by black people
living nearby, while still having access to a supply of cheap black
labor. Neville's solution was the remote agricultural colony at Moore
River, where up to a quarter of Western Australia's Aborigines congregated in an attempt to maintain contact with abducted children
and grandchildren. The children were kept hard at work in prepara-
tion for their future jobs as servants and agricultural workers for
the whites and were also expected to contribute to their upkeep, to
minimize the cost to the taxpayer.

The native colony functioned like the poorhouses of old. Spar-
ing use of public money was its guiding principle from the start.
In 1921, its budget was reduced still further. The teachers' wages
were cut. All "unnecessary" equipment such as toys and modeling

removed and the curriculum was reduced to nothing but
cal labor. The need to be economical also had an impact on the
tritional value of the food. A worryingly large number of Aborigines in Moore River began to suffer from tuberculosis. Doctors were
only called out in rare, special cases, dentists never. Anyone with
toothache had their teeth pulled by the camp director.[109]

Children were in a particularly vulnerable position. They often
had no idea where they had come from or where their parents and relations were. The administrative routine was to allocate the children
new names when they arrived at Moore, which made it difficult for
parents to make contact with them. The staff told the children that
their parents had lost interest in them, and told the parents their
children didn't want to see them.

The staff weren't allowed to discuss conditions in the camp with
outsiders. Breaking the rule meant instant dismissal. The staff read
and censored all outgoing and incoming post. The camp director
decided himself whether any complaints about his regime would be
dealt with by him or forwarded to the Native Affairs department. In
either case, it was rare for any action to be taken.

weren't allowed to advertise the reality of
these settlements

70

The only person who dared to take issue with the great maker of
policy on native affairs, Octavius Neville, was Mary Bennett. In a
speech to the Commonwealth Conference of 1933 she condemned
everything Moore River stood for, demanding that:

- Children of white fathers should not be taken from their black
  mothers to be brought up in institutions
- Young women should not be sent out as unpaid maids and risk
  being sexually assaulted by white employers
- Those appointed as the girls' guardians should be women, not
  policemen, who abused their power and turned a blind eye to
  other men doing the same
- The root of the native problem was that white and black male
  domination combined to produce dual oppression of women.

The speech prompted an official inquiry. For the first time ever, Aborigines from all over Western Australia came forward to give evidence. But since the testimonies came from "natives," they had no official weight as evidence according to Australian law, so were never published. The truth remained in the archives.

The Aboriginal witnesses particularly criticized conditions at Moore. Visiting unannounced, the head of the inquiry found the buildings overcrowded and crawling with vermin. The children received no training for their future jobs. Their diet lacked fruit, vegetables, eggs, and milk, with detrimental effects on their health. He concludes that the practice of locking small children up in detention was barbaric.

But in spite of all this, the final report was brief and glossed over many aspects. The head of the inquiry found no proof of maltreatment of the Aborigines. Neville triumphed, and the Native Administration Act of 1937 legalized a number of his earlier practices. The Chief Protector was given the explicit right to designate absolutely anyone, usually a white policeman, to carry out medical examinations of both sexes. Those who refused to be examined by the designated person could be punished by up to two years in prison. This enshrined in law the right of the police to harass and humiliate.

In order not to find themselves "under the Act," children with parents of different races had to sever all contact with indigenous parents and kin. They could only marry with the Protector's permission. Neville had thus ensured he had the legal instruments to "breed out" the Aborigines of Western Australia, which he saw as "the final solution" to "the race problem." [110]

Mary Bennett untiringly continued her campaign. She was there in 1938 when the Aborigines marked the 150th anniversary of the white invasion with a Day of Mourning, when she took the opportunity to voice further sharp criticism of Neville.

Neville retired in 1940, but the institution at Moore River remained open until 1951 and was later run by the Methodist Church under the name of Mogumber Mission. Today it is called Mogumber Farm, and the Aborigines run it themselves. It became widely known through Doris Pilkington's documentary novel *Follow the*

Rabbit-Proof Fence (1996) and the film *Rabbit-Proof Fence* (2002). Today there are plans to turn the former reform camp into a memorial to a dark era in Aboriginal history.

71

Moore River Native Settlement north of Perth had its equivalent to the south of the city in Carrolup Native Settlement. The official justification for the two institutions was the education they offered mixed-race children.

The school at Moore had just one teacher to teach more than a hundred children of different ages. Play was considered inappropriate, and the teacher was severely criticized by the camp director for taking the children on nature walks after school. The children were to be set to work instead, then locked in their dormitories at 7:30. The children slept and worked in the same clothes all year round. None of them had shoes. Their food consisted of porridge for breakfast, soup for lunch, and tea with bread and jam for supper.[111]

At Carrolup there was a schoolhouse of sorts, a concrete bunker with minimal equipment. The teacher's house was a tin hut with no kitchen or bathroom and a paraffin lamp as the sole source of light. Nobody who could possibly get employment anywhere else took a job like that. At times when there was no teacher, the children hung about aimlessly all day and were locked into their dormitories at five o'clock, summer or winter.

In 1945, a couple named White heard about this "dumping ground for human refuse,"[112] and applied for the teaching post. Noel White had an unusual way of winning the children's confidence. He played the flute for them and began with singing, drama, games, and drawing. Looking in the school archive at the children's exercise books from before White's arrival, one finds nothing to indicate any hint of talent. For that reason, many outsiders believed that White was doing their drawings himself. But White couldn't draw, only inspire. He accustomed the children to drawing pictures of everything they learned about. The results were both comical and remarkably vivid.

At the children's request, White continued their schooling even after dark. No more being locked in their dormitories at five. By the light of the paraffin lamp, White told them about black people who had been guides for Eyre and other white "discoverers" and about other contributions the Aborigines had made to the history of Australia. He encouraged them to listen to their old folk and learn as much as they could about their people's myths and legends. He taught the children to be proud of their black ancestry.[113]

The result of this teaching was a stream of increasingly interesting drawings, which created a stir in Perth and were a great success in London, where they were exhibited in June 1950.

What does one do with children who win international acclaim though they are nothing but refuse? They can never become real artists, after all. Maybe they should be taught to draw advertisements? Or take other jobs and pursue their artistic interests in their free time? And who actually owned the artwork that had already been produced and sold? The children? Or their parents, or maybe the Education Department or the Native Affairs Department?

The girls were sent to a Catholic missionary school, where they were taught sewing instead of art. A few particularly gifted boys were given jobs as office boys in the Education Department in Perth. They soon got bored and longed to get home to White and their classmates in Carrolup. But there the media interest in the young artists had provoked a power struggle between White and the new school management, which was doing all it could to lure the boys away from the teacher's influence. Art was pushed aside to make way for sport and scouting. It took the new director a year to have Noel White fired, the school closed, and the children dispersed.[114]

72

The girls from Carrolup became maids or prostitutes; the boys often got work at local vineyards. Part of their wages was paid in wine; before long they would have committed some crime while under the influence and begun their careers as jailbirds.[115]

Australia's first Aboriginal novel, Colin Johnson's *Wild Cat*

Falling (1965), tells the story of a talented, proud, and touchy young man, just released from prison in Fremantle.

His whole childhood and adolescence has been a struggle for acceptance as a white by the whites, a struggle to be white although he wasn't. So he was forbidden from playing with black children. He had to eat up his nice food like a good little white child. White was what you had to be. If you had the slightest hint of black in you, the Welfare would be down on you. "You know what that'll mean."

He knew all right. The Welfare wanted to take him away from his mother. The Welfare was always on the lookout for children who weren't white enough. The Welfare wanted to take them from their homes to put them in "homes." And sure enough, at the age of nine he's caught, ends up in a "boys' home" and then at Carrolup. And here he stands now, just out of prison.

He's scared. At least prison was a sort of refuge. He won some respect there, he was somebody. But out here?

The first person he meets is a white girl who advises him to start again. Which means: try to be white again. He plays it cool.

—I am too old now.
—How old?
—Nineteen.
—Practically Methuselah.
—Too old to laugh or cry any more. So old my bones ache . . .
—That's up to you.

I feel the old bitter taste of resentment in my mouth. Nothing is ever up to them. Only up to us, the outcast relics in the outskirt camps. The lazy, ungrateful rubbish people, who refuse to co-operate or integrate or even play it up for the tourist trade. Flyblown descendants of the dispossessed erupting their hopelessness in petty crime . . .[116]

He's soon back with the old gang, planning a new theft to prove prison hasn't "reformed" him. They steal a car and make themselves scarce, go back to his old hometown. But the break-in is discovered, they have nothing to show for their pains, and a shot is fired in the turmoil.

He flees into the woods and comes across an old black rabbit catcher he remembers from his childhood. He is told that his mother now lives in the Aboriginal camp.

She got nobody, only them, son.

Mum, with her phoney pride, dependent on the kindness of the people she reared me to despise. They brawl and bash each other up, gamble the shirts off their backs and make fools of anyone who tries to help them, but they have a warmth and loyalty to each other and a sort of philosophy of life that whites will never know or understand.[117]

He sleeps in the old man's hut and, seeing his chance, steals some money from a bowl. As he's leaving, he is given a gift by the old man: the very money he has just stolen.

"I feel the blood flushing up my neck and over my face and I hang my head. No one has ever made me feel that way before. No one."

For the author, as for the novel's narrator, *Wild Cat Falling* means he stops trying to be white and accepts his Aboriginal identity. Colin Johnson was the name the author used for his first novel, but it was as Mudrooroo that he became the leading novelist of Aboriginal literature.

73

How did it begin? Where did it begin?

The train rattles south through fertile, green agricultural land. There's a soft drizzle and all the furrows, hollows, and depressions are full of water.

This is how green and inviting the country appeared to Captain James Stirling when he first stepped ashore in Western Australia in 1827. He thought he'd found paradise. He threw in his lot with young landowner Thomas Peel and set up a company that promised every immigrant twenty acres of land for £3. He was unaware of, or paid no heed to, the fact that the land was already owned and looked after by a people that knew all its secrets. For him, the whole lot was *terra nullius*.

The first settlers arrived in 1829—with wholly unrealistic expectations of the life that awaited them. They got no farther than the beach, freezing through the storms of winter, plagued by sandflies and mosquitoes in summer. Their dining room furniture rotted in the rain as the allocation of land proceeded at an unbearable snail's pace. After a few years in tents by the beach, most had tired of it all and moved on to Sydney. One of the few who remained was Thomas Peel himself. He sat alone in a stone hut on his estate of four hundred square miles.

I'm the only one who gets off at Pinjarra. Opposite the station lies the Premier Hotel. A bridge leads over the long valley of the Murray River. Then comes the little town, threaded along its main street like wild strawberries on a stalk of straw—post office and bank, police station and courthouse, café and pizzeria, tires and gas, Food Land and Farm Mart, newspaper shop and real estate broker. Oh, and the churches, of course: the Anglican St. John's, the Roman Catholic St. Augustine's, plus Pinjarra Unity Church, the Alliance Church of Pinjarra, and the Open Faces Christian Ministry.

The tourist office has its premises in Edenvale, a grand house in the classical style. Its brochure recommends a "History Walk" through the town but doesn't say a word about the only thing for which the place is famous. Only those who make a point of asking get the special little brochure produced in conjunction with the Murray District Aboriginal Association.

I look through the brochure over my lunch of cheese sandwiches and a pot of tea, then walk across the narrow, swaying suspension bridge over the river and follow the route along the bank through the park. According to one version of history, this was the site of the "Battle of Pinjarra." The other version calls it the "Pinjarra Massacre." Fifteen black warriors fell, says one story. According to the other, about a hundred black people, mostly women and children, were buried in three mass graves and thirteen individual graves.

In 1834, the first settlers had just begun taking possession of the rich areas of land in the Murray River valley. The Nyungar people resisted, under their local leader, Calyute. Peel had invested his fortune in this huge area of land, which risked becoming worthless if the natives succeeded in scaring away the settlers. He called for military assistance from Governor Stirling.[118]

When Stirling seized the *terra nullius* on behalf of the British crown, he had declared the few (so he believed) Aborigines to be British subjects, with all the rights this implied. Now, five years later, ownership of the territory was disputed and violence seemed necessary, even commendable.

On October 27, 1834, Stirling left Thomas Peel's estate with eleven soldiers and five mounted policemen, as well as Peel himself and a pack of dogs. The ford at Pinjarra was known as a crossroads and meeting place for the natives. Stirling spent the night at a suitable distance from the ford and attacked at dawn. Some eighty black people were taken completely by surprise. When they tried to run away, they came under fire from the main force, located higher up on the opposite bank. Those trying to escape downriver were shot by men stationed at the next ford.

The massacre was all over in an hour but was followed by a protracted hunt in the surrounding brush. On the whites' side, one man had been injured and one other thrown from the saddle by native spears. According to the Aborigines, half the Nyungar people were killed, and its existence as a social entity was destroyed.

Once the two top men of the colonization project had given the lead, there was nothing to stop the rest of the settlers from following their example. The Pinjarra massacre unleashed a wave of terror that virtually annihilated black people the length of the Murray River valley.

The Smell of White Man

74

Early morning. I glide slowly and quietly out of Perth's urban landscape, into the farming belt—pale green autumn wheat and fields of gray stubble-edged with white-trunked eucalyptus. Each tree is its own copse. Some are multistoried, with different levels of foliage stacked one on top of the other, often with a cheeky little penthouse at the very top.

Road, railway, and pipeline run alongside each other. The water isn't running down from the mountains to the city with its million-plus inhabitants but being pumped from a reservoir in Perth up to the mines in the goldfields on the desert rim.

I spend the night at Hotel Australian in Kalgoorlie, in a town center where the renovated fin de siècle buildings still maintain the extravagant mood of the gold rush.

I go for a beer at the Exchange Hotel & Pub, opposite the Australian. It turns out to be the favored haunt of the miners from New Zealand. For men with dreams of being cowboys, there are bar stools in the shape of saddles. Electronic horses offer virtual rodeo.

There's not a woman in sight apart from the waitresses, who wear body stockings and are known as "skimpies."

Just around the corner is Paddy's Pub, where all the Irish go. An electronic disc jockey coordinates the blaring music with the gigantic video screen and a dozen smaller TV screens showing various sports channels, mostly boxing and racing. Then there's a billiard table and one of those old-fashioned but clearly hugely popular table football games where you flick the handles with your own bare hands to get the players to "kick" the ball, without any interference from computer power or even electricity.

I ended up at Bodington's. The men's toilets there aren't marked "Gentlemen" or even "Gents," but "Miners."

75

The coldest night of the year in Kalgoorlie. The temperature fell below freezing. I slept with my outdoor clothes on. But the clear weather that made the night cold also makes the day warm.

In the course of today's drive I saw six black emus picking their way with great gravitas among pewter-gray tussocks of grass and silvery bluebushes that look as though they have a coating of hoarfrost. Also five wild camels, one of them creamy white, grazing on the white grass. But no kangaroos, or at least no live ones—I've seen more than enough dead ones, there must have been about thirty bodies, victims of a permanently ongoing traffic massacre.

Depressions with clumps of red grass in red sand. Rounded green bushes. Little balls of green thrown aloft by spindly tree trunks. The wooded landscape gradually thins, the ground is bared, the plains open up—but it's not a proper desert, not yet.

Bacon and eggs at the Grand Hotel in Leonora. The smell of the food is so greasy you could fry the eggs in it. As I'm eating, the wind gets up from the west and heavy rainclouds fill the sky. I drive on with the wind at my back, and soon it's no longer cold but warm and humid.

At Laverton I check into the only hotel, the Desert Inn Hotel Motel. The narrow main entrance in the windowless wall makes me happy. Hotel entrances don't usually look like that. Hotels usually announce their names in huge letters over doors wide enough to admit the fattest of wallets. Not here. Here there's just a narrow door and above it simply the word "Entrance."

The door leads straight into the bar, which although it's only three in the afternoon is full of rowdy, quarrelsome, drunken men with hats grafted to their heads. A fat girl opens the top half of the door to the "office," which consists only of a board with keyhooks. I'm given the key to room 10, which is furnished with a hard bed, a hard chair, a bedside table, and a glass for a toothbrush. And a number of tree branches for the wind to scrape endlessly to and fro over the tin roof.

Whites are drinking with whites in the bar, blacks with blacks. They pretend not to notice each other. The black people are watching dog and horse racing on television, faithfully staking their money in a betting machine before the start of every new race. By about six, Thursday evening in Laverton has begun. Only the hotel, the liquor store, and the police station are still open.

A glance at the map shows me to be at about the same longitude as Fitzroy Crossing and the same latitude as Geraldton on the west coast. Between me and Coober Pedy to the east lies the Great Victoria Desert, Australia's largest. It has no water at all running on its surface, but beneath the sand dunes the bedrock is crisscrossed by riverbeds and drainage canals. The heart of the desert is so inaccessible that it has never been grazed by cattle, nor does it have any nonnative flora.[119]

Laverton is at the end of a little appendix in the road network: I've reached "the end of the road." Just seeing a place like that on a map gives me an adrenaline rush. And to actually be here, to see map and reality coincide for a moment—what does it matter that the room is shabby, the lights dim, the food inedible? It matters not at all. I'm happy.

76

Cold morning. Ground frost on the bathroom floor. All the moisture from here to Alice Springs seems to have been collected together and released on to the dripping car. But the sun is close. Why does it always seem so much closer here than in Sweden? The sun in Australia never seems more than a couple of blocks away.

The roads into Leonora are all adorned with big notices exhorting truck drivers to clean their wheels before they drive into the town. Like little boys, they're told to wipe the mud off their boots before they come rushing in. When you see the deposits the truck wheels leave on the tarmac, you understand why. Everything is obliterated by the red dust: the broken line down the middle, the unbroken lines at the sides—it all disappears in the same red dust-dream and blends into the verges and surrounding land, making a homogeneous red universe without boundaries or direction. In the midst of it all there's a pub calling itself "The Pub with No Beer."

Slowly south through lovely forests around Lakes Lefroi and Cowan. Could they be described as shallow? Somehow, a certain depth is required for something to be shallow. Here, the lake is so utterly without depth that the moisture seems to have been licked over the ground as over the back of a postage stamp. These are lakes as thin as a covering of ice formed overnight. But to the eye they still make a glittering surface that from a distance looks like an ocean.

Norseman is a crossroads with well-kept roadhouses and a mine that has created a vast, gray-black slagheap above the town. It looks as if it could start to slip at any moment, come crashing down, and wipe out the town.

We're used to equestrian statues with riders. In Norseman the statue features not the rider but the horse; that is, the horse which according to legend found gold here in 1893.

In my dream that night the polar bears gave a party for their human friends. They weren't aggressive at all, but of course you had to be careful. It's well known that white bears are more dangerous than brown ones. I spent most of my time up on the table or on a shelf that ran around the wall. A polar bear in a uniform cap was acting as a policeman but not unaided—behind him walked another police officer, a white person, to make sure the bear beheaded himself.

77

After Norseman, the road turns east. Between Belladonia and Caiguna comes the longest straight stretch in Australia and presumably the world: one hundred miles without a millimeter's deviation sideways or up and down.

The coastal desert is called Nullarbor, "No Trees." All you see are occasional dried-up trees along the wayside, like those marker buoys with brooms sticking up. The last forest disappeared during a period of drought fifteen thousand years ago.

The history of Nullarbor goes back to the time when Australia was part of Antarctica.[120] When the two continents went their separate ways hundreds of millions of years ago, the landscape was broken in two. Rivers that once ran from Antarctica into Australia continued in their previous course. Australia became unique in that the flow of water in its whole interior and on large parts of its south coast is not toward the sea but inward to the basin floor. What were once rivers are now chains of thin salt lakes. The water from the irregular rains vanishes down into the limestone in this karst desert with its winding, undrained cirques.

When the world oceans rose and the sea level reached its highest point, 116 million years ago, Nullarbor and the whole interior of Australia were flooded. Fifty million years ago, the sea invaded again, creating layers of sediment. Thirty-six million years ago the sea receded, only to return twenty million years ago. Now the whole area was covered in limestone.

Nullarbor is the world's largest limestone plateau, 150,000 square miles in size. Beneath the plateau there are caves large and small, some eroded by the sea, others by streams of water from torrential rain in the interior of Australia. All caves breathe to some extent, and in Nullarbor the breathing of the caves is particularly lively. They breathe in when the air pressure rises and out when it falls. Air speeds of up to forty-five miles an hour have been recorded.

The openings through which this breathing occurs are called "blowholes." Their sighs and groans have been the source of legends that the caves are inhabited, stories of subterranean cities and secret passageways to undiscovered gold deposits, of ancient peoples living on underground, defying time.

The desert is at its most desolate between Nullarbor Roadhouse and Yalata. In the middle of the day, a red dust-storm comes sweeping along the coast. Wild gusts of wind tug at the car, the red vortex lifts debris from the ground and tosses it up in the air in whirling spirals. Trees and houses are shrouded in red mist. It's scarily beautiful; my heart contracts sharply in my chest, but nothing happens, and seconds later the vortex has moved on.

At Nundroo Roadhouse, where I stay the night, you're only permitted entry to the bar if you meet strict criteria for neat, tidy, clean dress, good personal hygiene, appropriate footwear, sobriety, and unripped clothing. The management moreover reserves the right in each individual case to deny admission to those deemed to be behaving inappropriately.

I am woken several times during the night by violent cloudbursts beating on the tin roof. Will the rain make the road impassable? Have I, in this area of extremely sparse rainfall, managed to coincide with the only day of the year when water floods the road out into the desert?

78

Heavy black clouds hang like udders from the sky; the ground is covered in pools of water and there's a light drizzle. I drive the thirty miles to Yalata in the dramatic lighting of the sunrise.

Then I turn north through Yalata Community, an Aboriginal settlement, where the tarmac gives way to a washboard-like surface. The buzz is like driving across an endless cattle grid; the hard suspension makes the car body vibrate like a pneumatic drill.

After a long, bumpy stretch, the sand comes as a delightful, treacherous relief. The car is suddenly floating agreeably, like cream on top of milk. You're suspended. But that's also when you run the greatest risk of getting stuck, as your tires dig into the sand. The potholes are easier to negotiate. You drive around them, of course, if you can. Otherwise you take your foot off the accelerator and let yourself swing down into the hole and up again.

I don't meet a soul on this stretch. I pass a score or more of wrecked cars at intervals along the road, showing it's not without its dangers. I carry on north through the ever more naked landscape I love. And suddenly I'm there. It's the railroad. There's the first little signpost. It points west, to Watson, the next station. Straight on, heading north, the road goes up to Maralinga, a prohibited zone. A few hundred meters east stands the station sign: OOLDEA. The station house and the platforms have gone, all that remains is a little shunting yard with rusty rails and a small pile of concrete sleepers.

And there inside a ring of white stones is a white-painted lump of concrete bearing the words "1859–1951 Mrs Daisy Bates CBE. Devoted her life here and elsewhere to the welfare of the Australian aborigines."

No flowers, just thistles. The sun is shining and the wind is bitterly cold.

79

Nullarbor is only the coastal strip of the vast Great Victoria Desert.[121] There are no springs. All life is dependent on a hundred or so watering places: depressions and hollows where the rainwater collects in natural dishes of hard clay. Some of these dishes are small and shallow and quickly dry out. The biggest and most reliable was Ooldea. For that reason, Ooldea became one of the most important meeting points in the desert, a place on which all paths converged, where you could find refuge from the drought, where ceremonies with several hundred participants could be held without the water running out.

The supply of water also led to Ooldea becoming a junction on the transcontinental railway that was built in 1912–17. That was where the railway construction project advancing from the east met the one coming from the west. That was where the locomotives filled their water tanks, whether they were eastbound or westbound. The railroad used forty-five metric tons of water a day. As the wells ran dry, new and deeper ones were dug, until one day in 1922 the company engineers bored down into the bowl-like cavity that retained the water and cracked it. It had taken modern technology ten years to destroy a natural resource many thousands of years old.

The water now had to be transported in tank wagons as rail freight, primarily for railroad use, secondarily for the needs of white settlers along the railroad. In third place, and only if supplies permitted, it was provided for the black people whose watering places had been destroyed. They congregated around the station in their hundreds to beg for water. Soon enough, they were begging for food and money too. Soon enough, the rail passengers realized that they could invite little black girls on board, get them drunk, abuse them, and throw them off farther down the line—where they had no choice but to prostitute themselves again for a free ride back to Ooldea. Within a few years, alcohol and syphilis broke down the Aborigines who had come from the desert healthy and well nourished.

Daisy Bates was convinced the indigenous peoples of Australia were bound for extinction.[122] Her time as Radcliffe-Brown's scientific handmaid on the Islands of the Dead had strengthened her in that conviction. Back in Perth, she set out to look for the surviving remnants of the once numerous Bibulmun people. In Hopetown there was no hope left: they had already died out. In Esperance things didn't look hopeful either: there was just one old pair of brothers left, known as Dib and Dab. Everyone said, "*Jangga meenya bomunggur*"—"The smell of white man is killing us."[123]

She applied for a position as the natives' Protector, but the post was considered too hazardous for a woman.[124] Instead, she immersed herself in the Aborigines' world unpaid and unprotected. Her tent could be observed at Eucla and Yalata as the First World War raged and media attention was directed elsewhere. During the visit of the Prince of Wales in 1920, his train stopped at Ooldea to take on water, and Daisy found herself briefly front-page news. Then she disappeared into obscurity again for over a decade.

But the easterly sirocco hadn't forgotten her. It carried on storing sand between her sheets and under her eyelids. "A geologist could have made a study of the landscapes I have seen using the dust they have left in my eyes." [125]

When she returned to the white world at the age of seventy-six, she prepared herself carefully for the transition. "It had to be done in stages, like a diver in one of those metal capsules being slowly raised from the depths of the ocean, lying still while he gets used to the unaccustomed weight of the air around him." [126]

Daisy Bates had never been to the cinema; she refused to speak on the telephone and pretended to be deaf when the radio was on. But after all those years in the desert, she loved interviews and photographers. She wanted to be the center of attention. Well into her eighties, she would flirt wildly with the men around her. [127]

She brought with her a ton of paperwork, which was deposited in the library of the *Advertiser*, the newspaper that sponsored her return. The journalist Ernestine Hill tried in vain to retrieve anything publishable from the chaos. The diaries generally petered out after the first few months of each year, ending in heat and urgency, burden of work, and lack of events. All the material was already old. They had to start all over again and proceed orally. Bates told her story; Hill made notes. "All the material was hers; only the arranging, formulation and the writing itself was mine," said Hill half a century later.

How did she bear it, year after year in the monotony of the desert, through winter storms and summer heat? What did she really do for the natives? What was the value of her research? How could she reconcile her belief in the extinction of the indigenous people with her belief in the benevolence of the empire and the white woman's burden? What were the origins of her less than healthy tendency to share with other people and give away everything she had?

Her book *The Passing of the Aborigines* (1938) offers no answer to these crucial questions. More than forty years after her death, Daisy Bates remains an enigma.

80

The authorities viewed Daisy Bates's activities in Ooldea with the utmost suspicion and came up with a constant stream of imaginative excuses for ordering her to leave. But when the United Aborigines Mission opened a mission station on the ritual site beside the former water hole, they received full backing from the authorities. The missionaries were authorized to hand out state rations of flour, sugar, tea, and tobacco to the natives. The natives were also attracted to the school, although the girls were locked in their dormitories each evening and could only see their parents for a few hours a week. The parents had to adhere to a strict code of dress—no Aborigine could approach the mission unless dressed like a white person.

It was the missionaries' stated intention to break down the traditional culture, which in their eyes was heathen superstition. Their first aim was to undermine the authority of the clan system. One method employed was to take lantern slides of holy objects and symbols, which the old men had loaned out on the condition the missionaries kept them confidential, and then show the slides to the schoolboys with comments such as "Look how stupid this is! Just some old bits of wood! How can anyone think they're important! Don't listen to those silly old men, they don't know anything."

The missionaries saw themselves as saviors when they "protected" the boys from the horrors of circumcision and the whole barbaric cultural heritage surrounding it. They urged the boys to marry before their people considered them mature enough for such responsibility.

The missionaries saw themselves as saviors when they "protected" the girls from being married off as third concubine to some old man their uncle had chosen for them. They urged the girls to break their tribal laws and marry one of the boys who had "seen the light" and whom the missionaries had chosen for them.

Catherine and Ronald Berndt, who later became well-known anthropologists, carried out their first fieldwork in Ooldea in 1941. In their report *From Black to White* (1951), they criticize the mission for confusing Christianity with European middle-class mores. The

missionaries didn't realize how coercive their practices were. The
youths growing up in the dormitories were subjected throughout
their most impressionable years to a barrage of propaganda against
the culture of their own people. Their ultimate aspiration was supposed to be conversion to Christianity and marriage that contra-
vened the laws of their people.

"Last Sunday there were great preparations, for we had the joy of
marrying in our little church yet another Christian couple: Albert
Amunga and Meda Odewa were joined in the Lord after yet another
hard struggle against the customs and laws of the tribe. Everything
went very well, photographs were taken and the young couple drank
tea with all the missionaries. It was a pleasant evening." [128]

But the next day there was trouble, and a few days later Odewa's
parents took her down to the coast, out of reach of the missionaries,
who could only hope she would one day be reunited with Amunga.

It simply wasn't possible to pick and choose between elements of
the two cultures. Saying no to traditional marriage meant breaking
with your family, kin, and nation. Saying no to Christian marriage
meant forgoing the social and economic advantages the mission and
its wider society had to offer.

Behind both alternatives, catastrophe loomed. Both seemed to
be on a collision course with the railway and everything it brought
with it. Both whites and blacks were convinced the collision would
lead to the destruction of the blacks. The mission saw cultural destruction in a positive light, as salvation from physical destruction.
The two anthropologists hoped instead for cultural renewal. But in
what form?

81

Len Beadell, who in the 1940s had transformed the Great Victoria
Desert into an enormous missile-firing range, was given a new task
at the start of the 1950s: to find a suitable location for the testing of
British atomic weapons.

What was required for white culture to live out its suicidal ten-
dencies was a site about six miles in diameter, free from obstructing

sand dunes and far enough away from the launchpads for the radiation from the test bombs not to interfere with the missile
experiments.

The place initially chosen was Emu, where a ten-kiloton atomic
bomb was detonated on October 15, 1953. The radioactive cloud rose
to a height of 4,500 meters and then moved across the continent
for forty-eight hours. At the press conference, someone said the
bomb cloud looked like an Aborigine: "A perfect portrait of a myall
blackfellow written with atomic dust; the new and the old have come
together today." [129] The words were front-page headlines in all the
papers.

It was the natives whose lives were put most at risk. It was their
land that was contaminated. The problem then was to keep them
away from their old paths and ritual sites and warn them of an invisible danger that could only be measured by Geiger counters.

The most urgent step was to close down the mission in Ooldea.
The missionaries were evacuated in 1952; the Aborigines stayed. A
Lutheran missionary from Koonibba was given orders to travel there
and bring fifty dormitory children back with him. Only six came.
Of the three hundred adults he had orders to transport to Yalata,
only sixty-five came voluntarily. The rest were evacuated by force or
vanished into the vast "prohibited area" into which the former reservation was transformed.

After two large and numerous smaller atomic-weapon tests,
Emu had become too dangerous. Len Beadell was sent out to look for
a new location and happened upon Ooldea, now abandoned. There,
the clear-felled sand dunes had begun to shift and bury the buildings. Drifts of sand were blocking the outer doors and getting in
through the windows.

A new town was laid out just west of Ooldea: Maralinga, with
a thousand inhabitants, a hospital, and an airport. At the test site
a short distance away, seven British atomic bombs were set off in
1956–57. What the British called "minor trials" continued until
1963, in spite of the Nuclear Test Ban Treaty. The minor trials were
of three different kinds: "Kittens" tested different methods of setting off an atom bomb; "Rats" tested different materials used in

atom bombs; and finally "Vixens" studied the consequences of nuclear accidents, such as fires in nuclear-weapon stores or the crash-landing of a plane carrying an atomic weapon.

It was these six hundred or so "minor trials" that had the most serious repercussions. Over twenty kilos of plutonium was spread over large areas in the form of fine dust. The particles are dangerous if eaten or inhaled. People who go naked and barefoot, live in the open air, drink from open water holes, and gather their food from the ground or just under it are, of course, particularly vulnerable.

82

We don't know how much dangerous material is left today in Maralinga and its environs. Seven tons of uranium, 830 tons of atomic waste, and 1,120 tons of contaminated sand are buried in twenty-six protective pits in the area. Of the ninety-nine kilos of beryllium that was dispersed in Maralinga, less than two kilos has been retrieved and removed.[130]

Repeated decontamination projects were undertaken in the mid-1960s; in 1968 an agreement was signed freeing the British government from further liability for any results of the atomic tests.

Ten years later, the area was reexamined. The British decontamination was found to have consisted of plowing the plutonium a few decimeters below the surface of the ground, where it had soon been laid bare by the fierce desert winds.

The Australian Nuclear Veterans' Association was set up in 1979. Hundreds of experts and others involved in the experiments told of their experiences. The British sent three Hercules planes to continue the decontamination process but only managed to retrieve half a kilo of plutonium. At least nineteen kilos remained lying in the desert sands.

By the Maralinga Land Rights Act of 1983, the new Labor government gave the indigenous people back the land that had been requisitioned from them in the 1950s. But how safe was it to move back there?

A Royal Commission was appointed in 1984. It heard 311

witnesses and drew 201 conclusions, leading to seven recommendations. The commission made the British solely responsible for
the decontamination of the ground and demanded that the area be
made safe for permanent settlement by the native inhabitants.

While the commission was at work, fences and warning signs
were erected. They were still there at the beginning of the twenty-
first century. The half-life of the radioactivity in the plutonium is
280,000 years.

And the nuclear weapons that had been developed had a combined destructive power equivalent to a million Hiroshima bombs.
On a single order, the entire world can be turned into *terra nullius*.

The Ground

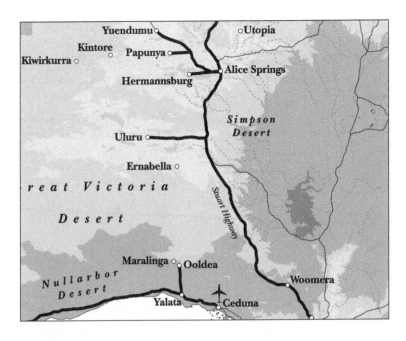

I see black fern patterns in light sand. I see light ribs on a dark background—an opened chest cavity. I see salt lakes lathered like half-scrubbed wooden floors.

I'm aboard a taxi plane, taking the shortcut across the Great Victoria Desert from Ceduna to Alice Springs. It saves me three days covering a route I've already driven. Above all, it gives me a new vantage point.

I look down over a dry inland lake, bluey-white with salt that could almost be ice. I see an archipelago of red islands in an Antarctic of salt.

The ground is striped and fingered, full of riverbeds without rivers. Crisscrossed by innumerable runnels that aren't running anywhere, traces of water events that used to happen once but aren't happening any more. A history wholly characterized by its landscape. A landscape wholly characterized by its history or, to be more precise, its water history. You feel you could read the ground as Sherlock Holmes reads the scene of a crime.

The bulldozers have left behind a few straight red tracks in the ash-gray sand and white salt. Wind and water have left behind innumerable meandering tracks, branching and rejoining each other, in nature's marshaling yard.

Little spots of yellow sand in the salt, like the yolk in a fried egg. Furrows, plowed by water. Ditches, dug by wind. Salt warp in the woven fabric. The shapes recur at regular intervals, as if in a wallpaper design.

From up here, it can be hard to see where the desert ends and the sky begins, when the sand cover and the cloud cover are the same color. The horizon seems to be lying sometimes right at your feet, so you almost stumble over it, sometimes way up at the zenith.

The trailing light of evening accentuates the sandy ridges; the edges grow sharper, the shadows deeper. But the clarity of focus only lasts a moment. Then the colors pale and fade out. Everything is erased in a froth of deep pink dusk.

We've arrived.

84

Why weren't the Aborigines who had been evacuated to Yalata content to stay there? Why was it so desperately important for them to return to exactly the same lands where they had lived before, although those were the very areas that were now contaminated with radioactivity?

The white authorities could understand that farmers might be attached to the soil. But the Aborigines weren't farmers. They were nomads. Who ever heard of a deeply rooted nomad? No, unlimited mobility was part of the nomad concept.

So the Aborigines were constantly being moved, not only to allow for atom bomb tests, but also because the whites' cattle needed a particular pool of water or because the whites' company had found new mineral deposits—or simply for their own good, so they could be looked after and learn the whites' table manners, the whites' good home cooking, the whites' working hours. The new policy after the Second World War was aimed at "assimilating" the Aborigines, which didn't imply white people thought they had anything to learn from black people but meant black people were to be trained to be steady wage earners and consumers on the fringes of white society.

Out in the desert, Aborigines were rounded up by police patrols that took them to mission stations like Ernabella or Hermannsburg or to state internment camps like Papunya and Yuendumu. One nigger was as good as another; nobody was bothered that they belonged to different nations and spoke dozens of different languages. After all, no proper person could tell those languages apart.

It was equally incomprehensible that every Aborigine had custody of particular places out in the desert and had to return to them to carry out their religious ceremonies—though the "place" to white eyes looked just the same as all the other places in the desert. Employers and camp directors suspected that all the talk of "holy places" was just an invention of incurable vagabonds and deserters from the settled lifestyle the internment camps were trying to teach.

85

White society was constructed on the presumption that Australia at the time of the British invasion had been "no one's land." Along the coasts, where the British first arrived, the continent was admittedly populated, but deeper inland they visualized vast uninhabited tracts. Countless explorers traversed Australia in all directions, vainly seeking the no man's land that was needed to legitimize the invasion.

In the end, only the deserts at the heart of the continent were left. Clearly there was little appetite for admitting that even here, where the land was least accessible and hospitable, even here every stone, every bush, and every water hole had its specific owner and custodian, its sacred history and religious significance.

The main thrust of white research on the subject of the Aborigines therefore avoided sacred geography. Spencer and Gillen took an interest in how people related to animals, Radcliffe-Brown in how they related to one another. No one showed an interest in the relationship between the people and their land.

Spencer and Gillen let the subjects of their study move to the backyards of the telegraph station, so they were easily accessible. Radcliffe-Brown found the subjects of his study among the involuntary inpatients languishing on the Islands of the Dead, far from their homelands. No wonder they missed the significance of place. The vantage point they had selected made place invisible.

86

Theo Strehlow (1909–78) chose a different vantage point.[131] He was the only white child in Hermannsburg, where his father, Carl Strehlow, was a missionary. Theo grew up in the borderland between two languages and cultures. His black playmates ran about naked and free, played wherever they wanted, and were never beaten. He himself had a strict German Lutheran upbringing. Children were little animals who must be tamed by a lovingly brutal father figure. If he said anything wrong in German, he was punished. The language of his playmates and the maids, Arrernte, became his true maternal tongue.

After Strehlow's father died in 1922, mother and son moved to Adelaide, where Theo's unique linguistic skills aroused attention at his school and then at the university. In 1932, his professor sent him back to Hermannsburg to study the phonetics of the Arrernte language. After a period of scientific fieldwork, he got a job as a mounted policeman, spending a total of fifteen years in the wilds. He was the only white man who could speak to the tribesmen in their own language, the only one who had no need of an interpreter to understand their songs and stories.

He sought them out wherever they happened to be, in situ, amid the geography that also contained their history. For a people without documents, history soon turns into fairy tale and dream. But the geography remains. You can't travel through history, but you can go to the place where the past happened. Soon you don't know anymore when it happened, only where it happened and where it goes on happening.

"It cannot be stressed too strongly that Central Australian mythology did not concern itself with the sky but with the ground," said Strehlow toward the end of his life, when he drew together his knowledge of what he called the "totemic landscape." [132]

Here, as so often, he is in dialogue with his father. Carl Strehlow had always looked for an equivalent to the heavenly God of Christianity in the natives' songs and tales. But his son emphasizes a human being's connection with the ground in his place of origin and with the supernatural beings that created it and still live there. Mythology is an imprint of the landscape and can be understood fully by someone who has experienced the places described in the myth.

This "ground-based religion" was the motor of economic life. Without ceremonies, the ground would dry out, animal prey would disappear, roots and seeds would shrivel. A religious leader's function was similar to that of a minister of agriculture and food: to ensure growth, to prepare the ground for small-scale enterprises in family groups, to create the right business climate for gathering and hunting.

Theo Strehlow also investigated the network of tracks and pathways that crossed the Simpson and Victoria Deserts. The Aborigines' constant migrations in their forefathers' footsteps enabled them to exploit local resources that would soon have been exhausted by permanent settlements. The intersections on the network had great economic importance as trading places. But above all they were holy places where historical myths were kept alive.

The holy sites of the Christian religion, from Bethlehem to Golgotha, are for most Christians very distant. In central Australia, the holy places have an uncommonly personal intimacy. The eternal truths of religion are expressed in the surrounding landscape. One can go to these truths, set up camp among them, become pregnant by them, draw them on the ground, dance them, and sing them, in the very spot where they once occurred—and thereby keep them alive and, along with many other people, contribute to keeping the whole universe alive.

87

Theo Strehlow saw himself as the Homer of the Arrernte people.[133] His ambition was to combine the countless song fragments he had collected into a single poetic work. He transposed oral tradition into a written language he had created himself. The tunes were of no interest to him. It was the text, the words, the great poem he wanted to highlight. In the course of the 1930s he amassed over four thousand verses, mostly two lines in length, which he edited and translated into English during the decade that followed.

But by 1950, the Aborigines of Australia were no longer the height of fashion in the European cultural world. Strehlow had trouble getting anyone even to flick through his manuscript. And those who did were startled by what they found. For most of the songs lacked any precise details about when, where, and from whom they had been collected. And how reliable, in fact, were the transcripts that claimed to be "condensed versions" of longer songs or perhaps amalgamations of several different songs?

Instead of using accepted scientific techniques, Theo's book contained innumerable alleged parallels between the songs of the Arrernte people and Western literature, from the medieval Icelandic *Hávamál* onward. It was a monster of a book, which had to wait several decades before it was finally published, with a print run of just a thousand, in 1971.[134]

By then, most of the old singers were already dead. Theo felt himself to be the sole remaining custodian of a treasury of songs nobody remembered. And perhaps he himself had contributed to that loss of memory. Just as an actor remembers his lines by associating the words with particular movements and spatial positions, one of the roles of ritual is to act as a memory bank for the myths and songs of the people. Rite is a living national library in which poetry is enveloped and preserved through action. The poetry dies if it is separated from the rite.

The Arrernte people believed in a connection between cultural and biological survival. If the songs die, the land dies, if the ground dies, the people die. The old Arrernte men contemplated with horror a future in which their songs, rites, and everything that kept the universe alive had sunk into oblivion.

This sense of doom permeates Theo Strehlow's entire life's work. His father at least had an alternative: God. Spencer believed in evolution, of which extinction was simply the inevitable reverse side. Strethlow had nothing but the bitterness of doom. His last words were: "Oblivion that has no end." [135]

88

In my dream I am lying on the ground under a tree. The crown of the tree is the memory of the Arrernte people. I see the brain stem disappearing into a huge mass of foliage. But the leaves begin to turn yellow, and in an autumnal storm of thoughts, they suddenly fall to the ground. This frightens me. But those that have fallen are the transient ones. In the remaining tracery of branches, new thoughts are alive; in fact when I look more closely, the twigs are already covered in buds.

89

A few years after Strehlow's death, the transistor radio created a new audience for the desert peoples' treasury of songs. In the 1970s and '80s, a hundred or so little radio stations sprang up. They became an important source of news and entertainment in the various Aboriginal languages and mediated knowledge of those cultures. [136]

Radio proved in many ways to be the ideal medium for desert conditions. The technology is simple and cheap, the running costs are low. Newspapers and letters call for literacy and take a long time to reach the recipient. Radio builds on the spoken or sung word, which can reach the recipient the moment it is broadcast—or be saved for an audience scattered not only in space but also in time.

Production of audiocassettes developed into production of video cassettes, which in turn led to the first illegal television broadcasts in Yuendumu in 1985. They were broadcasts of protest meetings, concerts, and local sporting events. A specialty developed in personal greeting messages to distant kinsfolk. Face after face pops up on screen, greets Uncle This or Cousin That and asks if they are well. These programs are tremendously popular—if the best thing you know is socializing with your relations, maybe the next best thing is seeing them on TV.

Other specialties include sand stories, documentary reports from holy places, and food programs about how to prepare grubs, seeds, roots, and other traditional bush dishes. But above all the television broadcasts are facilitating a renaissance of traditional rites, dances, and songs, enabled by the new technology to reach out to an audience many times greater than before. Songs Strehlow believed sunk in oblivion with no end are now living on, on everybody's lips.

90

The Aborigines' pictures perplexed Australia's European "discoverers" even more than their songs.

When early explorers found impressive cave paintings and rock carvings, they sometimes thought the images had been made not by the natives themselves but by some other, perhaps almost white race that had come in from outside, and that they thought they could glimpse among the blacks.[137]

But the more usual approach was to dismiss indigenous art as a kind of graffiti. As the German ethnologist Richard Andree wrote in 1888 with reference to Australian rock art: "If a drawing is done at a street corner, some imitator will soon come along and do another, and so school desks, outlook points and public toilets are soon filled with names and pictures."[138]

Another German ethnologist, Erhard Eylmann, surmised that the strange patterns came about because it is easier to make lines and dots into some sort of pattern than to scatter them randomly over a surface. The natives' painting was a development of the makeup they used—the men paint themselves to be attractive to women. Eylmann himself favored a different, more direct approach: "It is my conviction that it would do most women good to receive a sound thrashing at least once a week."[139]

George Grey discovered this cave painting in Kimberley and thought it must have been done by some other, almost white, race that had come in from outside and that he imagined he could detect among the blacks.

Spencer and Gillen wanted clear and unambiguous indications from their informants of the significance of particular pictorial elements. It irritated them that a figure was said to be wholly without meaning when drawn in the sand but assumed a very specific significance when it occurred on a holy object, and perhaps a differ-ent meaning again at a ceremonial site.[140]

But was this really so strange? Four numerals on a piece of paper might mean somebody was trying out their pen, but it could also be a date a schoolboy hopes to use for cheating on an exam, a code that opens locked doors, or even a PIN number allowing you to empty someone's bank account.

In their second book, Spencer and Gillen defined the pictorial elements as "decorations" and regretted the fact that the natives of-ten had no idea of their meaning. It didn't occur to them that their informants might have been keeping certain things secret to protect their bank accounts.

Ignorance hides behind condescending comments: "Apparently, from the artistic point of view, the Central Australian savage has been very little influenced by his natural surroundings, and delights in the production of wavy lines, circles and spirals . . ."[141]

Hardly an appropriate judgment of an art more deeply rooted in its local terrain than any other.

Even Spencer, an experienced map reader, can't see that the cir-cles and spirals of the "savages" are a different, non-depictional way of reproducing the reality around them. Not even when he is at those locations does it occur to him that there are few objects in the desert that lend themselves to direct, realistic depiction. A central perspec-tive generally only shows a small piece of ground which quickly dis-appears with distance and a huge sky above the horizon. Flat ground looks like a mere line, unless viewed from above.[142]

The status of Aboriginal art in that period is perhaps most clearly illustrated in the Rautenstrauch-Joest Museum in Cologne. There the hierarchy of the collections was built into the very build-ing. Enthroned on the top floor were Asia, Africa, and Indonesia. On the mezzanine below came the art of the more primitive Na-tive Americans. Another flight of stairs down: Melanesia, Polynesia, and the rest of Oceania. On the ground floor: New Guinea. But the art from Australia, the continent in which "the lowest forms of cul-ture are preserved," was placed in the basement.[143]

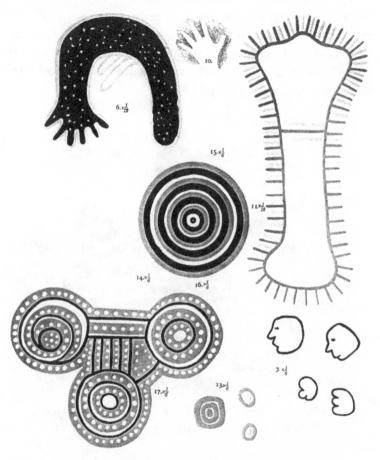

It irritated Spencer and Gillen (1899) that informants could
not give clear and unambiguous information about the
significance of the various elements of their pictures.

91

"As in the tale of Sleeping Beauty, the Australian peoples have fallen asleep," writes Herbert Kühn in *Die Kunst der Primitiven* (*The Art of the Primitives*, 1923). "But for them, the prince of deliverance will never come, and they may not even wish to awaken from their slumber. Because for them, European culture implies not liberation but ruin." [144]

But who in fact was sleeping and needed to be awoken? The black people or the white people?

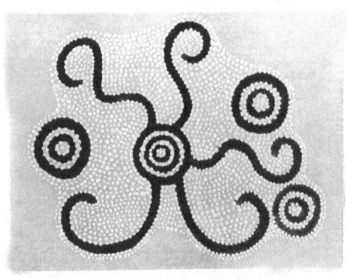

In their second book (1904), Spencer and Gillen classed the Aborigines' ground paintings as meaningless decoration.

Margaret Preston was the first to wake up. She "discovered" Aboriginal art in 1925 and was seized by a passionate belief that the whole set of native forms could be transposed into Western culture and be the starting point for a national art of Australia. Just as Braque and Picasso had used elements of African forms to create modern European art, Australian artists would use the Aboriginal idiom to renew their own art.

Preston's enthusiasm was infectious but also arrogantly colonial-
ist. She saw the Aborigines' pictorial world as a *terra nullius* lying in
wait for discovery and exploitation by white artists. She wasn't interested in the links between Aboriginal art, ground and myth, religion
and society. She wasn't interested in art as the desert peoples' last
chance of rescue from the brink of extermination. She discovered
the aesthetic potential of Aboriginal art but saw it solely as an open
treasure chest from which white artists could help themselves.[145]

92

Ten years later, Rex Battarbee woke up.[146] He was known for his watercolors and often painted scenes from the area around Hermannsburg. His camel keeper, Albert, kept asking if he could learn to use
watercolors. Within a few weeks, he was producing paintings virtually indistinguishable from those of the white artist. Battarbee took
a couple and exhibited them in Melbourne. They sold within three
days. A few years later, the National Art Gallery of South Australia
acquired one of Albert Namatjira's watercolors. That was the first
time a leading art gallery had bought work by an Aborigine.

Namatjira's work continued to sell well, and he was soon a pros-
perous man. Accustomed to sharing, he taught his techniques to
his relatives, and before long all Hermannsburg was busy painting.
A people that had been considered the world's artistically most im-
potent proved capable of unprecedented collective productivity in a
branch of the arts that already had the full approval of the whites.

Albert Namatjira became the ultimate role model for the policy
of assimilation. He was constantly held up as an example of how the
Aborigine, by learning from the white man, could quickly become
his cultural equal. No wonder Battarbee saw himself as the prince
who had awoken Sleeping Beauty from her slumbers.

93

In 1957, Namatjira's artistic achievements were rewarded with Australian citizenship. Namatjira was formally already an Australian

William Dargie, Australia 1921–2003, portrait of Albert
Namatjira, 1956, oil on canvas, 102.1 × 76.4 cm, purchased
1957, collection of the Queensland Art Gallery.

citizen by virtue of the 1948 Nationality and Citizenship Act that ostensibly made all Australian Aborigines citizens—but citizens without the right to vote or any other civil rights.[147]

In 1948 the Aborigines of the Alice Springs area could still be interned against their will; they were not allowed into white hotels, hospitals, or other "prohibited areas" and could not travel or leave employment without permission. They were outside the social security system and did not receive old age pensions, maternity allowances, or any other social benefits. Marriages were prohibited across racial boundaries, except by special permission from the authorities.

The 1953 Welfare Ordinance (NT) replaced all earlier Aboriginal Ordinances and substituted the word "ward" for "Aborigine." The criteria for being declared a "ward" were ostensibly racially neutral. They included lifestyle, behavior, and personal associations. According to these criteria more than 99 percent of the Aboriginal population were declared "wards" of the state.

In 1959 the Director of Welfare decided to prohibit marriage between Mick Daly (white) and Gladys Namagu (black). The incident attracted international attention and after the intervention of the UN Secretary-General, the Director changed his decision. The global decolonization process had made the racial laws of Australia increasingly conspicuous, and the government came under considerable international pressure to change the rules.

In 1962 Aboriginal people acquired the right to vote in both state and commonwealth elections. Two years later the concept of "ward" was abolished and the Aborigines became "persons who in the opinion of the Director are socially or economically in need of assistance." The change in terms changed little in the authorities' practice of power. In 1966 Aboriginal people were included in the Australian social system. Their social benefits, however, were often not paid out to them personally but to their employer or to the institution in which they were confined.

Finally, in a 1967 referendum, 90 percent of Australians voted "yes" to changing the Constitution in order to include Aboriginal people in the national census. The referendum had great symbolic significance, but the fight for full citizenship rights went on well into the 1980s.

Under this protracted process, what did "citizenship" mean in Namatjira's case?

When the 1953 Welfare Ordinance came into operation in 1957, Namatjira was not on the list of Aborigines declared "wards of the state." This meant that he could vote, be served in restaurants, and treated in hospitals reserved for white people. He was free from all restrictions governing the life of "wards."

In Alice Springs, many thought this was too great an honor for a "black ape." Namatjira came under intense small-town scrutiny.

Did he have his children with him after dark? He wasn't allowed to do that, because only Australian citizens were allowed to be in Alice in the evenings, and Albert's children weren't citizens. Had he been drinking with his relations? He wasn't allowed to do that, because offering Aborigines alcohol was prohibited.

Of course, innumerable white people broke these rules and went unpunished. They earned good money illicitly supplying alcohol to black people and kept their black mistresses in their beds well after nightfall. But when the police caught Namatjira and a fellow family member drunk in a taxi, the full force of the law was brought to bear. The local court sentenced Namatjira to six months' hard labor for supplying his relative with intoxicating beverages.

Taking account of the criminal's age and failing health, a superior court reduced his sentence to three months. The Supreme Court in Canberra confirmed the sentence on March 12, 1959. The local correspondent of *The News* got the first comment from a shattered Namatjira: "Why don't they kill us all? That is what they want."[148]

He was taken to the internment camp at Papunya, 125 miles northwest of Alice Springs, where he was kept isolated from the other inmates. But naturally they still drew their conclusions. Assimilation, even at its most successful, could only ever end in humiliation and disaster.

Albert Namatjira served his sentence and died of a heart attack soon after his release. After two years as an Australian citizen, he was buried on August 9, 1959.

94

Those ethnologists who first took an interest in Aboriginal images in the 1930s made quick forays into the desert, handed out brown paper and chalks, collected the drawings and the explanations of them, and then sat down to count up the different elements of form. The collection method was one-sided, the analysis superficial.[149]

The first person to study the desert peoples' imagery in depth was the American researcher Nancy D. Munn. She came to Yuendumu in 1956 and remained with the Warlpiri people for over a year. She was interested in the links between images and dreams, between songs and tracks.

Songs and tracks arose simultaneously in the dreams of the Warlpiri's ancestors. They dreamed their tracks. When they woke up, they gave material form to their dream by singing the song and drawing the track. As they were traveling, they sang their journey; they sang the names of the places and the song for each place; they sang about their journey and events along the way. And these events left their tracks in landscape as well as in song. The whole desert became a statement of their ancestors' dreams and exploits.

The structure of the travelogue binds action, dream, and song to specific places in space—actual, existing places that can be visited even when the dreamer is awake. Since all the ancestors are linked to specific places, they can be represented by pictures of these places. The ancestors have left their traces at these locations, and that's not all: the place *is* the trace. The place would not exist and be as it is, if the ancestor had not arrived there and left the place behind as a trace of his or her visit. The land the whites called *terra nullius* was the ancestors' work, and it was the task of the living to maintain it.[150]

Some songs, Nancy D. Munn writes, consist exclusively of place-names, and the word for song itself, *yiri*, also means "name," "visible mark," or "trace." The Warlpiri people call a series of songs a "song-line," and it is an exact equivalent of a series of places that exist in the real world.

It was these "songlines" that were made famous a quarter of a century later by Bruce Chatwin's book of the same name.

95

The scholars up to that point, all men, had been interested predominantly in the men's pictures, particularly the secret pictures that only men were allowed to see. Nancy Munn, on the other hand, ignored the high-status ceremonies of the men and approached things from a different direction. She observed the variations in the way the two sexes used pictures.

Warlpiri of both sexes draw in the sand when they are telling stories or arguing. But not in the same way. The men seem to put an overhead projector picture down in the sand at intervals, as if to illustrate some specific point in their presentation. The picture is used as a storeroom for knowledge that also exists in other forms. The picture can be unrolled verbally and the words can then be rolled back up into a picture. Women, by contrast, draw a whole stream of pictures, what Munn terms "a continuous running graphic notation." The Warlpiri women have made storytelling to the accompaniment of pictures into a unique art form: *djugurba*, the sand story.[151]

A sand story consists of rhythmically hummed words and accompanying gestures which explain the essence of the story: a sort of manual choreography in the sand. The movements of the hand as it shapes the pictures are what represent the action of the story. The ground itself "has" the story, the hand merely performs it in the sand, before the ground reclaims it.

"And they all lived happily ever after." That's how our traditional stories end. But the Warlpiri's sand stories end with everybody disappearing into the sand. The female storyteller draws a circle and makes all her characters enter it and go down into the ground. The words she says as they vanish are always the same: *Lawa-djari-dja-lgu*, "And so they became nothing."

Most Warlpiri women have a wide repertoire of such stories, which they perform using mime, voice, gestures, and signs in the sand. Any little girl of about eight or nine can make up a sand story and bring it to life. She tells it to other girls or younger boys. An older boy, however, won't listen to sand stories because they are part of the female role.

The Warlpiri people's sand stories end with everyone disappearing into the sand. The female storyteller draws a circle and makes all her characters enter it and go down into the ground, with the words *"Lawa-djari-dja-lgu"* (And so they became nothing). Illustration from Munn, *Walbiri Iconography*

Tracks left by animals and people are common in sand stories. The tracks are made with the hand, which is held in different positions to produce the prints left by birds, animals, and people. Making hand tracks like these is a game adults often play with children. The art of tracking animal prey is naturally vital for the desert folk's traditional food supply. But more important still are footsteps and other things a body may leave behind, as intersections between human being and ground.

The ground is the desert people's religion. A footprint in the sand is the key to their imagery.

96

Marcel Réja is the first, and most overlooked, theoretician of modern art.

If anybody remembers him today, it's for being nice to August Strindberg. They met in Paris in 1897. Strindberg was out to conquer Paris and wrote a novel in French, *Inferno*. Réja helped him, wrote a preface for the book, and arranged for it to be published by his own publishing house, Mercure de France.

The pseudonym Marcel Réja concealed a young doctor, Paul Gaston Meunier, who a few years later received his PhD for a dissertation on psychiatry. Under his own name he wrote a thick book on the interpretation of dreams: *Les Rêves et leur interprétation* (Dreams and Their Interpretation, 1910).

But Marcel Réja's most creative contribution to scholarship was the book *L'Art chez les fous* (The Art of the Mentally Deranged,

1907). The book was published in two editions the same year Picasso painted *Les Desmoiselles d'Avignon*. Among the twenty-six illustrations there are many that anticipate Picasso, such as a child's drawing of a face seen simultaneously from the front and the side.

Réja links the art of the mentally ill with children's drawings and the fetishes of "savages," and finds in these three forms of expression a primitive originality and power that were lacking in the conventional art of the period. He refers to the pictures as "ideogrammatic scripts," calling them "hieroglyphic drawings that express their ideas through bold distortions."

An African fetish "has no need to be beautiful"; it lacks "the seduction of art." A crudely carved idol from the Niger River gives a highly simplified idea of the human face: three cylinders of different sizes placed one on top of the other, one forming the forehead, another the nose, a third the rest of the face. The fetish represents the human being in "toute sa nudité géométrique," all its geometric nakedness.

By the Ogooué River in Gabon, Marcel Réja writes, we find a number of geometric works in which simplicity has been taken to its limits. The face is depicted with willful simplification as a flat surface with only the nose protruding. Interpreting this as proof of incompetence would be unjust. This is a different kind of art, an art that scorns representation and seeks to reproduce not the outward form of reality but its concept.

"Reduction to the geometrically abstract however remains the general principle of all this art," concludes Réja—thereby providing the formula Picasso and Braque set about putting into practice in the first Cubist paintings a few months later, opening the door to the modern era in Western art.

The artists reacted immediately, but it took half a century for Réja's ideas to filter through to public consciousness.

In the vanguard was the Museum of Modern Art in New York, which mounted exhibitions of African art in 1935, Mexican art in 1940, Native American art in 1941, South Pacific art in 1946, and more African art in 1953. In 1957 the Museum of Primitive Art in New York opened, and in 1971 the decision was taken to move the collections to a new wing of the Metropolitan Museum of Art. Thus "primitive" art became firmly anchored in the world's most exclusive museum environment.[152]

97

But Australia still wasn't represented. Why?

There's a mutual connection between "art" and "collecting art," wrote Shelly Errington in 1998. "Art" has to exist in order for people to collect it, and if no one collects it, then it isn't "art."

For artifacts to be collected, they have to be permanent and portable. The Aborigines' ground paintings could be neither preserved nor transported. They were danced down into the ground. Body paintings washed off or wore away. The drawings of the sand stories disappeared into the sand. They were all part of a combined art form in which the picture was incomplete without story, song, and dance. They were all components of unique happenings that would never happen in exactly the same way again.

In order to become "art," the picture had to be lifted out of this context, lifted from the ground and the skin and attached to a new backing, made permanent, and cut into rectangular pieces that could be demarcated from their surroundings in frames.

Packaged like this, the picture could be sold on a market and become part of a collection. Cut out like this, it could demand entry into new contexts, such as the Metropolitan Museum in New York and art galleries in other cities around the world.

It took something as radical as a Caesarean section, but only that one single cut, to make the inhabitants of the Australian deserts once again the best-known, the most interesting, and most debated indigenous peoples in the world.

98

At the end of the nineteenth century, Spencer and Gillen saw themselves as the "discoverers" of the Arrernte people. It has subsequently become clear that the Arrernte people consciously selected

Gillen, to try to break through the wall of white incomprehension. Theo Strehlow likewise saw himself as the Homer of the Arrernte people. But it was the Arrernte who entrusted him with their treasury of songs. And it was Namatjira who actively persuaded Battarbee, not the other way around.

Namatjira had shown that Aborigines, too, could create Western art. Margaret Preston had shown that Aboriginal art, too, could inspire Western artists. The questions remained: why did the idiom of the blacks only become art when imitated by white artists? Why did the Aborigines become artists only when they imitated the art of the whites?

It was in Papunya, Namatjira's place of detention, that the answer to these questions suddenly became evident.

99

Papunya was the jewel in the crown of the little gulag of native internment camps set up to implement the policy of assimilation.[153] There the Aborigines were to learn to live settled lives in corrugated-iron huts, in nameless, symmetrical rows of streets. They were to learn to keep to times, dress respectably, and blow their noses in handkerchiefs.

The department had patrols out in the desert, which rounded up small groups of nomads and herded them to Lajamanu, Yuendumu, or Papunya, where they were kept while their culture was soaked off them, like removing paint from old wooden furniture with lye. The result was apathy, intense homesickness, and a feverish interest in their own culture.

One day, a new schoolteacher arrived. He said hello to everyone he met, even black people. This caused amazement.

The new teacher took his food and went to sit in the black section of the dining hall. No one had ever done that before.

The new teacher, Geoffrey Bardon, had a small grant to look into the possibility of making cartoons in the style of Aboriginal art. He needed to know how the shapes would look when enlarged on to the big screen. He and his interpreter painted a few clumsy Aborigine motifs on a wall in an odd corner of the school.

The school caretakers, Bill Stockman and Long Jack, saw at once that this was something they could do much better than the teacher. Could they join in and help? Of course! More and more walls in the school were decorated with paintings, more and more of the respected old men took an interest: Old Tom Onion, Old Mick, Old Walter, Old Bert, Old Tutuma.

This happened in the period May–August 1971. First the small surfaces were covered with paintings; eventually only the large ones were left to do. The grand finale was a painting ten meters by three, which dominated the whole school and its surroundings. It made a powerful impression, first because of its shameless size, second because it set an Aboriginal stamp on a European building.

Filling the wall with *The Dream of the Honeybee* was an audacious challenge to the camp's program of indoctrination, and emphatically announced: "We've got our own culture. And we intend to hang on to it."

100

Tensions in Papunya had led to rioting and damage on several previous occasions. Now the men had found a way amid all the degradation of the camp to re-create something of what had made their lives in the desert meaningful. Soon they were queuing up to get brushes and acrylic paints from Bardon.

When the school walls were all used up, they found new things to paint on: worn old linoleum boards from the staff accommodation blocks (they had just been replaced by new ones and left lying outside the buildings).

Linoleum boards were something usually seen from above and walked on, like the ground. The boards were a kind of ground, but transportable. The boards turned out to be saleable ground, too. Bardon took some of them to Alice and got almost $100 each for them. The following weekend, boards were sold for a total of $1,300. It caused a sensation in Papunya, where money of your own meant a dramatic increase in personal freedom.

In the months that followed, there were at least five large cash transactions involving six hundred paintings by twenty-five different artists. The internees were already starting to dream of buying an old car to visit their former homelands in the desert.

Was it a coincidence that the desert happened to bloom that year, 1971? After several years of drought, the rains finally came. They not only filled the usual water holes and underground streams but also flowed across the land in rivers tens of miles wide. Nature burst its banks and gave its human inhabitants the courage to do the same.

The camp authorities lost control of the workforce and were furious. They refused to pay out the usual "training allowance" if the men didn't chop wood. What they had earned from their art would be confiscated for the Crown. The camp director came to the painting room and announced that the art was "government property." Government "expenses" would be subtracted from the latest sales profit of $700, leaving the remaining $21 to be divided between the artists as a bonus for diligence.

When Bardon entered the painting room, forty accusing faces met his gaze. The expectations he had aroused had proved unrealistic. Paints and brushes were thrown down into the sand; nobody would paint without payment. They all chanted in unison, "Money, money, money . . ."

Bardon writes: "I was finished, truly finished, I knew; and I drove out of Papunya in July 1972 with a despair and a fury I had never known before, toward Alice Springs, for I had truly lost the game." [154]

101

At that point, the Geoffrey Bardon episode could have run into the sand like so many other sand stories. That was the fate of Noel White and his wife in Carrolup in the 1940s and of various others who tried: "And so they became nothing."

But in 1972, the situation was rather different. A Labor government with new Aborigine policies came to power at the end of the year. The aim was no longer to eradicate native cultures but to highlight and preserve them. The Aboriginal Arts Board was set up, with the task of supporting and encouraging artistic initiatives. A series of successors to Bardon dealt with the finances, organized exhibitions, and marketed Papunya art.

Local opposition was still fierce. While the Papunya painters were holding a highly acclaimed exhibition in Sydney in 1974, the camp authorities seized their chance and whitewashed over the offending murals on the walls of the school.

Even within Aboriginal society there was some opposition. It was felt that the artists were selling the secrets of their people and trading in holy symbols. The criticism led to a gradual disappearance of ritually "dangerous" motifs. The ethnological content of the art was watered down. Traditional forms were used in a much freer, more personal way.

When the first wave of enthusiasm had died down, opposition also hardened among white art critics. What was this they were being asked to admire? A two-headed calf—one head in the Stone Age, the other in modernism? It couldn't be considered anything but a transient curiosity. "Curiosity art," it was dubbed. "Souvenir art." "Tourist art."

And naturally not all the thousands of paintings produced in Papunya were epoch-making. Most of what gets painted is rubbish, even in Paris or New York. The remarkable thing was rather that a small place with only 1,500 inhabitants, living in total isolation from the rest of the art world, could produce twenty or more great artists.

The breakthrough came in 1980, when the National Art Gallery in Canberra bought their first acrylic painted by an Aboriginal artist. In the same year, a large private collector bought some hundred works by the leading Papunya artists. Perhaps even more significantly, the South Australian Museum bought Clifford Possum's "Man's Love Story" and hung it not in ethnic isolation but along with work by other contemporary modern artists.[155] The painting immediately dominated the huge room, making all the other art-work nearby seem anxiously insignificant.

The international breakthrough came ten years later, as the *Dreamings* exhibition toured New York, Chicago, and Los Angeles in 1988–90.[156] It was now quite clear that the Papunya artists were not mining some little ethnological deposit that would soon be exhausted. No, this was a group of independent artists, each developing in his or her own way from a common starting point.

102

I met Geoffrey Bardon in his home in Taree, on the east coast of Australia. Sadly, I was too late. The cancer already had him in its grip. He could only say a few words. A couple of weeks later, he was dead.

"How did you come to get interested in the Aborigines?" I ask.

"Geoff wasn't particularly interested in Aborigines until he got to Papunya," says his wife, Dawn.

As she speaks, Geoff is summoning up the strength to answer:

"I met some severely oppressed human beings."

And he adds: "The nurse in Papunya said, 'They come here healthy. After three weeks they're all sick.' "

And a while later: "I've always been for the underdog."

Now he was death's underdog. He knew it, he said it, and his eyes often dulled. He was slipping away. But before he disappeared, he was intensely present in his look, still shining with the fire of the miracle in Papunya.

"What pictures did you bring with you to Papunya? What did you show them? Picasso? Klee?"

"I didn't have any pictures. I read poetry. I had poems."

"Which poems?"

"The Spanish poets. Lorca, above all."

Tall trees and birdsong. A cockatoo chatters in its cage, a dog barks at the back of the house. Geoff is sitting with his eyes closed and seems to have fallen asleep. But suddenly his eyelids open and his gaze is clear and straight.

It's my own gaze that flinches from the solemn truth of death. At the edge of my field of vision I see a Turner reproduction and some watercolors. I get up and take a closer look. They're Bardon's own watercolors from his years in Papunya. Sensitive but conventional. And above all horizontal, in fact almost exclusively horizon—as the desert is, until you start seeing it from above.

Amazing! So this was how Bardon was perceiving the world, while a totally different reality was breaking through in Papunya. The art he was encouraging was the polar opposite of the one he practiced himself.

Geoffrey Bardon wasn't one of the "Bardon Men," as the Papunya painters were called. Artistically, where subject matter and technique were concerned, he was still in Hermannsburg. Like White in Carrolup, he himself would never have been able to produce the pictures that were being created in Papunya. It wasn't a case of Bardon showing the Aborigines what to do.

103

"I didn't have any pictures. I had poems," Geoffrey Bardon said. I wonder if he'd read Theo Strehlow's *The Songs*, which was published in 1971, just when it was all happening in Papunya.

Both Strehlow and Bardon won the confidence of the desert peoples. Both were destined to be instruments in the survival of the desert peoples. They did the same thing in opposite ways.

In 1971, the Aborigines of Central Australia had neither "art" nor "poetry" as we understand them. They had ceremonies in which body-painting and ground-painting were bound up with dance, music, and song.

Strehlow took away everything except the words of the songs, the words as written down by him, presumably colored by his own Lutheran emotionalism. Strehlow distilled the "poetry" from the rite.

Geoffrey Bardon took away everything except the picture, the picture as he pulled it free and enlarged it on to walls, and presumably colored by his own knowledge of modern, abstract art. Bardon distilled the "art" from the rite—and the Bardon Men immediately seized the opportunity that this created.

Strehlow made printable text in written language out of the ritual songs. The Bardon Men made permanent, portable acrylic paintings out of the ritual body and ground paintings.

The difference was that Strehlow exercised complete control over the text and vainly attempted to control its interpretation, too. Bardon, by contrast, gave full rein to creative chaos.

The result was that the acrylics found a market, something the texts without tunes failed to achieve. The acrylics were constantly developing new painters, whereas the text could not liberate new poets or theater. Strehlow's project was a one-man business. Bardon created a popular movement that spread all over the deserts of central Australia.

104

In Yuendumu, horror mingled with delight as they observed the new route to respect and income opening up in their sister colony, Papunya.[157] The menfolk were afraid the ritual secrets on which their power rested would be revealed. The women of Yuenduma had no such secrets. Their sand stories belonged to anyone and everyone. Their ceremonies were open. For them, the step from rite to art was a shorter one.

The initiative came from a circle of ritually active women who routinely met early in the mornings to narrate and discuss their dreams. This group decided in 1984 to follow Papunya's example. The aim was to buy a Toyota to bring the holy places of their people within reach. Economic and religious objectives were from the outset closely intertwined.[158]

Just as in Papunya, their pictures were of the ground. Or rather, the history of the ground. A geologist sees the landscape as the result of historic and prehistoric processes: the Precambrian rock has been folded, fault lines have opened, sediment has built up. Events that have been in progress for hundreds of millions of years lie exposed in the present moment. The landscape carries with it the narrative of its creation. In a similar way, the ground speaks to the Aborigines of a permanently present mythical history, which shapes their lives and society.

In rite, you painted the ground. In art, you painted images of the ground. The images were designed to be seen from above, any way up. They were made not for the wall but for the floor, or rather for the ground, themselves a sort of concentrated ground, a surface removable from the ground.

The women who were leaders in the rite also became leaders in the art movement. Only they had the capacity to mobilize the collaboration that supports both rite and art. Even if there is a single name at the bottom of the picture, most works of art are the result of collaboration. Someone has shared their knowledge, someone has done the actual painting, others have made adjustments and additions. All those who played a part have a right to remuneration, so the price of the artwork is distributed within the kinship group. Since they are building on the knowledge of the elders and need their approval, the elders' position is strengthened. In Yuendumu it was predominantly the women's position that was boosted, because the initiative had been theirs.

A few months later it was the men's turn. In Papunya, the men had painted the school walls; in Yuendumu, they painted the school doors. Yuendumu had waited twelve years. Now, thirty-six doors were painted in one go. The men painted with the audacious speed of graffiti artists, with broad brushes, big brushstrokes, and vibrant colors. The result was a concentrate of the desert people's wealth of myths, assembled in one place, captured in a single moment: the quintessence of a culture.

105

The 1980s saw the art movement spreading like wildfire from Papunya and Yuendumu to the other desert settlements: Kintore in 1981, Kiwirkurra in 1983, Balgo in 1985, Lajamanu in 1986, Utopia

Dorothy Napangardi with winning work *Salt on Mina Mina*, synthetic polymer paint on linen, 2001, 244 × 168 cm, at the 18th Telstra National Aboriginal and Torres Strait Islander Art Award 2001. Courtesy of the Museum and Art Gallery of the Northern Territory.

in 1987. Both men and women were involved, and altogether over a thousand new desert artists were painting. Their work was analyzed and discussed in a flood of art books all over the world.

Once Papunya had broken the ice, the other groups soon gained entry to the big museums. In Darwin I heard white people going skeptically around the galleries. Art? This? Twenty years ago these were just the darkies' doodlings!

But the prices speak a language even the whites in Darwin must understand. Paintings that once sold for a hundred now cost hundreds of thousands of dollars. A high point was reached in 2001, when a painting by Rover Thomas was sold for over three-quarters of a million dollars.[159]

Today there is a score of painting communities in the desert. Many of the artists are old women who have never even been in Alice Springs. Most of them don't speak English. But their pictures reach the whole world via satellite. They exhibit in Tokyo and New York.

106

Is there any other example of a whole people turning to art as a route to liberation?

Inuits and Aborigines were "discovered" about the same time. Edward Nelson's standard work *The Eskimo* (1899) came out the same year as Spencer and Gillen's *The Native Tribes of Central Australia*. Fifty years later, the Canadian James Houston saw the artistic potential of Eskimo sculpture and created a market for it—just as Geoffrey Bardon, a quarter of a century after that, would find a market for Aboriginal art.

By the time another twenty-five years had passed, the Aborigines and Inuit were internationally acknowledged and above all as artists. Art was their major export, and there were villages in which nearly 80 percent of the adult population earned their living as artists.

Such concentration of artistic talent in just two peoples ought not to be possible—if we assume talent is distributed fairly equally across humanity. But perhaps that assumption of equal distribution is too hasty? Hot springs and volcanic activity aren't distributed evenly across the earth's crust, so why should creativity be?

Perhaps eruptions of creativity are associated not so much with peoples as with particular situations in history? When Picasso brought the African and European traditions together in *Les Demoiselles d'Avignon*, he opened the floodgates of creative force not just among his own people but spanning his whole age. A new way of painting prompted a new way of looking at and defining art, which in turn broadened the spectrum of artistic talent that could win acclaim.

In the final analysis, maybe it's the assumption of the rarity of artistic talent we should be questioning? In my day, the accepted view was that only a few scholarly pupils would benefit from higher education. Today, most young people go on to university or further study.

Both the Inuit and the Aborigines live in extremely inhospitable terrain in extremely harsh climatic conditions. Both have had their conception of the world and their lifestyle demolished. Both have repeatedly been declared doomed to extinction. Both have high death rates from illness, drug use, depression, and suicide. Art is often their only salvation. Art is none the worse for coming from the very brink of the abyss.

Both Inuit and Aborigine traditionally lived in cultures without any division of labor other than that between the sexes. All the men were expected to be able to hunt; all the women were expected to be able to find roots or prepare sealskins. Everyone was expected to be capable of doing everything, within the traditional sex roles. Art was no exception. There was an underlying assumption that anybody could produce art if they just knuckled down to it.

Both cultures have a tradition of everyone taking part. All the Warlpiri women tell sand stories to their children; all the Inuit women practice "story-knifing," in which the plot is drawn with a knife on the frozen crust of the snow. All Inuit men help to bring down their quarry when hunting; they all draw their ancestors' exploits in blood from their own noses. All Aborigine men paint the ground and their bodies, celebrate in song their ancestors' feats and play their part in maintaining the world order.[160] Everyone can take part in the holy rites—so why shouldn't they take part, too, when the images detach themselves from the rite and become what we call art?

If one of us can, everyone can. On that basis, it turns out that whole villages can produce superb works of art that win them acclaim from the world and raise them out of misery and dependence.

107

When Bardon arrived at Papunya in 1971, the Aborigines' history was as unknown as their art.

The fiction of Australia as a *terra nullius* demanded a mental suppression of the Aborigines. White historians wrote nothing of the Aborigines' achievements or even of their existence. In white historiography, the Aborigines long remained an inferior race doomed to "fade away" on contact with Western culture.[161]

There was no investigation of the violence that precipitated this "fading." Historians spoke of violence in general terms, without concrete examples. "[This] mental block has by no means disappeared," wrote C.D. Rowley in *The Destruction of Aboriginal Society* (1970–71), a pioneering work which tried for the first time to see Australian history from an Aboriginal point of view.

Rowley shows that the living conditions imposed on the Aborigines actually meant it was far easier for them to die than adapt to the new circumstances. "White consciences were salved by romanticizing high death rates as a graceful making way for the higher race in the inevitable contest for survival." [162]

"Those involved in their killing naturally enough were ready to equate them with forms of life less than human," Rowley wrote. Those Aborigines who survived in the remnants of a defeated society lived in a hopelessness and apathy that seemed to confirm the settlers' worst prejudices.[163]

In some parts of the Australian outback, those prejudices are still very much alive. But in modern Australia, in Sydney,

Melbourne, and other cities an educated minority questions the old attitudes. People are recognizing that the only Australian culture that time and again has made an international impact is the Aborigine culture. They are recognizing that this supposedly doomed ethnic group is actually displaying exceptional powers of survival. Contempt gives way to admiration as they see the consistency with which the Aborigines have held fast to the foundations of their traditional culture and the flexibility with which they have been able to adapt it to modern technology and modern society.

The question is: how will the new Australia face up to the crimes committed by the old one, the effects of which are still having a major impact on the living conditions of the Aborigines? How will modern-day Australia come to terms with its past?

The perpetrators in the majority of cases can no longer be put on trial. By which laws would they be judged? How can the dead be punished? Neither perpetrators nor victims can live their lives over again. It's the survivors who have got to devise a new way of dealing with the aftereffects of the crimes.

One very important aspect of this is the distribution of land—that land which is so fundamental to the desert peoples' economic, social, and ritual lives.

It's a problem not just in Australia but in many other countries, Sweden among them. ILO Convention 107, Article 2, establishes the duty of all states to acknowledge "the right of ownership, collective or individual, of the members of [indigenous] populations concerned over the lands which these populations traditionally occupy." Sweden, which doesn't want to acknowledge the injustice done to the Sami, has refused to ratify the Convention.[164] Australia, which does not want to acknowledge the injustice done to the Aborigines, has not signed either.

108

Three hundred million human beings on this planet are members of indigenous peoples who have been, or are on the way to being, robbed of their land. They are generally among the poorest and most scorned minorities in the countries where they live. Not long ago, they were considered doomed to die out. But in recent decades, the indigenous peoples have seized back the initiative on a global scale.

July 1990 saw the first Continental Indigenous International Convention, held in Quito. There were four hundred delegates from 120 nations. The meeting was hosted by one of the most active movements in South America, the Confederation of Indigenous Nationalities of Ecuador, which considers itself to represent 30 percent of its country's population. The Convention's central demands concern land and education. The overarching vision is to gather the indigenous peoples into a new, transborder, "multinational nation."

In Australia, less than a generation ago, white civil servants were busy stripping the Aborigines of their original culture, while other white civil servants had the task of trying to "save" the remains of a dying people. They were all caught equally unaware by the artistic vitality that suddenly came bubbling up from this culturally devastated land. The artistic renaissance went hand in hand with a political and legal reappraisal.

Australia began a decade-long process of reconciliation between white and black by declaring 1991 the Year of the Indigenous Peoples. Prime Minister Paul Keating inaugurated the year with the words: "It was we who did the dispossessing. We committed the murders. We took the children from their mothers. We practiced discrimination and exclusion."[165]

On June 3, 1992, the Australian High Court outlawed the concept of *terra nullius* and ratified Aboriginal rights to the land where they lived and had always lived. The so-called Mabo Decision revised the whole historic and legal basis of Australia as a nation.

But in 1996, Labor was voted out of power, partly for its pro-Aboriginal rights policy. Then the Aborigines felt the impact of severe budget cuts. In the new political climate, even the Mabo decision proved to be worth less than initially hoped. The new government countered the decision with amendments to the Native Title Act, preventing claims over large tracts of pastoral and mining land. In order to make a claim, the Aborigines have to show a continuing connection to the land. Since most of them have been robbed

of their land, or forced into cities and towns by unemployment, or
abducted from their parents as children, many have lost the right to
the lands of their fathers.

109

Australian race relations have become a major theme in both academic research and popular accounts of the country's history. This
disturbs many white Australians. They used to see themselves as
peaceful and law-abiding settlers, who had brought the blessings
of civilization to the indigenous inhabitants of Australia. They are
understandably reluctant to let historical research rob them of this
beautiful picture and substitute a history of mass killing, land theft,
rape, kidnapping, and other outrages. Many prefer to turn a blind
eye to the growing mountain of evidence of their forefathers' violence and racism.

Others go on the offensive and scrutinize the evidence for mistakes. Never have historians had their footnotes so closely perused
as in contemporary Australia. A missing comma here, a misspelled
name or a wrong date there—in hundreds of scholarly publications
there are bound to be some mistakes, and the attackers use them to
discredit the whole profession.

Foremost among the attackers is Keith Windschuttle. According
to his *The Fabrication of Aboriginal History, Volume One* (2002) no
genocide was committed, the massacres were legitimate police actions, and there was no reign of terror based on widespread violence.
Windschuttle rejects practically everything academic historians
have found out about Aboriginal history during the last thirty-five
years. It is all a gigantic forgery, intended to deprive Australians of
the right to be proud of their history.

Another revisionist, Michael Connor, maintains that Australia
as a nation was not founded on the fiction that the land was empty
and belonged to no one, or at least to no one who wasn't doomed to
extinction. In *The Invention of Terra Nullius* (2005) he alleges that
the *terra nullius* doctrine was created in the 1970s by a conspiracy of
politicized historians and ignorant judges.

The tone is astonishingly vituperative. Every argument is accompanied by an insult. According to the attackers, when professional historians started to research Aboriginal history in the 1970s, they were suddenly transformed into bitter academics, frozen moralists, power-hungry careerists, self-flattering elitists, and latte-stained conformists. They were said to gag history and torture their sources in order to produce trendy results, applauded by corrupt colleagues lobotomizing themselves in public.

The goal of the revisionists, in the words of Prime Minister John Howard, is to make Australians "comfortable and relaxed about their history." Their method is denial. They deny the obvious fact that before the British arrival the country belonged to the indigenous population. They deny that the Aborigines resisted British occupation. They deny that settlers killed large numbers of Aborigines on the frontier and terrified others to submission. They deny the role the British invasion played in the catastrophe that annihilated some nine-tenths of the Aboriginal population, extinguishing several hundred peoples, each with its own language and culture.[166]

110

"History," said I.A. Richards, "is simply a record of things which ought not to have happened."[167]

Recent decades have seen the history of elites being increasingly replaced by the history of ordinary peoples. When the rich and victorious are replaced as the principal figures of history by the poor and defeated, history turns out to consist largely of a series of injustices. As historical memory is gradually democratized and globalized, we have to get used to being seen not just as pioneers and benefactors but also as oppressors and perpetrators of outrages, sometimes of continent-wide crimes.

The new historical perspective has set off a growing avalanche of claims for damages all over the world. The victims of history's crimes have been given the courage to make demands.

Not even the victims of the Holocaust had the right to damages at the start. Former Gestapo and SS men, by contrast, received full pensions. Old Nazis stood laughing at their windows, looking down at the former owners of what had once been Jewish-owned houses. The Jews' demand for $12 billion in compensation for lost property was ignored by the Allies, apart from a few million from frozen German assets abroad.

It was therefore groundbreaking when West Germany in 1951 declared itself willing to pay financial compensation to the Jewish people and to individual Jewish victims of Nazi crimes.

The sufferings of the Jews were still not well known then, as they are today through research, diaries, documents, and feature films. The Jews were seen as one group among many stricken by the war. Why did they particularly deserve compensation?

East Germany did not admit any liability whatsoever for the crimes of the Third Reich. The West Germans too, both individually and collectively, were reluctant to admit guilt and responsibility.

Is there any such thing as collective guilt or debt? Can collective debt be inherited?

It's self-evident that specific collectives, such as companies or states, can have *economic* debts. Debts of that nature carry responsibility for repayment.

But can a collective, such as a company or a people, also have a moral debt? What responsibilities does it carry, if so? Must they admit having committed an injustice? Must they say sorry? Perhaps even give back what's been taken? And if something can't be given back, like life or good health—must there be economic compensation instead? Can even moral debt imply responsibility for repayment?

Such questions are answered differently in different countries. I read in my newspaper that an American diagnosed with a brain tumor is suing a mobile phone company for several billion dollars. Seven families who lost relatives in the September 11 attacks are demanding $100 billion in compensation from bin Laden. Enormous damage claims are the norm in the United States.

Another day, the newspaper informs me that the asbestos workers in Lomma have had to make do with a pathetic few thousand

kronor in compensation for their lungs. And yet it was the greatest workplace health and safety scandal in Swedish history. When
the asbestos cement sheeting factory in Lomma closed in 1977, five
hundred workers had been affected, a hundred and fifty had become invalids, and fifty-one had died of asbestosis. Since that time,
asbestos has continued claiming new victims.

Thus history lives on in the bodies of living people. When the
dead body is opened up, you find history in the form of glittering
silver fibers—the last remains of the air people inhaled in factories
and workers' accommodations in the 1950s and '60s.

And when the votes are counted at the boardroom meetings of
today's companies, the same history is there—the profits from that
time still entitle their owners to power and dividends. Just as the asbestos workers' children have inherited the fibers, so other children
have inherited the blocks of shares. Shouldn't they also have inherited the responsibility for the working conditions that once gener-
ated those profits?

And that applies not just to company shareholders but to all of
us who have reaped the benefit of unacceptable conditions in the
past. I can hear the voice of the Norwegian great-grandmother in my
head. She was right. I'd had my share of the booty. So I had to take
my share of the responsibility, too.

III

The Australian Aborigines' demands for redress and compensation
are part of a global movement that sometimes succeeds, sometimes
fails.

Of the two hundred thousand women who were forcibly recruited into Japanese military brothels during the Second World
War, only a couple of thousand are left today. Public opinion in Japan
views them as prostitutes. They have therefore received only half-
hearted apologies and risibly meager compensation payments.[168]

By contrast, many of the Americans of Japanese origin whom
the United States interned without any justification during the

same war are today influential members of society. On the basis of
the precedent set by the damages Germany is paying to Israel, they
were granted full redress and compensation in 1988.

The prestige enjoyed by a particular ethnic group seems to be
the major factor in deciding the level of damage payments they
achieve. It's a sign of the lack of respect of society at large that the
Aborigines in Australia and the Sami in Sweden so often fail in
their attempts to demand back the land taken from them. And it's
certainly no coincidence that the very Aboriginal settlements that
have won international acclaim for their art are also among those
who have pursued the most successful campaign to regain control
of their lands.

In the United States, a series of Native American nations has demanded that the agreements broken by the American government
in the nineteenth century be reinstated. One particularly dramatic
story is that of Black Hills, which is holy ground for the Sioux Indians. The U.S. government considered the land worthless, and so let
the Indians keep it. Six years later, gold was found and the land was
confiscated. The Sioux have been insisting on their rights of ownership for more than a hundred years. In 1980 the U.S. Supreme
Court offered them the largest sum in damages in Native American
history, $122 million. But they refused the money and are continu-
ing to demand their land back.[169]

In other cases demands for compensation are aimed primarily
at financial redress. The Herero people of Namibia are demanding apologies and compensation for the German genocide of 1904.
African Americans are demanding compensation for slavery and
discrimination. In 1995, the 60 million black people in Brazil demanded $6,000 billion in compensation for slavery. In Africa, the
countries from which the slaves were taken are formulating similar
claims.

These are just a few examples among many of a general tendency to translate moral demands into financial ones. They are often put as counterdemands to the financial debt currently enslaving
the Third World.

Many see these demands as moral blackmail and the

globalization of a grotesque American compensation culture that
keeps the lawyers and insurance companies rich and ultimately
results in increased costs to consumers. Others see them as a
practicable route to reconciliation with the past.

Can financial compensation provide release from guilt for historical crimes? Can punitively high financial dues paid to victims
also prevent new victims emerging? Can they in fact lead to a new
global redistribution policy?

One advantage of this method is that it doesn't seek to achieve a
single, definitive solution to all these problems but is a way of negotiating through the problems one at a time. The more governments
that acknowledge their responsibilities and compensate the victims,
the easier one hopes it will become for other governments to do the
same.

Is negotiation over historic debt a generally applicable method
for conflict resolution? That's a question posed by historian Elazar
Barkan. Can it even generate a new relationship between the powerful and the powerless? Between the rich and the poor? Can the
admission of historic debt or guilt foster new cooperation between
the perpetrator and the victim, to throw off the curse of the past?

Hitherto it has at least proved possible to find a few individual,
temporary solutions to questions of debt and compensation in a
deeply unjust world.[170]

112

"It's no use crying over spilt milk," people say when someone's be-
moaning losses in the past. "Let the dead bury their dead." Getting
indignant about crimes of the past is a waste of energy. Paying compensation is "throwing good money after bad." Countless sayings
exhort us just to forget and move on, in the knowledge that once
something has happened it is beyond recall. "What's done is done.
You can't turn back the clock."

Countering the wisdom of the proverbs is the conviction that
even the past can be changed. When the misdeeds of the past are
brought to light, when the perpetrators and their heirs confess and

ask forgiveness, when we do penance and mend our ways and pay the price—then the crime committed has a new setting and a new significance. No longer the inescapable extinction of a people, but its ability to survive and ultimately to have the justice of its claim acknowledged.

CHRONOLOGY

The events of the book organized chronologically, with the chapter in which an event is mentioned given in brackets.

600 million years before modern chronology The sandstone in Uluru begins to be formed from coarse gravel of gneiss and granite coming from the south (16).

100 million years before modern chronology Australia breaks free from Antarctica (77).

30 million years before modern chronology The silica in the groundwater accumulates in the porous sandstone and crystallizes into opals (12).

20 million years before modern chronology Australia is flooded by the sea and large areas of the south coast are covered by the world's largest limestone plateau, covering 150,000 square miles (77).

70,000 to 40,000 years before modern chronology The Aborigines arrive in Australia.

13,000 years before modern chronology The last forest disappears from the limestone plateau, leaving the most recently formed desert, Nullarbor (77).

1770 James Cook claims eastern Australia for Great Britain.

1788 The British invasion of Australia begins. Eastern Australia becomes a penal colony.

1827 Captain James Stirling finds paradise in the Murray River valley in Western Australia (73).

1829 The first British settlers reach the Murray River (73).

1834 The Pinjarra massacre (73).

1837 A British parliamentary committee reports that the indigenous peoples of the empire are en route to extinction (6).

1839 John Eyre finds paradise in Moorundie (5). George Grey arrives at the islands of Bernier and Dorré, where no tree or blade of grass grows (58).

1841 Massacre of the Aboriginal population in Moorundie. Eyre becomes District Chief (5).

1862 McDouall Stuart is successful, at the third attempt, in crossing Australia from south to north. He is elevated to the peerage—and dies an alcoholic in obscurity in London four years later (8).

1871 In *The Descent of Man*, Charles Darwin presents the extermination of native peoples as a natural part of the process of evolution (20).

1877 In *Ancient Society*, Henry Morgan concludes from the Aborigines' forms of address that human beings originally lived in group marriages (34).

1884 Friedrich Engels develops Morgan's idea further: the transition from animal to human being occurred when the males relinquished their claims to sexual monopoly and began sharing females with one another (34).

1887 Baldwin Spencer becomes a professor in Melbourne, Émile Durkheim a university teacher in Bordeaux, and Sigmund Freud a doctor in Vienna (26).

1888 German ethnologist Richard Andree likens Australian rock art to graffiti in public toilets (90).

1890 Catherine Martin describes the contrasts between white and black child-rearing in *An Australian Girl* (36).

1891 Frank Gillen, Justice of the Peace, intervenes in a case of routine police murder of Aborigines. The officer responsible, William Willshire, is acquitted but transferred out of the area (19).

1895 Ernest Favenc publishes *The Secret of the Australian Desert* (17, 18).

1896 The report of the Horn expedition sentences the Aborigines to extinction (21). The Arrernte people respond with one of the most successful publicity campaigns in history. Spencer and Gillen are invited for seven weeks of ceremonies in the backyard of the telegraph station at Alice Springs (22).

1899 Spencer and Gillen's *The Native Tribes of Central Australia* creates a scientific sensation in Europe (22). Later in the year, Freud makes his name with *Die Traumdeutung* (*The Interpretation of Dreams*) (26). Edward Nelson's standard work *The Eskimo* is published (106).

1900 "If the workforce of a colony cannot be disciplined into producing the profits rightly expected by the mother country," writes Henry C. Morris in his *History of Colonization*, "the natives must then be exterminated or reduced to such numbers as to be readily controlled." Many scholars defend or advocate what we today term genocide (20).

1901 Australia ceases to be a British colony and becomes a self-governing federal state under the British Crown. One of the first laws the federation passes is the Immigration Restriction Act (10).

1902 Petr Kropotkin publishes *Mutual Aid*, which argues that natural selection leads not to conflict and competition but to a search for ways of avoiding conflict. Animals become humans through cooperation (25).

1903 In Jeannie Gunn's *The Little Black Princess of the Never-Never*, a white housewife tells the story of her black maid in a benevolently condescending tone. The first full-length portrait of a young Aboriginal woman in Australian literature (31).

1904 In *The Northern Tribes of Central Australia*, Spencer and Gillen dismiss the Aborigines' art as incomprehensible decoration (90).

1907 A young doctor, Paul Meunier, publishes under the name of Marcel Réja a program for Cubism, which Picasso and Braque begin putting into practice in the autumn of the same year (96).

1908 On Bernier and Dorré, two hospitals are opened for the forcible treatment of Aborigines alleged to have sexually transmitted diseases (58).

1911 In the Northern Territory, the Aboriginals' Ordinance gives a protector appointed by the whites authority to take any Aborigine or "half-blood" into custody at any time. The ordinance remains in force until 1957 (33). Eric Mjöberg, leader of a Swedish expedition to Australia, robs Aboriginal graves and takes the skeletons home with him (48, 49). Radcliffe-Brown studies the social organization of the Aborigines by questioning patients on Bernier and Dorré (59).

1912 In *Les Formes élémentaires de la vie réligieuse* (*The Elementary Forms of Religious Life*), Émile Durkheim reinterprets Spencer and Gillen's data in the light of his own view of society. The experience of society is the real-life basis of all religions (26).

1912–13 In *Totem und Tabu* (*Totem and Taboo*), Sigmund Freud reinterprets Spencer and Gillen's data in the light of his patients' neuroses. Patricide is the creative act that leads to the genesis of civilization (27).

1912–17 A transcontinental railway is built, linking Adelaide and Perth. The Aborigines' ceremonial site at Ooldea becomes a water reservoir for the railway (79).

1913 Borislaw Malinowski's *The Family Among the Australian Aborigines* reevaluates the reliability of the sources of many statements about Aboriginal families and finds one fact incontrovertible: they are deeply attached to their children (35). Baldwin Spencer establishes Kahlin Compound in Darwin as an internment camp for children taken from black mothers (41). Radcliffe-Brown begins publishing the results of his genealogical studies of the patients committed for treatment at Bernier and Dorré (60, 61).

1914 In *Gudstrons uppkomst* (The Origin of Faith in God), Nathan Söderblom retells the Luritja people's stories of the initial helplessness of mankind (14). A new doctor discovers that most of the patients forcibly detained on Bernier and Dorré do not have sexually transmitted diseases. Incorrect diagnosis, wrong treatment, unnecessary internment (58).

1915   A black boy finds the first opal at Coober Pedy (12).

1918   The hospital on Bernier and Dorré is closed down. All that remains on the "Islands of the Dead" are the graves of the patients who died during treatment (58). The buildings are pulled down and taken to Moore River Native Settlement, a new reform school for children taken from their black mothers (69).

1919   Daisy Bates pitches her tent in Ooldea (79).

1921   "Unnecessary" toys are removed from Moore River Settlement and the timetable is restricted purely to physical labor. The nutritional value of the food is reduced; tuberculosis becomes increasingly common (69).

1922   While boring for more water, the railway engineers split the rock beneath the water reservoir in Ooldea (79).

1923   Catherine Martin's book *The Incredible Journey* tells of two black women's search for an abducted child (38).

1925   Margaret Preston "discovers" the Aborigines' art, seeing it as an open treasure chest from which white artists can help themselves (91).

1927   A gang of police officers and settlers enter the Forrest River Aboriginal reservation in Kimberley and kill all the Aborigines they find. Pastor Gribble reports the mass murder and an investigation finds at least eleven of the Aborigines had been shot while in chains. No white people are prepared to testify against the perpetrators, who boast openly of their deed. The officers return to duty; Pastor Gribble is sent elsewhere (64).

1928   Severe drought leads to water disputes. The Aborigines attempt to stop white people letting their cattle drink and pollute the water they need for survival. A white dingo hunter called Brooks is murdered. The police respond by killing Aborigines indiscriminately: the Coniston massacre (64).

1930   Mary Bennett's *The Australian Aboriginal as a Human Being* is published (64).

1932   Theo Strehlow returns to the Hermannsburg of his childhood to study the phonetics of the Arrernte language. He spends fifteen years in the wilderness, collecting songs and seeing himself as the Homer of the Arrernte people (86, 87).

1933   Mary Bennett attacks official policy on native peoples, particularly the situation at Moore River. An inquiry uncovers extremely bad conditions but makes only vague recommendations (70). The United Aborigines Mission opens a mission station on the ritual site at Ooldea (80).

1935 Xavier Herbert arrives in Darwin as acting head of Kahlin Compound (41). The Museum of Modern Art in New York exhibits African art (96).

1936 Daisy Bates leaves Ooldea (79). Camel keeper Albert Namatjira learns to paint in watercolor (92).

1937 The Native Administration Act gives the Chief Protector legal instruments with which to "breed out" the Aborigines, the "final solution" to the race problem in Western Australia (70).

1938 Australia's first modern novel, Xavier Herbert's *Capricornia*, is a furious attack on white racism and an impassioned defense of abandoned children (39–42). The Aborigines mark the 150th anniversary of the white invasion with a Day of Mourning (70). Daisy Bates's *The Passing of the Aborigines* attempts to reconcile faith in the benevolence of the empire with a conviction that the Aborigines are doomed to extinction (79).

1939 Kahlin Compound is closed down (41).

1940 The Museum of Modern Art in New York exhibits Mexican art (96).

1941 Catherine and Ronald Berndt carry out their first fieldwork in Ooldea (80). The Museum of Modern Art in New York exhibits Native American art (96).

1945 Little Millicent is born in a sand dune behind the hospital in Geraldton (65). Noel White takes up a teaching post at Carrolup Native Settlement, "a dumping ground for human refuse," and starts to stimulate the children through games, singing and drawing (71).

1946 The Museum of Modern Art in New York exhibits South Pacific art (96).

1947 In Woomera, launchpads are constructed for a missile firing range 1,500 miles in length, mainly on land formerly allocated to the Aborigines "in perpetuity" (9).

1948 The artist James Houston "discovers" the art of the Inuit (106).

1948 The Nationality and Citizenship Act ostensibly gives Australian citizenship to all Australian Aborigines—but without the right to vote or any other civil rights.

1949 H.E. Thonemann's *Tell the White Man: The Life Story of an Aboriginal Lubra* relates further adventures of the little black princess, narrated in the first autobiography of an Aboriginal woman (32). The police take four-year-old Millicent from her mother and six siblings and place her in a children's home (65). In *Les structures élémentaires de la parenté* (Elementary Structures of Kinship), Claude Lévi-Strauss shows that Aboriginal culture finds its fullest expression in its family relationships (65).

1950   Drawings from Carrolup Native Settlement win praise when exhibited in London (71).

1951   The Moore River institution is taken over by the Methodist Church (70). West Germany begins paying compensation to the Jewish people and to individual Jewish victims of Nazi crimes (109).

1952   The mission station at Ooldea closes (80).

1953   On October 15, a ten-kiloton atomic bomb is set off at Emu, just north of Ooldea. The radioactive cloud rises to a height of 4,500 meters and moves across the continent for two days and nights (81). The Museum of Modern Art in New York mounts a further exhibition of African art (96).

1953   The 1953 Welfare Ordinance (NT) substitutes the racially neutral word "ward" for "Aborigine." More than 99 percent of the Aboriginal population are declared "wards" of the state (93).

1956   Nancy D. Munn arrives at Yuendumu and begins researching the uses and meanings of the Warlpiri people's pictures (95).

1956–57 Seven British atomic bombs are exploded near Maralinga, just west of Ooldea (81).

1957   Namatjira is rewarded for his artistic achievement with Australian citizenship (93). The Museum of Primitive Art opens in New York (96).

1957–63 At Maralinga, the British defy the Nuclear Test Ban Treaty by carrying out "minor trials," releasing at least twenty kilograms of plutonium that spread over wide areas in the form of fine dust (81).

1958   The Migration Act allows every foreigner without a visa to be interned (10). The Western Australian police defend the use of neck-irons by saying the natives want to wear them (58).

1959   Albert Namatjira is sentenced to three months' hard labor for having supplied a relative with intoxicating liquor and interned in Papunya. Having served his sentence, he dies of a heart attack. He is buried on August 9 after two years as an Australian citizen (93).

1962   Aboriginal people acquire the right to vote in both state and commonwealth elections. They are however still "wards" of the state and subject to the rulings of the Director of Welfare (93).

1962   Millicent is sent as a maid to a station where she is raped by her white employer. She seeks refuge at the children's home but is ordered back to the station, where she is tortured and raped again. She gives birth to a child who is taken from her (66).

1964 The Social Welfare Ordinance (NT) abolishes the concept of "ward" and replaces it with "persons who in the opinion of the Director are socially or economically in need of assistance." The change in terms changes little in the authorities' practice of power (93).

1965 Colin Johnson publishes his first book, *Wild Cat Falling*, Australia's first Aboriginal novel. Writing under the name Mudrooroo, Johnson soon becomes the leading novelist of Aboriginal literature (72).

1966 Inspired by the civil rights movement in the United States, the black workers at Wave Hill Station go on strike, first for wages, then for land (44).

1966 Aboriginal people are included in the Australian social security system. Their social benefits are, however, often not paid out to them personally but to their employer or to the institution in which they are confined (93).

1967 In a referendum 90 percent of Australians vote yes to changing the Constitution to include Aboriginal people in the national census. The referendum has great symbolic significance, but the fight for full citizenship rights goes on well into the 1980s (93).

1968 After repeated decontamination operations around Maralinga, an agreement absolves the British from any further responsibility for consequences of the atomic tests. The area is checked again. Plutonium is found to have been plowed only a few decimeters into the ground and exposed again by the harsh desert winds (82).

1970–1 Historian C.D. Rowley publishes *The Destruction of Aboriginal Society*, a pioneering work attempting for the first time to see Australian history from an Aboriginal point of view (107).

1971 Theo Strehlow publishes his magnum opus *The Songs of Central Australia* (86–89, 98, 103). So-called primitive art reaches the world's most exclusive museum venue: the Metropolitan Museum of Art in New York (96). Geoffrey Bardon arrives at Papunya. His interest triggers a flurry of artistic activity. The men begin translating their traditional pictorial idiom into modern acrylic paintings (99–103, 106, 107).

1972 Geoffrey Bardon leaves Papunya, convinced he has been defeated (100). A left-wing government takes office and implements new policies on Aborigines, and successors to Bardon handle the administration and marketing of Papunya art (101).

1973 Nancy D. Munn publishes her study of the pictorial world of the desert: *Walbiri Iconography* (94, 95).

1974 The camp authorities vandalize the wall paintings at Papunya (101).

1975 The strike at Wave Hill ends with the Gurundji people regaining 2,000 square miles of land they had lost.

1977   When the asbestos cement sheeting factory in Lomma, Sweden, closes, five hundred workers are suffering ill effects, a hundred and fifty have become invalids, and fifty-one have died of asbestosis. Since that time, asbestos has claimed new victims year after year (109).

1978   Theo Strehlow dies the same day his research institute is due to open. His last words are "Oblivion that has no end" (87).

1979   The Australian Nuclear Veterans' Association is formed; hundreds of experts and ex-soldiers start giving their account of events. The British resume the decontamination process but retrieve only half a kilogram of plutonium. At least 19 kilograms remain in the desert sand (82).

1980   The South Australian Museum hangs Clifford Possum's *Man's Love Story* with other works by contemporary artists. The painting immediately dominates the huge gallery (101). The U.S. Supreme Court offers the Sioux the highest compensation award in Native American history, $122 million. They refuse the money and continue demanding to be given back the Black Hills (110).

1981–83 The art movement spreads to Papunya's offshoots at Kintore and Kiwirkurra (105).

1983   Sixteen-year-old John Pat is taken into custody on September 28 after a clash between Aborigines and the police in Roebourne. He dies in his cell the same night. Five officers are accused of murder but acquitted (55).

1984   A royal commission demands that the British authorities make Maralinga safe for permanent resettlement by the indigenous population, who by the Maralinga Land Rights Act regain the land requisitioned from them in the 1950s (82). A group of ritually active women in Yuendumu follow Papunya's example and begin to paint (104).

1985   Uluru is restored to its original owners, the Anangu people—on the condition that the area remains accessible to tourists. Uluru becomes the central national symbol in the marketing of Australia as a tourist destination (16). The art movement spreads to Balgo (105).

1986–87 Aborigines at Lajamanu, Utopia, and a number of other desert settlements begin painting (105).

1987   The Stuart Highway is tarmacked all the way from Adelaide to Darwin (8). The "songlines" found by Nancy D. Munn among the Warlpiri people become world-famous through Bruce Chatwin's book *The Songlines* (94).

1988   Five years after John Pat's death, an investigation is launched; its final report, "Black Deaths in Custody," alerts the whole nation to racist police violence (55). Desert art makes its international breakthrough thanks to the *Dreamings* exhibition in New York, Chicago, and Los Angeles (101). Americans of Japanese descent, forcibly interned during the Second World War, are given redress and financial compensation (110).

1990 Four hundred delegates from indigenous peoples in 120 countries assemble for the first Continental Indigenous International Convention in Quito (108).

1991 Australia begins a decade-long process of reconciliation between white and black with a Year of the Indigenous Peoples. Prime Minister Keating says: "It was we who did the dispossessing. We committed the murders" (108).

1992 In the Mabo Decision, the Australian Supreme Court outlaws the concept of *terra nullius,* thus revising the whole historic and legal basis of Australia as a nation (108).

1995 Brazil's 6 million black people demand $6,000 billion in compensation for slavery (110).

1996 Millicent is reunited with her daughter Tony, taken from her thirty-three years earlier (66). Doris Pilkington's documentary novel *Follow the Rabbit-Proof Fence* describes the fate of children running away from the Moore River Settlement (70). A Conservative government comes to power and announces: "Australians of this generation should not be required to accept guilt and blame for past actions and policies" (108).

1999 Woomera (10) and Curtin (50) become internment camps for asylum seekers.

2001 A painting by Rover Thomas is sold for over three-quarters of a million dollars (105). Fences and warning signs still encircle Maralinga. It will take 280,000 years for half the radiation in the plutonium dust to subside (82).

2002 Thirty years of professional scholarship on Aboriginal history come under attack by journalist historians, who try to reestablish white Australians' pride in their history by denying genocide, mass killings, and forced dispossession (109).

2002 Hunger-striking prisoners at Woomera sew up their mouths (10). At Curtin, they burn down the camp (50). The Moore River Settlement is made internationally known by the film *Rabbit-Proof Fence* (70).

2003 Geoffrey Bardon dies in Taree after a long period of illness (102).

BIBLIOGRAPHY

For practical guidance I have relied on the Lonely Planet guides. My most important historical reference tool has been D.J. Mulvaney's *Encounters in Place*. I have studied issues of historical guilt principally in Elazar Barkan's *The Guilt of Nations*. My teacher on the subject of Australian nature study has been Mary E. White, in particular her *After the Greening*. My spiritual guide to the desert has been, and will remain, *Seeking the Centre* by Roslynn D. Haynes.

Amadio, Nadine, and Richard Kimber. *Wildbird Dreaming: Aboriginal Art from the Central Deserts of Australia*. Melbourne, 1988.
Anaya, James. *Indigenous Peoples in International Law*. Oxford, 1996.
Andree, Richard. *Ethnographische Parallelen und Vergleiche, Neue Folge*. Stuttgart, 1888.
Attwood, Bain. *Telling the Truth about Aboriginal History*. Sydney, 2005.
Attwood, Bain, and S.G. Foster. *Frontier Conflict: The Australian Experience*. Canberra, 2003.
Attwood, Bain, and Andrew Markus. *The Struggle for Aboriginal Rights: A Documentary History*. Melbourne, 1999.
Australian Dictionary of Biography, vol. 7. Melbourne, 1979.
Bardon, Geoff. *Aboriginal Art of the Western Desert*. Adelaide, 1979.
Bardon, Geoffrey. *Papunya Tula: Art of the Western Desert*. New York, 1991.
Barkan, Elazar. *The Guilt of Nations: Restitution and Negotiating Historical Injustices*. New York, 2000.
Barrett, Charles, and Robert Henderson Croll. *Art of the Australian Aboriginal*. Melbourne, 1943.
Basedow, Herbert. *The Australian Aboriginal*. Adelaide, 1925.
Bates, Daisy. *The Passing of the Aborigines: A Lifetime Spent Among the Natives of Australia*. London, 1938.
Battarbee, Rex. *Modern Australian Aboriginal Art*. Sydney, 1951.
Batty, Joyce D. *Namatjira: Wanderer Between Two Worlds*. Melbourne, 1963.
Beadell, Len. *Still in the Bush*. Sydney, 1965, 1999.
———. *Blast the Bush*. Sydney, 1967, 1999.

Bedjaoui, Mohammed. *Terra nullius, "droits" historiques et autodétermination: Exposés oraux devant la Cour internationale de Justice.* La Haye, 1975.

Bennett, Mary Montgomerie. *The Australian Aboriginal as a Human Being.* London, 1930.

————. *Christison of Lammermoor.* London, 1927.

Berndt, Catherine, and Ronald Berndt. *From Black to White in South Australia.* Melbourne, 1951.

Blackburn, Julia. *Daisy Bates in the Desert: A Woman's Life Among the Aborigines.* London, 1994.

Blakeway, Denys, and Sue Lloyd-Roberts. *Fields of Thunder: Testing Britain's Bomb.* London, 1985.

Bolinder, Gustaf. *Naturfolkens konst.* Stockholm, 1927.

Boulter, Michael. *The Art of Utopia: A New Direction in Contemporary Aboriginal Art.* East Roseville, NSW, 1991.

Brändström, Kjell-Arne. *Bilden av det samiska: Samerna och det samiska i skönlitteratur, forskning och debatt.* Umeå, 2000.

Bringing Them Home: Report of the National Inquiry into the Separation of Aboriginal and Torres Strait Islander Children from Their Families. Canberra, 1997.

Cambridge Companion to Australian Literature, Cambridge, 2000.

Caruana, Wally. *Aboriginal Art.* London, 1993.

————, ed. *Windows on the Dreaming: Aboriginal Paintings in the Australian National Gallery.* Canberra, 1989.

Chambers, Edward W. *Woomera: Its Human Face.* Adelaide, 2000.

Chambers, John H. *Historisk guide till Australien.* Falun, 1999.

Chatwin, Bruce. *The Songlines.* London, 1987, 1998.

Chesterman, John, and Brian Galligan. *Citizens Without Rights: Aborigines and Australian Citizenship.* Cambridge, 1997.

Clancy, Laurie. *Xavier Herbert.* Boston, 1981.

Clarke, Simon. *The Foundations of Structuralism: A Critique of Lévi-Strauss and the Structuralist Movement.* Brighton, 1981.

Connor, Michael. *The Invention of Terra Nullius.* Sydney, 2005.

Corbally Stourton, Patrick, and Nigel Corbally Stourton. *Songlines and Dreamings: Contemporary Australian Aboriginal Painting: The First Quarter-Century of Papunya Tula.* London, 1996.

Crandall, Richard C. *Inuit Art: A History.* Jefferson, NC, 2000.

Darwin, Charles. *The Origin of Species by Means of Natural Selection.* London, 1859, 1988.

————. *The Descent of Man.* Princeton, 1871, 1981.

Dawson, John. *Washout: On the Academic Response to the Fabrication of Aboriginal History.* Sydney, 2004.

De Groen, Frances. *Xavier Herbert: A Biography.* Brisbane, 1998.

Dewar, Mickey. *In Search of the Never-Never: Looking for Australia in Northern Territory Writing.* Darwin, 1997.

Dictionnaire de la terminologie du droit international. Paris, 1960.

Dixon, Robert. *Writing the Colonial Adventure: Race, Gender and Nation in Anglo-Australian Popular Fiction, 1875–1914.* Cambridge, 1995.

Dreamings of the Desert: Aboriginal Dot Paintings of the Western Desert. Art Gallery of South Australia, Adelaide, 1996.

Durack Miller, Mary. *Child Artists of the Australian Bush.* London, 1952.

Durkheim, Émile. *Les Formes élémentaires de la vie religieuse.* Paris, 1912, 1998.

———. *Selected Writings.* Cambridge, 1972.

Dussart, Françoise. "A Body Painting in Translation." In *Rethinking Visual Anthropology,* ed. Marcus Banks. New Haven, CT, 1997.

———. *La Peinture des Aborigènes d'Australie.* Paris, 1993.

———. *The Politics of Ritual in an Aboriginal Settlement: Kinship, Gender and the Currency of Knowledge.* Washington, DC, 2000.

Dutton, Geoffrey. *The Hero as Murderer: The Life of Edward John Eyre.* London, 1967.

Edwards, Hugh. *Port of Pearls.* Perth, 1984.

Elder, Bruce. *Blood on the Wattle, Massacres and Maltreatment of Aboriginal Australians Since 1788.* Sydney, 1998.

Engels, Friedrich. *Der Ursprung der Familie, des Privateigentums und des Staats.* Berlin, 1884, 1984.

Errington, Shelly. *The Death of Authentic Primitive Art.* Berkeley, CA, 1998.

Eylmann, Erhard. *Die Eingeborenen der Kolonie Südaustralien.* Berlin, 1908.

Eyre, Edward John. *Journals of Expeditions of Discovery into Central Australia,* vol. 2. London, 1845.

Favenc, Ernest. *Ödemarkens hemlighet, Äventyr under en upptäcktsfärd i Australien* (The Secrets of the Australian Desert). Stockholm, 1896, 1918.

Foy, Willy. *Führer durch das Rautenstrauch-Joest Museum der Stadt Coln.* Köln, 1906.

Freud, Sigmund. *Totem und Tabu: Einige Übereinstimmungen im Seelenleben der Wilden und der Neurotiker.* Frankfurt, 1912–13, 1974.

———. *Die Traumdeutung.* Frankfurt, 1899, 1972.

Gay, Peter. *Freud: A Life for Our Time.* New York, 1988.

Gill, Sam D. *Storytracking: Texts, Stories and Histories in Central Australia.* New York, 1998.

Glowczewski, Barbara. *Du Rêve à la loi chez les Aborigènes: Mythes, rites et organisation sociale en Australie.* Paris, 1991.

———. *Les Rêveurs du désert: Les Warlpiri.* Paris, 1989.

Goodwin, Ken. *A History of Australian Literature*. Basingstoke, 1986.

Graburn, Nelson H.H. *Ethnic and Tourist Arts: Cultural Expressions From the Fourth World*. Berkeley, CA, 1976.

Grey, George. *Journals of Two Expeditions of Discovery in Northwest and Western Australia . . . With Observations on the Moral and Physical Condition of the Aboriginal Inhabitants*. London, 1841.

Grosse, Ernst. *Die Anfänge der Kunst*. Freiburg and Leipzig, 1894.

Gunn, Mrs. Aeneas (Jeannie). *The Little Black Princess of the Never-Never*. Sydney, 1903, 1962.

———. *We of the Never-Never*. Sydney, 1908,1990.

Haebich, Anna. *For Their Own Good: Aborigines and Government in the Southwest of Western Australia, 1900–1940*. Crawley, WA, 1988.

Hallgren, Claes. *Två resenärer, två bilder av Australien: Eric Mjöbergs och Yngve Laurells vetenskapliga expeditioner, 1910–1913*. Uppsala, 2003.

Haynes, Roslynn. *Seeking the Centre: The Australian Desert in Literature, Art and Film*. Cambridge, 1998.

Healy, J.J. *Literature and the Aborigine in Australia, 1770–1975*. New York, 1978.

Herbert, Xavier. *Capricornia*. Sydney, 1938, 1999.

Hiatt, L.R. *Arguments About Aborigines: Australia and the Evolution of Social Anthropology*. Cambridge, 1996.

Hicks, George. *The Comfort Women*. Sydney, 1995.

Hill, Barry. *Broken Song: T.G.H. Strehlow and Aboriginal Possession*. Sydney, 2002.

Hill, Ernestine. *The Great Australian Loneliness*. Melbourne, 1940.

———. *Kabbarli: A Personal Memoir of Daisy Bates*. Sydney, 1973.

Hill, George Chatterton. *Heredity and Selection*. London, 1907.

Himmelheber, Hans. *Eskimo Artists*. Fairbanks, AK, 1993.

Isaacs, Jennifer. *Spirit Country: Contemporary Australian Aboriginal Art*. San Francisco, 1999.

Jebb, Mary Anne. "The Lock Hospitals Experiment: Europeans, Aborigines and Venereal Disease." *Studies in Western Australian History*, no. 8 (1984).

Johnson, Christopher. *Claude Lévi-Strauss: The Formative Years*. Cambridge, 2003.

Johnson, Colin. *Wild Cat Falling*. Sydney, 1965, 1995. *See also* Mudrooroo.

Johnson, Vivien. *Aboriginal Artists of the Western Desert: A Biographical Dictionary*. Roseville, NSW, 1994.

———. *The Art of Clifford Possum Tjapaltjarri*. East Roseville, NSW, 1994.

Jupp, James. *Immigration*. Oxford, 1991.

Kropotkin, Petr. *Mutual Aid: A Factor of Evolution*. Boston, 1902,1955.

Kühn, Herbert. *Die Kunst der Primitiven*. Munich, 1923.

Kuper, Adam. *The Invention of Primitive Society: Transformations of an Illusion.* London, 1988.

Lazarus, Edward. *Black Hills, White Justice: The Sioux Nation Versus the United States 1775 to the Present.* New York, 1991.

Leach, Edmund. *Claude Lévi-Strauss.* Chicago, 1970, 1978.

Lévi-Strauss, Claude. *Les Structures élémentaires de la parenté.* Paris, 1949.

Lindley, M.F. *The Acquisition and Government of Backward Territory in International Law, Being a Treatise on the Law and Practice Relating to Colonial Expansion.* New York, 1926.

Lindqvist, Sven. *"Exterminate All the Brutes": One Man's Odyssey into the Heart of Darkness and the Origins of European Genocide,* trans. Joan Tate. New York, 1996.

——. *The Skull Measurer's Mistake: And Other Portraits of Men and Women Who Spoke Out Against Racism,* trans. Joan Tate. New York, 1997.

——. *A History of Bombing,* trans. Linda Haverty Rugg. New York, 2001.

Lukes, Steven. *Emile Durkheim: His Life and Work.* London, 1973.

Lumholtz, Carl. *Among Cannibals.* London, 1890.

Lundmark, Lennart. *Så länge vi har marker: Samerna och staten under sex hundra år.* Stockholm, 1999.

——. *"Lappen är ombytlig, ostadig och obekväm": Svenska statens samepolitik i rasismens tidevarv.* Umeå, 2002.

Macintyre, Stuart. *The History Wars.* Carlton, VIC, 2004.

——, ed. *The Historian's Conscience: Australian Historians on the Ethics of History.* Melbourne, 2004.

Malinowski, B. *The Family Among the Australian Aborigines: A Sociological Study.* New York, 1913, 1963.

Manne, Robert, ed. *Whitewash: On Keith Windschuttle's Fabrication of Aboriginal History.* Melbourne, 2003.

Martin, Catherine. *An Australian Girl.* Oxford, 1890, 1999.

——. *The Incredible Journey.* London, 1923, 1987.

McCulloch, Susan. *Contemporary Aboriginal Art: A Guide to the Rebirth of an Ancient Culture.* Sydney, 2001.

McGregor, Russell. *Imagined Destinies: Aboriginal Australians and the Doomed Race Theory, 1880–1939.* Melbourne, 1997.

McMaster, Don. *Asylum Seekers: Australia's Response to Refugees.* Melbourne, 2001.

Michaels, Eric. *Bad Aboriginal Art: Tradition, Media and Technological Horizons.* Minneapolis, 1994.

Mjöberg, Eric. *Bland vilda djur och folk i Australien.* Stockholm, 1915.

——. *"Svenska Biologiska Expeditionen till Australien 1910–11." Ymer,* no. 4 (1912).

Molnar, Helen, and Michael Meadows. *Songlines to Satellites: Indigenous Communication in Australia, the South Pacific and Canada*. Sydney, 2001.

Morgan, Lewis H. *Ancient Society or Researches in the Lines of Human Progress from Savagery Through Barbarism to Civilization*. New York, 1877.

Morphy, Howard. *Aboriginal Art*. London, 1998.

Morris, Henry C. *The History of Colonization from the Earliest Times to the Present Day*. New York, 1900.

Morton, Peter. *Fire Across the Desert: Woomera and the Anglo-Australian Joint Project, 1946–1980*. Canberra, 1989.

Morton, S.R., and D.J. Mulvaney. *Exploring Central Australia: Society, the Environment and the 1894 Horn Expedition*. Chipping Norton, 1996.

Moses, Dirk, ed. *Genocide and Settler Society: Frontier Violence and Stolen Indigenous Children in Australian History*. New York, 2005.

Mountford, C.P. "Aboriginal Crayon Drawings from the Warburton Ranges of Western Australia Relating to the Wanderings of Two Ancestral Beings the Wati Kutjara." *Records of the South Australian Museum* 6, no. 1 (1937).

———. *The Art of Albert Namatjira*. Melbourne, 1944.

Mowaljarlai, David, and Jutta Malnic. *YorroYorro: Everything Standing up Alive*. Broome, WA, 1993.

Mudie, Ian. *The Heroic Journey of John McDouall Stuart*. Sydney, 1968.

Mudrooroo. *The Indigenous Literature of Australia*. Melbourne, 1997. *See also* Johnson, Colin.

Mulvaney, D.J. *Encounters in Place: Outsiders and Aboriginal Australians, 1606–1985*. Adelaide, 1989.

Mulvaney, D.J., and J.H. Calaby. *"So Much That Is New": Baldwin Spencer, 1860–1929*. Melbourne, 1985.

Munn, Nancy D. *Walbiri Iconography: Graphic Representation and Cultural Symbolism in a Central Australian Society*. Ithaca, NY, 1973.

Myers, Fred R. *Painting Culture: The Making of an Aboriginal High Art*. Durham, NC, 2002.

———. *Pintupi Country, Pintupi Self: Sentiment, Place and Politics Among Western Desert Aborigines*. Washington, DC, 1986.

Nelson, Edward. *The Eskimo About Bering Strait*. Washington, DC, 1899.

Oxford Companion to Australian History. Melbourne, 1998.

Oxford Literary Guide to Australia. Oxford, 1993.

Papunya Tula: Genesis and Genius. Art Gallery of New South Wales, 2000.

Phillips, Richard. *Mapping Men and Empire: A Geography of Adventure*. London, 1997.

Pierce, Peter. *The Country of Lost Children: An Australian Anxiety.* Cambridge, 1999.

Pilkington, Doris. *Follow the Rabbit-Proof Fence.* Brisbane, 1996.

Pitt-Rivers, George Henry Lane-Fox. *The Clash of Cultures and the Contact of Races: An Anthropological and Psychological Study of the Laws of Racial Adaptability with Special Reference to the Depopulation of the Pacific and the Government of Subject Races.* London, 1927.

Radcliffe-Brown, A.R. "Three Tribes of Western Australia." *Journal of the Royal Anthropological Institute* 43 (1913): 143–94.

———. *Social Organization of Australian Tribes,* vols. 1–3. Oceania, 1930–31.

Radford, Ron. Preface to *Dreamings of the Desert.* Adelaide, 1996.

Ray, Dorothy Jean. *Eskimo Art.* Vancouver, 1977.

Réja, Marcel. *L'Art chez les fous.* Paris, 1907.

———. *Les Rêves et leur interpretation.* Paris, 1910.

Report of the Parliamentary Select Committee on Aboriginal Tribes. London, 1837.

Report on the Work of the Horn Scientific Expedition to Central Australia, vol. 4: *Anthropology.* Melbourne, 1896.

Reynolds, Henry. *Why Weren't We Told? A Personal Search for the Truth About Our History.* Penguin, 1999.

Rivers, William Halse Rivers. "The Genealogical Method of Anthropological Inquiry." *Sociological Review* (1910).

Roberts, Tony. *Frontier Justice: A History of the Gulf Culture to 1900.* St. Lucia, QLD, 2005.

Rowley, C.D. *The Destruction of Aboriginal Society, Aboriginal Policy and Practice,* vol. 1. Canberra, 1970.

———. *The Remote Aborigines, Aboriginal Policy and Practice,* vol. 3. Canberra, 1971.

Ryan, Judith. *Images of Power: Aboriginal Art of the Kimberley.* Melbourne, 1993.

Ryan, Judith, and Geoffrey Bardon. *Mythscapes: Aboriginal Art of the Desert from the National Gallery of Victoria.* Melbourne, 1989.

Salomon, C. *L'Occupation des territories sans maître.* Paris, 1889.

Salter, Elizabeth. *Daisy Bates: "The Great White Queen of the Never Never."* Sydney, 1972.

Shapiro, Warren. *Social Organization in Aboriginal Australia.* New York, 1979.

Shephard, Mark. *The Great Victoria Desert.* Chatswood, NSW, 1995.

Söderblom, Nathan. *Gudstrons uppkomst.* Stockholm, 1914.

Southall, Ivan. *Woomera.* Sydney, 1962.

Spencer, W. Baldwin, and F.J. Gillen. *The Native Tribes of Central Australia.* London, 1899.

———. *The Northern Tribes of Central Australia.* London, 1904.

———. *The Arunta: A Study of a Stone Age People.* Oosterhout, 1927, 1966.

Stocking, George W., ed. *Observers Observed: Essays on Ethnographic Fieldwork.* Madison, WI, 1983.

Stokes, J. Lort. *Discoveries in Australia.* London, 1846.

Strehlow, T. "Geography and the Totemic Landscape in Central Australia: A Functional Study." In *Australian Aboriginal Anthropology,* ed. Ronald M. Berndt. Crawley, WA, 1970.

———. *Songs of Central Australia.* Sydney, 1971.

Sutton, Peter. *Dreamings: The Art of Aboriginal Australia.* New York, 1988.

———. "Icons of Country: Topographic Representations in Classical Aboriginal Traditions." *History of Cartography* 2 (1998).

———. "Aboriginal Maps and Plans." *History of Cartography* 2 (1998).

Symonds, J.L. *A History of British Atomic Tests in Australia.* Canberra, 1985.

Thonemann, H.E. *Tell the White Man: The Life Story of an Aboriginal Lubra.* Sydney, 1949.

Tindale, Norman B. *Aboriginal Tribes of Australia: Their Terrain, Environmental Controls, Distribution, Limits and Proper Names.* Berkeley, CA, 1974.

Torpey, John, ed. *Politics and the Past: On Repairing Historical Injustices.* Lanham, 2003.

Tyler, Heather. *Asylum: Voices Behind the Razor Wire.* Melbourne, 2003.

Warlukurlangu Artists. *Kuruwarri, Yuendumu Doors.* Canberra, 1992.

Watson, E.L. *But to What Purpose: The Autobiography of a Contemporary.* London, 1946.

White, Mary E. *After the Greening: The Browning of Australia.* East Roseville, NSW, 1998.

Windschuttle, Keith. *The Fabrication of Aboriginal History.* Sydney, 2002.

Woodcock, George, and Ivan Avacumovic. *The Anarchist Prince: A Biographical Study of Peter Kropotkin.* New York, 1950, 1970.

Worsley, Peter. *Knowledges: Culture, Counterculture, Subculture.* New York, 1997.

Worsnop, Thomas. *The Prehistoric Arts, Manufactures, Works, Weapons, Etc. of the Aborigines of Australia.* Adelaide, 1897.

Wright, Alexis. *Grog War.* Broome, WA, 1997.

NOTES

To Moorundie

1. Salomon; Lindley; *Dictionnaire*; Bedjaoui; Anaya.
2. Tindale, 214; Mulvaney, chap. 12.
3. Eyre, 147ff.
4. Dutton, 66, 71, 157–65.
5. Mulvaney, chap. 12.
6. Report of the Parliamentary Select Committee on Aboriginal Tribes, 1837.
7. Eyre, chap. 1.

The Secret of the Desert

8. Mudie.
9. Morton, chap. 4–6; Southall; Beadell; Chambers.
10. Immigration Museum, Adelaide; Jupp, chap. 5.
11. McMaster, Preface, chap. 3, 4, 6; Immigration Museum, Adelaide.
12. McMaster, 95.
13. White, chap. 4.
14. White, chap. 18, 23.
15. Söderblom, chap. 4.
16. White, chap. 7.
17. Favenc, chap. 4.
18. Favenc, chap. 5.
19. Favenc, chap. 7.
20. Favenc, chap. 8. See also Phillips, chap. 4; Haynes, chap. 5.
21. Favenc, chap. 25.
22. Mulvaney, chap. 18.
23. Dewar, chap. 2.
24. Mulvaney, chap. 18.
25. Darwin, chap. 6; Lindqvist, *"Exterminate"*; Lindqvist, *Skull Measurer's Mistake*, chap. 10, 12, 18.
26. George Chatterton Hill, chap. 5.
27. Morris, 20ff.

28. Pitt-Rivers, chap. 3.

29. *Report on the Work of the Horn Scientific Expedition to Central Australia*, vol. 4, iv.

30. Spencer and Gillen called them "Arunta," and various other forms of the name occur in the literature. I use throughout the name that the Aborigine peoples themselves use today.

31. Stocking; Mulvaney and Calaby, chap. 9.

32. Malinowski, quoted in Gill, chap. 2.

33. *New Territory News*, March 24, 2003.

34. Kropotkin; Woodcock; Hiatt, chap. 5.

35. Hiatt, chap. 6.

36. Gay, chap. 1.

37. Lukes; Kuper, chap. 6.

38. Freud, *Totem und Tabu*, pt. 4, chap. 5.

39. Freud, *Totem und Tabu*, pt. 4, chap. 7.

40. Gay, chap. 7.

41. Lukes, chap. 23.

To Kahlin Compound

42. Wright, chap. 6.

43. Wright, chap. 3.

44. Wright, chap. 3.

45. Wright, chap. 5

46. Wright, chap. 4.

47. Gunn, chap. 3.

48. Gunn, chap. 11.

49. Gunn, chap. 9.

50. Dewar, chap. 2.

51. Thonemann, chap. 1.

52. Thonemann, chap. 10.

53. Thonemann, 66.

54. *Bringing them Home*, chap. 7.

55. *Bringing them Home*, chap. 9.

56. Hiatt, chap. 3.

57. Engels, 39–55; Kuper, chap. 3; Hiatt, chap. 4.

58. Kuper, chap. 6.

59. Malinowski, chap. 1; cf. Engels, 49: "Not the individuals but the whole group are married to each other, class with class."

60. Malinowski, Introduction.

61. Martin, *Australian Girl*, chap. 16.

62. Pierce, Introduction.

63. Martin, *Incredible Journey*, chap. 8.
64. Martin, *Incredible Journey*, chap. 26.
65. Quoted in Dewar, chap. 4; Haynes, chap. 10.
66. Herbert, chap. 3.
67. Herbert, chap. 4.
68. Herbert, chap. 7.
69. Herbert, chap. 10.
70. Herbert, chap. 11.
71. Herbert, chap. 14.
72. McGregor, chap. 4.
73. De Groen, chap. 6.
74. De Groen, chap. 10.
75. Herbert, chap. 32.

The Dead Do Not Die
76. Rowley, *Remote Aborigines*, chap. 16; Attwood and Markus, sec. 124–28.
77. Mjöberg, *Bland vilda djur och folk i Australien*, chap. 18. Translations into English from the original Swedish by Sarah Death.
78. Ibid., chap. 21.
79. Ibid., chap. 22.
80. Ibid., chap. 25.
81. Tyler, chap. 1.
82. Ernestine Hill, *Great Australian Loneliness*, chap. 4.
83. Edwards, chap. 5.
84. *Bringing Them Home*, chap. 1, confidential evidence 821.
85. Attwood and Markus, sec. 165.
86. Eyre, entries for February 24 to March 1, 1839.
87. Jebb; Mulvaney, chap. 26.
88. Watson, chap. 15.
89. Radcliffe-Brown, "Three Tribes of Western Australia."
90. Bates, chap. 9; Salter, chap. 17.

To Pinjarra
91. Critique of Radcliffe-Brown in Shapiro.
92. Bennett, *Christison of Lammermoor*, chap. 7.
93. Bennett, *Australian Aboriginal as a Human Being*, chap. 3; Rowley, chap. 11.
94. Elder, chap. 14, 15.
95. Bennett, *Australian Aboriginal*, chap. 4.
96. *Australian Dictionary of Biography*, chap. 7.

97. *Bringing Them Home*, chap. 7, confidential submission 640.
98. Lévi-Strauss, chap. 11.
99. *Bringing Them Home*, chap. 7.
100. Christopher Johnson, chap. 2.
101. Leach, chap. 6.
102. Quoted in Clarke, chap. 2.
103. Quoted in ibid., chap. 4.
104. Lévi-Strauss, chap. 23.
105. Quoted in Clarke, chap. 4.
106. Ibid., chap. 5.
107. Haebich, chap. 5.
108. Ibid.
109. Ibid., chap. 6.
110. Ibid., chap. 10.
111. Ibid., chap. 6.
112. Ibid., chap. 4.
113. Ibid., chap. 5–7.
114. Ibid., chap. 10, 14.
115. Colin Johnson, Preface.
116. Ibid., chap. 4.
117. Ibid., chap. 10.
118. Rowley, *Destruction of Aboriginal Society*, chap. 4; Mulvaney, chap. 24.

The Smell of the White Man

119. Shephard, Introduction.
120. White, chap. 5, 7.
121. Shephard, chap. 6, 8.
122. Bates; Ernestine Hill, *Great Australian Loneliness*.
123. Ernestine Hill, *Kabbarli*, chap. 1.
124. Salter, chap. 18.
125. Blackburn, chap. 22.
126. Ibid., chap. 15.
127. Hill, *Kabbarli*, chap. 10.
128. Berndt, chap. 4.
129. Shephard, chap. 5; Beadell, chap. 16; Blakeway, chap. 6.
130. Shephard, chap. 9.

The Ground

131. Barry Hill.
132. Strehlow, "Geography and the Totemic Landscape in Central Australia."
133. Barry Hill, pp. 166ff, 441ff.

134. Strehlow, *Songs of Central Australia*.

135. Barry Hill, p. 752.

136. Molnar and Meadows.

137. Grey, vol. 1, p. 263.

138. Andree, p. 64.

139. Eylmann, chapp. 5, 23.

140. Spencer and Gillen, *Native Tribes of Central Australia*, chap. 19.

141. Spencer and Gillen, *Northern Tribes of Central Australia*, chap. 25.

142. Haynes, chap. 5.

143. Foy.

144. Kühn, chap.7.

145. Haynes, chap. 15

146. Barrett and Croll; Mountford, 1944; Battarbee.

147. Chesterman and Galligan.

148. Batty, chap. 13.

149. Mountford, 1937.

150. Munn, chap. 5.

151. Ibid., chap. 4.

152. Errington.

153. Bardon, *Aboriginal Art of the Western Desert*; Ryan and Bardon, *Mythscapes*; Bardon, *Papunya Tule*; Amadin and Kimber; Caruana, *Windows on the Dreaming*; Vivien Johnson, *Aboriginal Artists of the Western Desert*; Corbally Stourton; *Morphy*; *Papunya Tula*.

154. Bardon, *Papunya Tula*, p. 45.

155. Johnson, *Aboriginal Artists*, chap. 4; Radford.

156. Sutton, *Dreaming*; Myers, *Painting Culture*.

157. Warlukurlangi Artists; Ryan and Bardon, *Mythscapes*; Johnson, *Aboriginal Artists*, chap. 2; Dussart, *Body Painting in Translation*; Dussart, *Politics of Ritual in an Aboriginal Settlement*, chap. 3.

158. Dussart, *Politics of Ritual*, chap. 3.

159. Geoff Maslen, "Aboriginal Art Set to Top $15 Million," *The Age*, July 7, 2004.

160. Himmelheber; Graburn; Ray; Crandall.

161. Reynolds.

162. Rowley, *Destruction of Aboriginal Society*, chap. 2.

163. Ibid., chap. 3.

164. Brandström; Lundmark, *Så länge vi. har marker*; Lundmark, "Lappen är ombytlig, ostadig och obekväm."

165. Barkan, chap. 10.

166. This chapter has been added to the English edition. Records of the Windschuttle debate in Manne and Dawson. Attwood and Foster and

Macintyre and Attwood analyze the revisionist attack from historical and ethical perspectives. Meanwhile the scholarly discussion continues, for example in Moses.

167. Quoted in Torpey.
168. Hicks.
169. Barkan, chap. 8; Lazarus, chap. 16, 17.
170. Barkan, particularly the Introduction and Conclusion.

Publishing in the Public Interest

Thank you for reading this book published by The New Press. The New Press is a nonprofit, public interest publisher. New Press books and authors play a crucial role in sparking conversations about the key political and social issues of our day.

We hope you enjoyed this book and that you will stay in touch with The New Press. Here are a few ways to stay up to date with our books, events, and the issues we cover:

- Sign up at www.thenewpress.com/subscribe to receive updates on New Press authors and issues and to be notified about local events
- Like us on Facebook: www.facebook.com/newpressbooks
- Follow us on Twitter: www.twitter.com/thenewpress

Please consider buying New Press books for yourself; for friends and family; or to donate to schools, libraries, community centers, prison libraries, and other organizations involved with the issues our authors write about.

The New Press is a 501(c)(3) nonprofit organization. You can also support our work with a tax-deductible gift by visiting www.thenewpress.com/donate.